MAKING GLOBAL LEARNING UNIVERSAL

MAKING GLOBAL LEARNING UNIVERSAL

Promoting Inclusion and Success for All Students

Hilary Landorf, Stephanie Doscher,
and Jaffus Hardrick

Foreword by Caryn McTighe Musil

Copublished with

STERLING, VIRGINIA

Published by Stylus Publishing, LLC.
22883 Quicksilver Drive Sterling, Virginia 20166-2019

Library of Congress Cataloging-in-Publication-Data
Names: Landorf, Hilary, author. | Doscher, Stephanie, author. | Hardrick, Jaffus, author. | Musil, Caryn McTighe, 1944- author of foreword.
Title: Making global learning universal : promoting inclusion and success for all students / Hilary Landorf, Stephanie Doscher, and Jaffus Hardrick ; foreword by Caryn McTighe Musil.
Description: First edition. |
Sterling, Virginia : Stylus Publishing, [2018] |
Includes bibliographical references and index.
Identifiers: LCCN 2017050312 (print) |
LCCN 2018031690 (ebook) | ISBN 9781620363614 (uPDF) |
ISBN 9781620363621 (ePub, mobi) |
ISBN 9781620363591 (cloth : alk. paper) |
ISBN 9781620363607 (pbk. : alk. paper) |
ISBN 9781620363614 (library networkable e-edition) |
ISBN 9781620363621 (consumer e-edition)
Subjects: LCSH: Global method of teaching. |
Multicultural education. | Multiculturalism--Study and teaching.
Classification: LCC LB1029.G55 (ebook) |
LCC LB1029.G55 L36 2018 (print) |
DDC 371.9/046--dc23
LC record available at https://lccn.loc.gov/2017050312

13-digit ISBN: 978-1-62036-359-1 (cloth)
13-digit ISBN: 978-1-62036-360-7 (paperback)
13-digit ISBN: 978-1-62036-361-4 (library networkable e-edition)
13-digit ISBN: 978-1-62036-362-1 (consumer e-edition)

Printed in the United States of America

All first editions printed on acid-free paper
that meets the American National Standards Institute
Z39-48 Standard.

A copublication of Stylus Publishing, LLC. and NAFSA: Association of International Educators.

Bulk Purchases
Quantity discounts are available for use in workshops and for staff development.
Call 1-800-232-0223
NAFSA: Call 1-866-538-1927 to order

First Edition, 2018

We dedicate this book to the current and former staff of FIU's Office of Global Learning Initiatives, whose tireless efforts and constant innovation are the not-so-secret source of our success: Eric Feldman, Abhignyan Nagesetti, Melissa Livingston, Andrew Gomez, Bimal Soti, Connie Penczak, Sherrie Beeson, Ashwini Ramanna, Rippy Koul, Jared Leichner, Gregory Anderson, and Frank Rojas.

And we dedicate this book to all the students, faculty, staff, administrators, alumni, and local and global community members who have participated in the development of Global Learning for Global Citizenship and have engaged in the process of global learning over the past 10 years. The impacts of your efforts are more significant and farther reaching than we ever could have planned for, anticipated, or will know. We honor you through this book.

CONTENTS

**PART THREE: SUSTAINING AND EXPANDING
GLOBAL LEARNING**

Global Learning Without a Passport

It's almost impossible to dislodge a strong, long-held belief, however much the facts contradict it. This has been the case with default thinking about how to instill in college students a global consciousness and a more expansive understanding of individuals' and nations' responsibilities in a global ecology. For decades the autopilot response has been study abroad. *Making Global Learning Universal: Promoting Inclusion and Success for All Students* disrupts those assumptions and offers an alternative that is now institutionalized at Florida International University (FIU). FIU's educational design for universal global learning enables all students to engage in global learning without a passport. It's a blueprint that relies on moving minds, not bodies.

Let me be very clear. Study abroad is a high-impact practice that should be expanded and made widely and equitably accessible to all students. But the stark reality, widely glossed over, is how few college students ever study outside the United States. According to the Institute of International Education (2017), although the number of students studying abroad has more than doubled since 2000, only 325,339 college students studied abroad for credit hours in 2015–2016. That number pales in comparison to the total number of U.S. college students, which stands at about 16.5 million. Study abroad involves only 1.7% of college students. When alternative spring breaks, semester breaks, or summer noncredit opportunities are added, the percentage increases but remains lower than the digits on two hands. As a strategic investment to prepare the next generation of college graduates to shape complex financial, media, governmental, ethnographic, cultural, and ecological global systems, study abroad alone fails. It's a bit like trying to build a tunnel through a mountain with a spoon.

Although study abroad should be kept as part of the global learning portfolio, the time is long past to understand its limits and to implement more effective, scalable practices. FIU has done just that, and *Making Global Learning Universal* explains in careful, illuminating, practical detail how it was done. Administrators of FIU, an institution with international in its name, understand that a student can and must be able to investigate, interrogate, and learn about the world in collaboration with diverse others without ever physically crossing a geographic border. Hilary Landorf and Stephanie

Doscher took a courageous, creative stand by developing a transformative curricular and cocurricular model that touches every FIU student. Administrators at other institutions should rush to experiment with how this new theory, model, and set of practices can be adapted on their campuses.

After more than a year of study and conversations with colleagues across FIU's campus, Landorf and Doscher (2015) decisively shifted a working paradigm of global learning from internationalizing the curriculum to educating students for global citizenship. In turn, that shift drove their new definition of *global learning* to be "the process of diverse peoples collaboratively analyzing and addressing complex problems that transcend borders of all kinds" (para. 2). A problem-based curriculum thus became a necessary part of their educational design; diverse perspectives and people became inextricably linked to those ends; and making global learning possible for all FIU students, not a select few, became the norm. Their design underscored global learning not as optional but as indispensable, not as collecting frequent flyer miles but as learning how to collaboratively address global challenges that have no national borders. To be deprived of such learning puts graduates, the nation, and the world at risk.

Since 2002 the Association of American Colleges & Universities (AAC&U) has supported institutions of higher education as their administrators seek new ways to educate students in global knowledge and responsibility. The AAC&U (2017c) called the initiative Shared Futures: Global Learning and Social Responsibility, which was supported in part by a series of Luce Foundation and Department of Education Fund for the Improvement of Postsecondary Education grants and involved more than 80 colleges and universities. In its trailblazing work, FIU has broken free of earlier intellectual frameworks and practices to achieve global learning for all and has redirected the purposes of such learning.

Making Global Learning Universal records a remarkable institutional venture, provides extraordinary vision, and bolsters the reluctant to not hold back. The authors offer contemporary theories that undergird this new conception of global learning, the engagement with diversity as foundational, the nuts and bolts of how they proceeded and where they stumbled, the strategies that have involved more than 1,500 faculty in over 110 different professional development opportunities, and the leadership and infrastructure that have been critical to sustaining momentum. This book has redrawn the map for global learning. The authors not only recognize that the world is not flat but also reveal that it can be seen, understood, experienced, and engaged with right here on American soil.

Caryn McTighe Musil
Senior Scholar and Director of Civic Learning and Democracy Initiatives
Association of American Colleges & Universities

STATEMENT FROM THE PRESIDENT OF
FLORIDA INTERNATIONAL UNIVERSITY

As a comparativist and internationalist nurtured in language studies and as an area studies approaches specialist, I am particularly pleased to be a small part of this book on global learning prepared by my colleagues here at Florida International University (FIU).

The global learning framework they have developed gives our university an approach that enables us to study our broader environment and the behavior of its inhabitants. It also gives us a student-centered rationale to take responsibility and provide solutions to address the critical issues of our time.

The authors point out that we at FIU have an advantage in that our founders immediately sensed the potential, if not the imperative, of connections beyond local and national borders. Our founding president, Charles Perry, had this sensibility. He insisted our university should not be aloof from society's problems and urged us to find solutions to the most pressing issues of our age.

Our institution was formed in the late 1960s and early 1970s with an activist local and global mission. However, we were then focused on establishing a credible advanced learning center; crafting a portfolio of degrees sensitive to the needs of mostly place-bound, nontraditional learners; and building an internationally respected research portfolio. Achieving these goals alone has taken us more than 40 years, and of course, there is still more to do.

Then in 2007, our former provost, Ronald M. Berkman, and his senior administration challenged the university community to reach beyond the diversity that had characterized and flavored the international dimension of our institution. The commitment of open-minded and enterprising faculty, students, and professional staff, led by Berkman's successor, Douglas Wartzok, enabled the building blocks of our university-wide global learning initiative to be put in place. This process brought about deep soul searching and compromises, as is typical of any major organizational change or curriculum reform.

Global learning has galvanized our stakeholders into a proactive mindset that involves taking responsibility for local and global challenges.

This mind-set is illustrated by our medical school, which integrates preventive medicine with multicultural perspectives, community engagement initiatives with public and private organizations that involve win-win deep partnerships, and our being selected in 2016 as an Ashoka Changemaker Campus, the leading designation for colleges and universities that provide social innovation education and change-making opportunities on campus and beyond.

Our present era will undergo some of the most profound changes ever seen in higher education. Automation is accelerating, technology infuses all aspects of learning and living, and the structure of work is rapidly changing. The process of global learning will enable institutions of higher education to better respond and adapt to these developments that alternately nourish and crowd our well-being. I have great confidence in this, in part because of the creativity of the team that leads our global learning initiative. I commend this work to you.

Mark B. Rosenberg
Florida International University
July 4, 2017

ACKNOWLEDGMENTS

We are tremendously grateful to the following for their generous contributions to the making of this book: Bahia Simons-Lane, for her indispensible research and writing assistance; Chad B. Anderson, who provided valuable editorial feedback; Caryn McTighe Musil, for composing an encouraging and inspirational foreword; and to Florida International University President Mark B. Rosenberg, whose powerful statement serves as a model for high-level leadership of universal global learning.

INTRODUCTION

A map says to you, "Read me carefully, follow me closely, doubt me not." It says, "'I am the earth in the palm of your hand. Without me, you are alone and lost.'" (Markham, 1942, p. 245)

There's no map for you to follow and take your journey. You are Lewis and Clark. You are the mapmaker. (Soo, in Paulson, 2017, para. 11)

Conduct a Google image search for the term *global learning* and what do you think you'll find? You guessed it: world maps. Chances are, if your institution has a global learning program, the image of a map of the world is used to market it. Even the cover of this book features maps. A map seems to be a logical symbol for *global learning*; its meaning and relevance appear self-evident. Maps help people learn about the world. They enable us to position ourselves on the planet, reveal the existence of other environments, and help us travel from one location to another. Maps organize how we see relationships among different peoples and locales. World maps situate identity, suggest objectivity, and depict local details while simultaneously suggesting a broad view (Edsall, 2007). On the face of things, maps symbolize what global learning should be all about: discovering more about the world's peoples and places.

But is a world map really a good symbol of global learning? People use symbols as a shorthand to convey meaning, often selecting concrete objects to represent an abstract concept or phenomenon. The choice of an appropriate symbol assumes a clear understanding of the concept and the symbol. In this case, a common, easily recognizable object—a map—is frequently used to signify the meaning of global learning, a concept that's difficult to visualize and ill-defined in the literature. Colleges and universities use the term *global learning* to refer to all kinds of educational activities, from curriculum internationalization, study abroad, and area studies programs to foreign language courses, international collaboration online, and culturally diverse cocurricular programming. Given the broad range of meanings assigned to global learning, we think it is fair game to ask, What exactly is global learning, and are maps fitting symbols of its nature and significance?

Before we offer a definition of *global learning*, let's take a moment to explore the characteristics of maps. As representations of the world, all maps are symbols (Edsall, 2007). No map can portray everything there is

to know about the world, so each can offer viewers only selected information (National Geographic Society, n.d.). The mapmaker determines what
information to share based on the purpose for creating the map, and design
choices are influenced by standards in the field and the mapmaker's own
artistic style. Because maps are two dimensional and the Earth is a three-
dimensional sphere, mapmakers also need a means of projection, a method
by which they can translate points on a curved plane onto a flat surface.
Projections offset the correct appearance of selected data about the world
with the distortion of other information considered less important to the
mapmaker's objectives.

All maps must sacrifice accuracy for the sake of usability. For example,
the classic Mercator projection (Figure I.1) was created to enable sailors to
navigate the world in seafaring vessels. To accurately display the distance
between locations, the map widens land masses and oceans as they approach
the Earth's poles. As a result, the sizes of land masses are distorted: Countries
like Russia and Canada are outsized, whereas the entire continent of Africa
appears smaller than Greenland even though it's actually 14 times larger
(Thompson, 2017). The Gall-Peters projection (Figure I.2) was created to
correct Mercator's errors. This projection distorts the land masses' shapes but
accurately portrays their size relative to one another. Boston Public Schools
recently adopted the Gall-Peters projection for all secondary school classroom
maps as part of a three-year plan to "decolonize the curriculum" (Walters,
2017, para. 13). Hayden Frederick-Clarke, director of cultural proficiency
for Boston Public Schools, explained the reason for the change:

> Eighty-six percent of our students are students of color. Maps that they are
> presented with generally classify the places that they're from as small and
> insignificant. It only seems right that we would present them with an accu-
> rate view of themselves. (Shaffer, 2017, para. 9)

All maps mislead viewers somehow. No two-dimensional projection can
accurately display all the properties of our three-dimensional planet. Because
there's no limit to the number of projections that can be created, there's also
no limit to the ways maps can mislead. This characteristic of maps—their
inherent distortion of our worldview—seems inconsistent with the concept
of global learning, calling into question their symbolic validity.

What about globes, though? A globe is a kind of map frequently used
to symbolize global learning. At our institution, Florida International
University (FIU), a stylized globe is central to the logo for our university-
wide initiative, titled Global Learning for Global Citizenship. Spherical
globes overcome the distortion problem associated with two-dimensional

Figure I.1. Mercator projection.

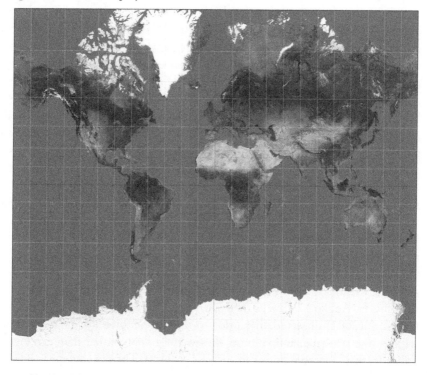

Figure I.2. Gall-Peters projection.

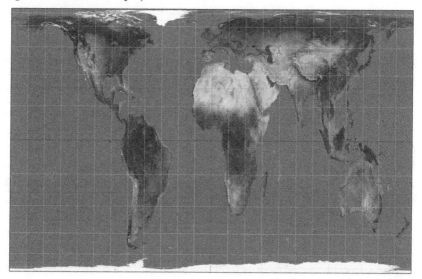

maps. Globes spin on an axis, just the way the Earth does, so they portray a world that can be viewed from multiple points of view. Three-dimensional globes provide exact representations of Earth's land masses, but like two-dimensional maps, they're limited in their capacity to display all there is to know about the world. There simply isn't enough room to show every city, town, and neighborhood or every road, river, and mountain. Globes and two-dimensional maps are also snapshots in time; they can't depict how human and geological dynamics influence political borders and physical topography (National Research Council, 2010). Furthermore, as symbols, globes are steeped in a long, complicated history. In Ancient Rome, a celestial globe, which depicts the sky's constellations, was associated with Caesar's claim to divinity. Medieval Christian leaders used a terrestrial globe to signify their divinely inspired imperial command over the Earth. Globes often adorn private homes and public libraries as symbols of scholarship, but in Baroque-era *vanitas* artworks they were used to indicate the worthless pursuit of worldly goods and enjoyment (Mokre, 2000).

On December 7, 1972, globes acquired a new layer of meaning with the arrival of the first full-view photo of the planet, the Blue Marble image, captured by the Apollo 17 crew as their spaceship left Earth's orbit for the moon. Cosgrove (2001) observed that prior to this image, globes were associated with geometry, shape, and volume; they were "graphic rather than experiential or textual" representations of the planet (p. 8). The photographic image of the whole Earth evoked an emotional, metaphorical response. It stressed "the globe's organic unity and matters of life, dwelling, and rootedness" (pp. 262–263). Divinity, power, vanity, erudition, geometry, unity: To what extent do some or all of these elements comport with how we wish to portray the meaning of global learning?

The truth is, we do think maps and globes represent our definition of *global learning*, but only under particular circumstances. Let us explain by showing rather than just telling you what we mean.

Take a moment to look at the cover of this book. Notice that maps aren't used as an embellishment or decorative element; they're the subject of a discussion involving a group of FIU undergraduates. The students are participating in a global learning strategy developed by one of our colleagues, Linda Bliss, a retired instructor of qualitative research in FIU's School of Education and Human Development. Bliss prompts participants to compare and contrast diverse maps of the world, interpret the information the maps present, and interrogate their symbolic meaning. Bliss begins by asking students to simply observe the maps she's placed around the room. Some maps were gathered during Bliss's travels; others were given to her by friends and former students. The maps were created for different purposes and use different projection systems. One places North America at the center, whereas others focus on different continents, and the United States appears at the periphery. There are physical maps, political maps, maps that use different color and symbol schemes, and maps written in different languages. Bliss asks students to circulate around the room and decipher what they see. She doesn't lecture about the maps or their design, but she answers basic questions about how or where they were acquired. For those unfamiliar with projection systems, she provides a brief explanation, if asked. When students are given ample time to discuss their interpretations, they develop a high level of curiosity. What accounts for the diverse ways our common planet is portrayed? At the height of interest, Bliss poses a critical question: What are the implications of different portrayals of maps for different people around the world? In the ensuing conversation, global learning begins.

Students quickly grasp that there is more to a map than meets the eye, and there is more to the world than any single map can help us see. Being used to visualizing the world in terms of the Mercator projection, students are shocked to discover that they've been operating under some significant misconceptions concerning Earth's geography. They often ask why the Northern Hemisphere is usually presented at the top of maps and the Southern Hemisphere at the bottom; does this create an unconscious perception that the north is better? A study by Meier, Moller, Chen, and Riemer-Peltz (2011) suggests that it does. Students question the existential implications of Mercator's perspective; residents of countries and continents placed at the center are conferred higher levels of power and influence, and those shown at the periphery vie for attention and resources. Some students notice their hometown or city does not appear on any of the maps, causing them to ponder whether they exist in the eyes of the rest of the world. This prompts them to inquire about people who don't have access to any maps or who are only exposed to one kind of map. How can people develop a sense of identity or seek equitable treatment if they don't understand their relationship to others or are presented with a distorted view of themselves? These questions cause students to see maps less as objective depictions and more as artifacts showing different mapmakers' perspectives on what's important to know about the world and how best to communicate that information. This explains why there is such a wide variety of maps. Students induce that there's no limit to the ways our Earth can be portrayed; there are as many projections and perspectives as there are mapmakers.

Together students slowly realize that the process of developing a more authentic, nuanced understanding of the world is a complex problem that needs to be solved. It's a problem that cannot be solved by one person or perspective alone. Because there are so many ways to interpret and portray our world, people need to exchange as many maps as possible to piece together an accurate, holistic conception of reality. This process of knowledge and perspective exchange involves a negotiation of differences and commonalities in meaning-making, not a simple transfer of facts from one mind to another. This is what global learning is all about—experiencing how complex problems transcend many kinds of borders of difference. Regardless of geographic location, citizenship, race, religion, gender, sexuality, socioeconomic status, or any other factor, everyone who wants to understand and address a complex problem must find a way to counterbalance his or her own limited, distorted knowledge and perspective, one's internal map of the world, with those of others. This process involves adapting one's worldview and generating new knowledge based on interconnections among diverse perspectives. "Maps are representations and no representation is identical to reality," Bliss said. "New maps can give us a different sense of ourselves in the world" (Tejedor, 2017, para. 8). Bliss's maps strategy usually ends with students reaching the following conclusion: Global learning involves a process of collectively analyzing information from diverse sources and perspectives and synthesizing that information into more comprehensive understandings, evaluations, and solutions.

In this sense, we think maps are terrific symbols of global learning because *global learning*, as we define it, is the process of diverse people collaboratively analyzing and addressing complex problems that transcend borders. Global learning strategies enable groups to determine relationships among diverse perspectives on problems and to develop more equitable, sustainable solutions for the world's interconnected human and natural communities. Whether the problem involves a group of students trying to develop a holistic worldview by viewing diverse maps or pertains to addressing a local public health crisis, the challenge of international refugee resettlement, or the effects of sea level rise, the way toward valid, equitable, sustainable solutions involves the process of global learning. No individual student or educator can accomplish global learning alone. To effectively decipher the complex problems facing our interconnected local and global communities, global learning must marshal the collective knowledge, perspectives, and experiences of as many as possible. We need all these stakeholders' individual maps to create new knowledge—new maps—that will lead toward new solutions. The opening epigraphs from Beryl Markham and Phillipa Soo are meant to illustrate this point. Global learning is a process that brings together individual maps to help piece together an understanding of a complex problem, but when it comes to charting a course toward a solution, there is no map that can help us find the way. This is when we ourselves must become map-makers. The process of global learning involves map reading and mapmaking alike.

We feel a strong sense of urgency to make the process of global learning part of every student's higher education. Global learning enables students to understand and make connections between local and global concerns and analyze pressing issues from multiple perspectives. It involves collaborative efforts to grapple with real-world problems influencing local and global communities.

Whether you believe that the purposes of higher education encompass career development, knowledge creation, personal fulfillment, or civic responsibility, global learning is essential. This book presents a model for enabling global learning for all. It addresses our research-based definition of *global learning*, which serves as the foundation for organizational change and curricular and cocurricular transformation. Susan Albertine, senior scholar in the Office of Integrative Liberal Learning and the Global Commons at the Association of American Colleges & Universities (AAC&U), has tied the need for a definition of *global learning* to the pressing need to solve today's complex local and global problems. In her opening address to the 2014 AAC&U Global Learning in College Conference, Albertine (2014) entreated attendees to employ global learning to help students start to address challenges while they are still in college and not wait until after they graduate:

> We have raised the theme of global learning and devoted resources to this series of conferences not because we think we know so well what global learning in college means. We genuinely don't. . . . We are here out of compassion and heartfelt tough-minded concern because there is urgency, a critical need to understand what global learning is, what our global moment and condition mean, and what to do as educators with that knowledge for our students—right now, and into the future. (p. 1)

We share Albertine's compassion and heartfelt, tough-minded concern for global learning. If you're reading this book, you probably share these feelings too.

Purpose and Audience

This book's premise is that global learning should be central to all students' higher education. We refer to the provision of global learning for all students as *universal global learning*. We believe that universal global learning should involve the curriculum and cocurriculum, and it should be integrative; that is, it should enable students to make connections among ideas, issues, and experiences and synthesize and transfer their learning to new and increasingly complex situations (AAC&U, 2017a). We further assert that universal global learning is integral to inclusive excellence, achieved when institutions "integrate diversity, equity, and educational quality efforts into their missions and institutional operations" (AAC&U, 2017b, para. 1).

Our purpose is to present you with a replicable model for achieving universal global learning. Just as our definition of *global learning* demands the involvement of diverse people's knowledge, experiences, and perspectives, our model involves virtually all institutional stakeholders. From senior leaders and midlevel administrators to faculty, staff, alumni, and community members, anyone interested in the conduct and outcomes of higher education will find something in this book that will help them contribute to all students' global learning.

The model emerges from our research and expertise in the fields of global education, curriculum reform, and organizational leadership; our experience developing, designing, and implementing a universal global learning initiative in one of the nation's largest and most diverse urban, public research universities; and our knowledge of challenges faced by those leading global learning initiatives in other colleges and universities in varying institutional contexts. The model consists of seven interconnected components:

1. A theory of organizational change that engages a broad spectrum of stakeholders
2. Global learning student learning outcomes (SLOs) that apply to all students and program goals that facilitate all students' achievement of those SLOs
3. A varied menu of professional development opportunities that enable faculty and staff to design and facilitate global learning experiences in the curriculum and cocurriculum
4. Human, physical, financial, and technological resources needed to support the common agenda
5. Strategies for promoting integrative global learning
6. Methods for assessing the extent to which all students are achieving global learning SLOs and evaluating the extent to which the institution is achieving its program goals
7. Processes for enabling continuous communication of assessment and evaluation data and facilitating continuous improvement of the initiative's activities, goals, and SLOs

Through the presentation of specific strategies and examples, we hope to transform how you think about global learning and its facilitation throughout the institution and the student learning experience. You may already be struck, however, by the fact that this far into the introduction you've yet to read the the word *internationalization*, a term frequently used interchangeably with global learning. We think these concepts are related but distinct. Here we quickly clarify the relationship among global learning, internationalization, and two other frequently interchanged terms, *curriculum internationalization*, also known as internationalization of the curriculum (IoC), and *globalization*. If you use these terms to describe your work, there's something in this book for you too.

Internationalization is the process of infusing "international and comparative perspectives throughout the teaching, research, and service missions of higher education" (Hudzik, 2011, p. 6). We agree with Hawawini (2011) that internationalization may be inwardly focused, outwardly focused, or both. Inwardly focused internationalization integrates "an international dimension into the existing institutional setting" (p. 5), whereas an outward focus aims to integrate "the institution into the emerging global knowledge and learning network" (p. 5). The Center for Internationalization and Global Engagement, a program of the American Council on Education (2012), identified six interconnected aspects of an institution that can be internationalized:

1. Articulated institutional commitment
2. Administrative leadership, structure, and staffing
3. Curriculum, cocurriculum, and learning outcomes
4. Faculty policies and practices
5. Student mobility
6. Collaboration and partnerships

Internationalization is primarily concerned with inputs and outputs such as increasing international student recruitment or funding for international research. Colleges and universities can internationalize to support students' global learning, but global learning doesn't necessarily result from internationalization. Global learning describes a specific kind of educational process in which students engage with diverse others, and this can happen at home, abroad, in person, or online. Olsen, Green, and Hill (2006) have said that internationalization refers to what institutions do, whereas global learning refers to how students learn.

Knight (1994) argued that the curriculum is "the backbone of the internationalization process" (p. 6). Leask (2015) defines *IoC* as "the process of incorporating international, intercultural and global dimensions into the content of the curriculum as well as the learning outcomes, assessment tasks, teaching methods and support services of a program of study" (p. 69). Institutions can engage in IoC through multiple approaches such as study abroad programs, foreign language courses, interdisciplinary or area studies programs, or courses with an international, intercultural, or comparative focus. But *global learning* as we define it and curriculum internationalization are not the same thing. Institutional stakeholders can choose to internationalize curricula by supporting students' global learning, or they may choose to support other approaches. Just because an institution's stakeholders want to internationalize curricula, it doesn't mean they are interested in facilitating global learning. In recent years, however, we've noticed a considerable uptick in interest in internationalizing curricula and cocurricula through global learning, which was a major impetus for this book.

Finally, we often hear people use *globalization* to describe their IoC efforts, for example, "I'm globalizing my course." We understand that these faculty want to communicate that they're infusing global issues and themes into their courses, but globalization is misapplied if it's used in reference to curriculum reform. According to the Levin Institute (2016),

> Globalization is a process of interaction and integration among the people, companies, and governments of different nations, a process driven by international trade and investment and aided by information technology. This process has effects on the environment, on culture, on political systems, on economic development and prosperity, and on human physical well-being in societies around the world. (para. 1)

All educational institutions across the world operate in the context of globalization, influencing what and how faculty teach and students learn. The process of global learning is not globalization. Globalization presents people and the planet with diverse challenges and opportunities to secure well-being; global learning assembles diverse perspectives to understand and address these challenges and opportunities. If globalization influences your life, your field of study, or the content of your course or student engagement activities, then this book will help you respond through the process of global learning.

When it comes right down to it, the creation of our own institution was a response to globalization. FIU was founded to address the issues faced by a rapidly growing and globalizing Miami in the mid-to-late 1960s and early 1970s. Having introduced you to our unique definition of *global learning*, we now switch gears and introduce you to the unique story of FIU to acquaint you with the context that gave rise to our commitment to universal global learning. We follow up with a broad outline of FIU's Global Learning for Global Citizenship initiative and conclude with a summary of the chapters.

About FIU

FIU opened its doors on September 19, 1972, to 5,667 upper-division juniors or seniors and graduate students, the largest opening enrollment in U.S. collegiate history. Charles Perry, at only 32, was the youngest university president ever selected in Florida and the youngest public university president in the United States. Only three years earlier, Perry gazed at what was then a sea of grass and envisioned a new kind of university emerging for new Americans living and working in an emergent global city. Although lacking old traditions, FIU was also be unshackled by them. "At FIU, we intend to make the most of newness by seeking out new ways to serve the community, the state, the nation, and yes, even the world" (Perry, 1973, pp. 9–10). Perry's vision was for a nontraditional institution that would take bold, experimental steps to achieve three founding goals:

1. Education of students—To provide a university education for qualified students that (a) prepares them for useful careers in education, social service, business, industry, and the professions; (b) furnishes them with the opportunity to become effective members of the society; and (c) offers them an appreciation of their relation to their cultural, aesthetic, and technological environments.
2. Service to the community—To serve the greater community, with a primary emphasis on serving the Greater Miami and South Florida area, in a manner which enhances the metropolitan area's capability to meet the ecological, cultural, social, and urban challenges which it faces.
3. Greater international understanding—To become a major international education center with a primary emphasis on creating greater mutual understanding among the Americas and throughout the world.

Perry insisted that FIU adapt its organizational structures to meet the needs of its students who were then, as now, highly diverse and historically underserved. He commissioned a sculpture, *The Four Races,* for the entrance of Primera Casa, FIU's first building, to serve as "a constant—and dramatic—reminder that Florida International serves all people—rich or poor, male or female, young or old—of all races" (Perry, 1972, p. 2). Perry also recruited and hired demographically diverse faculty members who possessed an inter-disciplinary, student-focused outlook:

> Faculty members at Florida International must be willing to and, hopefully, have demonstrated their abilities to work across disciplinary boundaries in dealing with issues central to the environmental, urban, and international missions of the University. Faculty members should also have a strong student orientation and an accompanying desire to enter into a composite learning-teaching-research experience. In short, the faculty will be challenged to be experimental, and to respond to the structure and mission of the University with an openness and awareness of its innovative nature. (FIU, 1970, pp. 47–48)

The term *global* was not fashionable during the late 1960s and early 1970s, but Perry's leadership perspective was distinctly so. He sought faculty who demonstrated "an attitude, a tone, a feeling, an understanding and a willingness to look at education beyond the traditional borders of the United States or Western Europe" and a personal "desire to be truly concerned about the problems of the world—not just the problems of this region, of this State, of this nation" (Perry, 1972, p. 7). Perry wanted to imbue the same perspective in students without making them leave home to acquire it. Prior to FIU's opening, Dade County high school graduates had to either leave South Florida or pay private school tuition at the University of Miami to receive a bachelor's degree. This challenge was overcome the day FIU opened its doors. As an urban public institution, FIU was charged with preparing students for life and work in the local community, so the university's master plan stipulated that every undergraduate must have work experience as part of his or her major program of study. Because international was FIU's middle name, the plan also called for every student "to have a formal international educational experience during [his or her] university career, if not by study involvement in another country, then in curriculum offerings, courses, or seminars on international affairs and understanding" (FIU, 1970, p. 51).

Although the work experience requirement was later dropped, FIU remained committed to preparing students for their personal and professional lives beyond graduation through student internships. The institution also maintained its commitment to provide internationalized learning experiences to all students, but there were roadblocks to fulfilling this pledge from the very start. The biggest problem concerned feasibility; internationalized learning wasn't built into programs of study, and students were simply encouraged to find and pursue opportunities that appealed to them. Also, faculty were not required to infuse international,

intercultural, or global perspectives into their courses. FIU's early oppor-
tunistic approach to internationalize learning for all resulted in participation of the very few. According to Thomas Breslin (1984), former associate
dean of FIU's International Affairs Center (IAC), "An initial survey in fall
1977 showed that only thirteen of the university's 120 degree programs had
an international or comparative requirement" (p. 145). The fact that the
university's main sources of students, Miami-Dade Community College
and Dade County Public Schools, had few if any programs with an international component was also a problem for FIU. Breslin bemoaned that
international offerings were frequently canceled due to lack of interest. He
also attributed anemic enrollment to FIU's demographic profile: The average student at the time was 28 and female and found it hard to travel or
take courses that didn't lead directly to a degree or certificate. By the early
1980s the IAC stopped addressing curricula and focused on other internationalization efforts, such as supporting faculty research and instruction
abroad.

The IAC continued to encourage degree programs that offered internationalized learning opportunities, but these withered on the vine because
"a clientele had to be developed" (Breslin, 1984, p. 145). To address the
problem, the IAC began a long-term collaboration in 1979 with the late Jan
Tucker in the School of Education to support global education in the K–12
pipeline through the Global Awareness Program (GAP). The hope was that
the GAP would encourage future FIU students to pursue international learning when they matriculated. In a remark foreshadowing the development
of universal global learning at FIU, Breslin (1984) reflected that if the university could find a way to permeate the curriculum with internationalized
learning experiences at home, it would "indeed have become Florida's center
for international education" (p. 146).

Fast Forward: Global Learning for Global Citizenship

Global learning and global citizenship are in FIU's DNA. Our stakeholders have always been acutely aware of the connection between the local and
the global and our institution's responsibility to bridge that connection.
Administrators, faculty, staff, students, alumni, and community members
alike agree that for students and citizens to understand and address local
issues, they must grasp that our locality is part of the wider world and that
our community is influenced by international, intercultural, and global
dynamics. Likewise, students and citizens become curious about the rest of
the world when they recognize that events elsewhere affect their local quality of life. It's part of our job as researchers and educators to help others

understand that their work and well-being are positioned at the intersection of the local and global; global learning is the process that enables this realization and prepares students to fulfill their roles and responsibilities as local and global citizens.

Because FIU is situated in South Florida, a global crossroads, we're particularly sensitive to our responsibility to facilitate global learning. The evidence of our local–global interconnectedness surrounds us daily. It's evident in our accents, architecture, and art, as well as our news, social networks, and neighborhoods. But neither our name nor our geography nor our demographics make us special in terms of our responsibility to provide universal global learning. All institutions of higher education in all communities operate at the intersection of local and global; although those in other types of institutions in other localities may find it more challenging to detect and analyze relationships with far-flung communities, these relationships exist nonetheless, and we bear a collective responsibility to understand them and to share this understanding with others. This is why we advocate for universal global learning and why we've worked to develop a replicable model for making this vision a reality.

Today FIU is still Miami's first and only public research university. Our colleges and schools offer nearly 200 bachelor's, master's, and doctoral programs in fields ranging from anthropology and accounting to hospitality, landscape architecture, law, medicine, social work, and theater. We currently serve more than 41,000 undergraduate; 8,700 graduate; and 6,000 non-degree-seeking students, making us one of the 10 largest higher education institutions in the country. As of fall 2017, our undergraduate demographics mirror those of our locality: About 64% of students are Hispanic, 13% Black or African American, 10% White, non-Hispanic, 7% international, 3% Asian, and 3% two or more races. The typical FIU undergraduate is a first- or second-generation American citizen and a first-generation college student living at home and juggling a full course load and a full-time job. About 58% of undergraduates fund their education through Pell Grants. Regardless of race, ethnicity, or socioeconomic status, every one of our undergraduates participates in multiple global learning experiences throughout his or her educational career through our Global Learning for Global Citizenship intiative.

From the student's point of view, the heart of Global Learning for Global Citizenship is a requirement to take at least two global learning courses and participate in integrative global learning cocurricular activities prior to graduation. Global learning courses and activities engage students in collaborative analysis and problem-solving and are aimed at developing three graduation-level SLOs:

1. Global awareness, knowledge of the interrelatedness of local, global, international, and intercultural issues, trends, and systems
2. Global perspective, the ability to construct a multiperspective analysis of local, global, international, and intercultural problems
3. Global engagement, the willingness to engage in local, global, international, and intercultural problem-solving

Students currently choose from about 200 global learning courses located in every undergraduate-serving academic department and embedded in every degree program of study. Global learning courses are offered in multiple modalities—on campus, online, hybrid or blended learning, and abroad—and come in two types, foundations and discipline specific. Foundations courses are first- or second-year courses open to all majors, and most of them also count toward general education requirements. Discipline-specific courses are upper-division courses that may or may not have prerequisites or be open to any major. Some departments housing multiple global learning courses, such as African and African diaspora studies and communication arts, group them into certificates and minors designated as global learning.

Global learning cocurricular activities serve all students, whether they live on campus, commute, or pursue a campus-based or completely online degree. Students can drop in for weekly face-to-face or online discussion series, volunteering opportunities, and international coffee hours; immerse themselves in internships or in the Global Living Learning Community; or join student-led clubs and organizations such as GlobeMed, which pairs college chapters with grassroots community organizations in developing countries to design and implement health improvement projects, and Alternative Breaks, which enables students to explore a social justice issue through hands-on service-learning trips supplemented by education and reflection. Students can also elect to go beyond minimum graduation requirements by pursuing FIU's Global Learning Medallion or the nationally recognized Peace Corps Prep certificate. Students in all majors can earn these graduation honors by taking additional global learning courses, accruing a certain number of cocurricular activity points, and completing capstone projects, eportfolios, and reflections.

From an administrative perspective, Global Learning for Global Citizenship began as our university's Quality Enhancement Plan (QEP), which is required by the Southern Association of Colleges and Schools Commission on Colleges (SACSCOC, 2012) as a condition of reaffirmation of reaccreditation. Although FIU administrators had made attempts over the years to internationalize the university's curricula, the QEP provided a high-stakes opportunity to realize that commitment. As a condition of approval, FIU (2010) had to demonstrate that its QEP had emerged from institutional assessment and a broad-based process of identifying a key issue that was aligned with the institution's mission and that addressed student learning. The institution also had to demonstrate that it had "sufficient resources to initiate, implement, sustain, and complete the QEP" (SACSCOC, 2012, p. 1), that the plan's development and implementation would involve a wide range of stakeholders, and that it included program goals and strategies to evaluate their achievement. The QEP's requirements, coupled with the oversight of our accrediting agency, provided the structure and pressure FIU needed to achieve its bold vision of universal global learning. The QEP's development was initiated in 2007 by a university-wide steering committee and was taken up in 2008 by the Office of Global Learning Initiatives (OGLI), founded and led by Hilary Landorf and Stephanie Doscher. The OGLI is charged with leading and coordinating the administration of the many moving parts of Global Learning for Global Citizenship.

As we explore our model for making global learning universal, we provide many tangible examples of how we've achieved it at FIU. We've worked hard to design and describe the model to make it replicable through customization. The model is meant to help you translate, not transfer, our initiative to your unique context. Although some of our examples may indeed work well at your institution, we encourage you to resist direct reproduction. Jack Ma, founder of the Chinese e-commerce conglomerate Alibaba, once cautioned that to innovate "you should learn from your competitor, but never copy. Copy and you die" (Kolesnikov-Jessop, 2007, para. 8). We aren't competitors, we're colleagues, but the same holds true in this case. Make this model your own. Use it to map your own journey toward universal global learning.

Organization of Chapters

The book's chapters are divided into three parts: Setting the Stage for Making Global Learning Universal; What Global Learning Looks Like: Mutually Reinforcing Activities; and Sustaining and Expanding Global Learning. Our model's elements are woven throughout the chapters, and many of the chapters also address essential questions we've grappled with during the development, design, and implementation stages of our initiative. You can use these questions to engage your stakeholders in the process of customization.

Part One: Setting the Stage for Making Global Learning Universal

This part's first two chapters define foundational terms, concepts, and theories. Chapter 1, "Defining *Global Learning*," takes you through the early days of the development of our QEP. It recounts how our stakeholders moved from wanting to internationalize the curriculum to committing to educating all students for global citizenship. We tell the origin story of the term *global learning* and examine the three central attributes of our definition: engagement with diversity, collaboration, and problems that transcend borders. Finally, we delve into the research and meaning behind FIU's three graduation-level global learning outcomes: global awareness, global perspective, and global engagement.

In chapter 2, "Universal Global Learning, Diversity, and the Practice of Inclusive Excellence," we argue that universal global learning makes student diversity essential to achieving higher education's mission of transmitting and producing new knowledge. What's more, universal global learning promotes a pattern of inclusion that supports all students' success as learners and citizens. In this chapter we lay out three conditions that characterize inclusive excellence and take a deep dive into three different ways of thinking about diversity in higher education: demographics, curriculum, and cognition. All three conceptualizations interconnect and pertain to the process of global learning, but they have differential impacts on the extent to which leaders can guide their institutions toward inclusive excellence.

Organizational leadership is the focus of chapter 3, "Making Global Learning Universal Through Collective Impact." Here we address the first component of our model, a theory of organizational change. Originally developed to enable a diverse set of community stakeholders to coordinate distinct yet interconnected efforts to solve complex social problems, collective impact (Kania & Kramer, 2011) can also be used to lead complex initiatives in multifaceted organizations such as colleges and universities. We chose collective impact because it involves the same attributes as those of global learning: diversity, collaboration, and complex problem-solving. We continue to use it because its five conditions address virtually all aspects of program leadership and administration, from planning and implementation to evaluation and improvement:

1. Common agenda, a shared vision for change
2. Backbone organization, a coordinating infrastructure with dedicated staff who plan, manage, and sustain the initiative
3. Mutually reinforcing activities, coordinated, differentiated activities as part of an overarching strategic plan
4. Shared measurement systems, a short list of common measurements of success and methods to analyze and report data
5. Continuous communication, methods to review formative and summative data and make incremental changes to increase success

In addition to providing a more detailed discussion of this theory of change, chapter 3 describes how we used the process of setting a common agenda for collective impact to fulfill the second component of our model: the development of universal global learning SLOs and program goals.

Chapter 4, titled "Resourcing Universal Global Learning," asks, What human, physical, information technology, and financial resources does your institution need to provide global learning for all, given your common agenda? We suggest methods for determining whether needed resources are already available and, if not, how you can acquire them. We take an in-depth look at human resources, providing some specific examples from FIU's OGLI, our initiative's backbone organization. With customization in mind, we offer different approaches to situating and structuring your backbone in the institution's broader organizational map. We also present the administrative and leadership functions your backbone will likely undertake and make specific recommendations regarding the knowledge, skills, and traits to look for when staffing a backbone organization for universal global learning.

Part Two: What Global Learning Looks Like

Part two addresses components of our model that mutually reinforce each other: professional development and integrative global learning in the curriculum and cocurriculum. We also describe how you can construct global learning pipeline programs with K–12 schools. Individually, professional development and curricular and cocurricular reform have a direct impact on universal global learning, and together they enhance their power to affect the common agenda.

Chapter 5, "Global Learning Professional Development," addresses three main questions: How do you get people to attend global learning professional development? What should global learning professional development entail? and How do you get participants to apply what they've learned? The chapter is grounded in research and enriched with specific examples from our experience supporting more than 1,500 faculty, staff, and graduate teaching assistants through coaching and more than 110 professional development events since 2009.

Chapter 6, "Global Learning Courses at Home and Abroad," presents five case studies of how faculty have used their professional development to infuse global learning into the curriculum and transform students' learning experiences. The cases cover face-to-face and online modalities and a range of disciplines: biology, health sciences, public administration, economics, and recreational therapy. Chapter 7, "Global Learning in the Cocurriculum," explores how activities outside the classroom intersect with classroom learning to promote integrative learning. We describe the ingredients that make up what we call *integrative global learning habitats*, or environments that provide students with prolonged global learning engagement. These habitats provide students with opportunities to make connections among their course work, cocurricular activities, personal lives, and the challenges they and others face in communities around the world.

Chapter 8, the final chapter in part two, "Global Learning in the K–12 Pipeline," addresses an important contribution to inclusive excellence. Begun in 1979, the groundbreaking GAP in Dade County Schools involved students in global learning before they entered our doors and laid the groundwork for Global Learning for Global Citizenship. Jan Tucker's work is carried on today through FIU's K–12 teacher preparation program and undergraduate student-initiated projects with K–12 students. This chapter describes these efforts and recommends principles for successful partnerships between K–12 schools and institutions of higher education.

Part Three: Sustaining and Expanding Global Learning

Chapters 9 and 10 are concerned with the remaining components of our model and of collective impact. We are convinced these components are critical to expanding the depth and breadth of your universal global initiative and to sustaining quality and impact over the short and long term. In chapter 9, "Student Learning Assessment and Program Evaluation," we describe how we see these two endeavors, often conducted by separate and unrelated institutional entities, as a shared measurement system. By this we mean that SLOs, which are statements that designate what students should "demonstrate, represent, or produce" as a result of an educational experience (Maki, 2010, p. 88), and program goals, which "establish criteria and standards against which you can determine program performance" (Centers for Disease Control, n.d.), should be completely interrelated. Your initiative's SLOs should drive the development of your program's goals, and your program goals should support all students' global learning and their achievement of global learning SLOs. Chapter 9 will help you determine when to collect and analyze student learning assessment and program evaluation data and how to choose data collection and analysis methods that will lead to effective shared measurement.

Chapter 10, the final chapter, "Continuous Communication and Improvement," addresses what to do with the data you collect. This is the step leaders often neglect or ignore entirely, rendering assessment and evaluation essentially meaningless and making it very difficult, if not impossible, to move the common agenda forward. We've endeavored to make this chapter as specific, practical, and feasible as possible, knowing that leaders sometimes lack energy or resources for this step. We offer concrete ideas for helping stakeholders exchange information across reporting lines in timely and engaging ways. You'll also take away from this chapter methods for enabling individuals and groups to reflect on results and use them to map more efficient and effective routes for providing high-quality global learning to all students.

Onward and Inward

As you proceed through the chapters of this book, please keep in mind that global learning is a process rooted in self-reflection and the acquisition of self-knowledge. As Dena Kaye (1981) once observed, "To travel is to take a journey into yourself" (p. 1). Whether *travel* is understood figuratively as seeing the world through another's perspective by walking in someone else's shoes or literally to mean walking through someone else's streets, global learning causes people to reinterpret their own lives and points of view in the context of others' perspectives and realities. Self-awareness is a stage in all humans' developmental journey and is also the foundation for global awareness, perspective, and engagement. We invite you to join us in mapping the terrain of universal global learning and helping students, faculty, and staff navigate their paths toward this destination.

PART ONE

SETTING THE STAGE FOR MAKING GLOBAL LEARNING UNIVERSAL

I

DEFINING *GLOBAL LEARNING*

A single word can have multiple meanings. It can also have different meanings for different people. In contrast, people can use different words to mean the same things. One's choice of words, then, is meaningful. As educational researchers, we understand the need to use precise terms and provide operational definitions to enhance validity and avoid confusion. But as educational leaders, we are sensitive to the transformative potential of allowing others to construct meaning for themselves. Discourse on the meaning of words and concepts can promote self-reflection and autonomous thinking (Mezirow, 1990, 1997). This process can also bring about transformative learning, a reevaluation of one's assumptions and actions, leading to new ways of being and doing in the world (Mezirow, 1990).

In this chapter, we offer a research-based definition for the term *global learning*. We also describe how an institution-wide discussion about its meaning was transformative for our university and our students. We contend that by using a similar process, your institution can experience these outcomes as well. But in the interest of full disclosure, although universal global learning is where we ended up, this wasn't our goal at the outset. For us, the transformation began with a paradigm shift—a transition from thinking about internationalizing our curriculum to educating our students for global citizenship. During the early stages of our discussions, we grappled with the following challenging questions:

- What is the difference between internationalization and global learning? Which of these makes sense for our institution?
- What is a global citizen? What is the relationship between global learning and global citizenship?

23

- Should all universities engage students in global learning? Should all students engage in global learning?

Feeling uncertain about the answers to these questions? At the beginning of our transformation process at FIU, we were uncertain too. As you read through this chapter and learn how our thinking evolved, we encourage you to periodically reflect on the development of your own answers to these questions. Consider how your beliefs, values, and assumptions about *global learning* may overlap or conflict with the definition we provide. Think about the ways different definitions of *global learning* may influence choices about what, how, and whom we teach. Think also about how these choices influence what, how, and with whom students learn. At the end of the chapter, we ask you to reflect on whether our process of defining *global learning* has led to a paradigm shift for you as it did for us.

Putting the *I* Back in FIU

For FIU the road to universal global learning began in late 2007 when the university set out to significantly enhance the quality and relevance of the education it provided to undergraduate students. Campus leadership resolved to accomplish this goal through an initiative to reinvigorate the international aspects of the university's curricula and cocurricula. A steering committee was formed to develop a vision for the project and initially dubbed Internationalizing the International University (FIU, 2010). Many of the committee members thought it would take only a little tinkering at the margins to put the *I* back in FIU. How much reform would be necessary for a university with international as its middle name?

Institutional research indicated that it might take more change than the committee members originally anticipated. A branding study conducted during the spring and summer of 2008 revealed that when stakeholders used the word *international* to describe FIU, they were primarily referring to campus demographics. Coded responses to an open-ended essay question revealed that large proportions of faculty, staff, board members, and students thought that our middle name referred to our campus diversity. Few respondents thought it also described FIU's teaching and learning activities, such as programs with an international or global base, diverse and multicultural experiences, or preparation for the global marketplace (see Table 1.1).

Observing that internationalization required the assistance of full-time personnel, the provost hired Hilary Landorf and Stephanie Doscher in August

TABLE 1.1

Perceptions of the Term *International* as It Relates to FIU

When Thinking About FIU, What Does the Term International Mean to You?	Faculty, Staff, and Board Members	Students
Refers to the diverse and multicultural campus population	56%	69%
Global or worldwide perspective or emphasis	10%	9%
A specific country or region	6%	4%
Programs have an international or global base	8%	3%
Culturally aware, embracing of, open to other cultures	6%	3%
Don't know, no answer	4%	3%
Study abroad, global opportunities	4%	3%
Language or multilingual	<1%	2%
Refers to the locations of the university	10%	2%
A detraction from what we really are, not true	5%	2%
Connected abroad, globally	<1%	2%
Diverse or multicultural experience	<1%	2%
Prepares students for the global marketplace	4%	2%
Attracts foreign students, marketing terms	3%	2%
Research is conducted in other countries	3%	<1%

Note. From FIU (2010).

2008 to guide the committee's work and create an administrative structure to carry out the group's recommendations. One of our first tasks was to conduct a review of undergraduate degree self-study reports to determine the extent of internationalization in academic program design. We found that although all programs touted one or more accomplishment related to international teaching, research, or service, only 30% reported an internationalized SLO, a statement that designated what students should "demonstrate, represent, or produce" as a result of an internationalized educational experience (Maki, 2010, p. 88). Assessment of internationalized SLOs was also conspicuously absent. We concluded that programs were experiencing an internationalization gap, that is, a disparity between the importance placed on internationalization and the level of its implementation, particularly in the curriculum.

Given the inconsistent ways committee members, board members, faculty, staff, and students used the terms *international* and *internationalization* to describe FIU, we assumed these stakeholders might also disagree on how the university should live up to the promise of its middle name. After we presented the committee with definitions other universities used for *internationalization* (Hudzik, 2011; Knight, 2003, 2004) and how they had approached the goal of internationalizing their campuses, members suggested that FIU just do something that seemed feasible, such as introduce a new diversity awareness or intercultural communication course into the general education curriculum. We responded that although this top-down approach seemed practical and expedient, it probably wouldn't be effective. An internationalization plan would stand little chance of enhancing student learning if it lacked support from those who were supposed to implement it and those who were supposed to benefit from it. Before the steering committee could develop a vision for change, it needed to know what stakeholders really wanted in terms of an internationalized FIU education. Did they want the institution to maintain or increase student diversity? If so, what was meant by the term *diversity?* International students? Domestic historically underserved students? Perhaps stakeholders wanted FIU to focus instead on internationalizing its academic programs. If this was the case, did they want more students to participate in study abroad programs, or were they looking for more on-campus opportunities such as area studies degrees or internationally themed cocurricular activities? The committee wasn't even sure of the best way to gather information from our thousands of faculty, staff, students, alumni, and community members. A survey? A town hall meeting?

The committee boldly determined to lead a long-term, broad-based, multimethod investigation into what the university community really wanted to accomplish through internationalization. What impacts did stakeholders envision for FIU students, the institution, the nation, and the world at large? The investigation began with some self-examination. In a review of steering committee meeting minutes, we discovered that members were using the word global to describe an FIU education much more than they were using international. This prompted us to wonder: Did the term *internationalization* accurately describe the committee's mission and vision? If the committee could not identify and use the right language, how could it effectively facilitate the creation and implementation of a new plan for the institution? Successful strategic plans for change are grounded in a strong collective rationale. As Morrill (2013) argued,

Institutions and their major units need above all to define a compelling sense of purpose that authentically reflects their narratives of identity and core capabilities, and that translates into an ambitious agenda for action. The work of strategy is always about integrating the powerful intrinsic values and motivation that come from a strong sense of educational purpose with the need to gain advantage in a competitive and precarious world of limited resources. (p. 12)

Although international was part of our birth name, and greater international understanding was one of our founding goals, did that word fully express our current sense of identity? Even FIU's founding president, Charles Perry, used rhetoric that revealed a distinctly global orientation:

We realize that solutions to the problems of pollution, urbanization, and population growth which beset us can only be approached by a consciousness of their relation to the global human environment. It is this consciousness which led to the commitment of Florida International University not only to the traditions of higher education, but also to innovation in response to the changing needs of the citizens of the world. (FIU Interama Campus Planning Office, 1974, p. 1).

The steering committee endorsed the launch of a university-wide dialogue exploring which term faculty, students, staff, alumni, and community members thought better described an FIU education—*international* or *global*—and what meanings stakeholders ascribed to these terms. The goal was to arrive at overlapping consensus concerning the initiative's purpose, goals, SLOs, and actions to be implemented—a condition reached when stakeholders agree on fundamental elements, although perhaps for slightly different reasons (Rawls, 1987). Chapter 3 provides detailed descriptions of the consensus-building methods we used, but here we describe the change in perspective that resulted from this dialogue.

From Internationalizing the Curriculum to Global Learning for Global Citizenship

Through nearly 18 months of discussion, we found that stakeholders wanted FIU to capitalize on its demographic diversity to enhance teaching and learning inside and outside the classroom. FIU is located in Miami, a global crossroads, and the U.S. city with the largest proportion of foreign-born residents (Florida, 2015). The majority of our students come from south Florida, and most of our alumni spend their working lives in the region. Significant numbers of FIU students are undocumented or hold dual citizenship. Many identify themselves as multiethnic, biracial, or multilingual. It isn't uncommon to hear first-generation students talk about returning to their country of birth for the first time as young adults on service-learning trips or choosing to study heritage languages that had been ignored at home or disavowed in public. With all this in mind, administrators, faculty, students, and alumni all agreed they wanted FIU to help students make sense of their complex identities rather than emphasize assimilation. In addition, they wanted students to be able to discern the many implications that identity and perspective hold for personal, professional, and civic decision- making. Students in particular talked about developing a global consciousness, an understanding that well-being transcends geographic borders. In the words of one undergraduate,

> We're taking a global perspective here. That means that everybody will have to be concerned with everyone else's welfare as far as the environment is concern[ed], not necessarily the US having their own environmental issues and say Africa having their own environmental issues and Asia having their own environmental issues, but instead saying that if South America is having a problem, everybody is having a problem. And so that's where the global aspect comes in. (Landorf & Doscher, 2013b, p. 167)

Stakeholders repeatedly expressed a desire for FIU students to think of themselves as cosmopolitans or citizens of the world. Originating in classical Greece, the concept of global citizenship has taken on new relevance in the context of globalization (Appiah, 2006a). Unlike national citizenship, which is a legal status, global citizenship is a disposition that prompts individuals to assume rights and responsibilities not necessarily conferred by birth or naturalization (Steenburgen, 1994). According to Nussbaum (2004), global citizenship is developed through education, and

> cultivating our humanity in a complex interlocking world involves understanding the ways in which common needs and aims are differently realized in different circumstances. This requires a great deal of knowledge that American college students rarely got in previous eras. . . . We must become more curious and more humble about our role in the world, and we will do this only if undergraduate education is reformed in this direction. (p. 45)

Global citizens have a complex sense of affiliation that causes them to see their own well-being and that of others as interdependent. Understanding that humanity and the natural world are deeply interconnected, global citizens accept shared responsibility for solving problems that may only affect them indirectly (Falk, 1994; Hanvey, 1975). In essence, global citizens view themselves as change agents (Sen, 1999). They are active rather than passive inhabitants of the global community.

Participants in our various discussions broadly agreed on several key points that eventually became part of the bedrock of our initiative. First, they wanted students to study and analyze global problems as a significant component of their undergraduate education. Global problems were described as those that transcend borders of geography, culture, and discipline, that is, "socio-spatial distinctions between places, individuals, and groups" (Kolossov & Scott, 2013, p. 3). Second, stakeholders were firm in their conviction that students shouldn't stop at learning about global problems, nor should they wait until after they graduate to begin effecting change. FIU's culture should encourage students to find small and large ways to address global problems as undergraduates. There was also broad agreement that the university should not try to predetermine individual students' values or choices; rather, students should be presented with multiple paths of entry and ways forward as change agents throughout their undergraduate careers. Finally, stakeholders committed to making education for global citizenship—global learning—universal. All FIU students should be prepared for global citizenship as part of a quality twenty-first-century education. To accomplish these lofty goals, FIU needed to develop a much better understanding of the oft-used but ill-defined term *global learning*, namely, what it is, how it's accomplished, and the learning outcomes it should produce.

What Is Global Learning?

We started our exploration of the meaning of global learning with Hovland (2006), who identified the concept as the educational process by which students are prepared for citizenship in a diverse and interconnected world. Hovland differentiated global learning from "narrower efforts to 'internationalize' the curriculum" (p. 19), which generally focus on inputs and outputs such as the number of area studies or study abroad courses available or the number of international students enrolled in the institution. Alongside this publication, the AAC&U's Shared Futures: Global Learning and Social Responsibility initiative (2017c) was designed to help select institutions shift their focus from programmatic accomplishments toward SLOs. The AAC&U recommended colleges and universities should execute this change by implementing purposeful curricula that challenge students to reflect on the relationship between their identity and their sense of responsibility to address "large unsolved global problems" (Hovland, 2006, p. 19). What the Shared Futures initiative and its connected publications did not specify, however, were the unique attributes of such curricula, nor did it define the specific components of global learning as an educational process. We wanted to know just how global learning was supposed to work: What does it look like, and how is it different from other approaches to teaching and learning? To gain this guidance, we cast our gaze farther back in time and into the literature to the first usage of the term *global learning*, which began with the founding of the United Nations University (UNU).

The Origin of Global Learning

The UNU opened its doors in 1975 as an international network of research and teaching scholars engaged with "pressing global problems of human survival, development, and welfare" (Soedjatmoko & Newland, 1987; United Nations, n.d.-a). When Secretary General U Thant first proposed the creation of the UNU in 1969, the world was evolving rapidly in its understanding of global interdependence and its implications. People were becoming much more aware of the transnational sociocultural and political impacts of the arms race, nuclear proliferation, overpopulation, poverty, and environmental degradation. These impacts extended to the education sector as well. Leaders called for new modes of teaching and learning that would prepare youths to respond to increasingly complex, dynamic, and interconnected local and global challenges. To this day, the UNU operates without a campus, degree-seeking students, or a permanent faculty. Unlike a traditional brick-and-mortar university, the decentralized UNU was formed to tear down intellectual barriers by engaging students and scholars throughout the world in interdisciplinary, problem-centered studies and research (Soedjatmoko & Newland, 1987).

The UNU's 1981 annual report committed the institution to addressing global problems in the following areas:

- peace, security, conflict resolution, and global transformation
- the global economy
- hunger, poverty, resources, and the environment
- human and social development and co-existence of peoples, cultures, and social systems
- science and technology and their social and ethical implications (p. 14)

To achieve a multilayered understanding of these issues, UNU scholars were categorized according to analytical and methodological approaches rather than discipline. These approaches were grouped into three divisions: Development Research, Global Studies, and Global Learning (Soedjatmoko & Newland, 1987; United Nations, 1981, n.d.-b). The Global Learning

Division focused on defining the nature of global problems and determining learning processes that would initiate change by causing progressive solutions to develop, take hold, and spread (Ploman, 1986). The UNU's leadership contended that such learning would need to be social, in that it would involve learning with others, as well as integrative, meaning it would need to enable people to exchange and synthesize information by crossing borders of difference (Botkin, Elmandjra, & Malitza, 1979; Soedjatmoko, 1985). The Global Learning Division's name had a deliberate double meaning,

> meant to convey both the sense of learning as a global process that must include all levels of society, and the sense of learning to think globally, in the recognition that the world is a finite, closely interconnected, global system. (Soedjatmoko & Newland, 1987, p. 221)

We learned from this history that from inception, global learning's purpose has been to enable people to understand and determine solutions to global problems. To accomplish this, people's diverse perspectives are essential. Global problems transcend borders, so participation in global problem-solving must do so as well. Edward Ploman, an international communications researcher and the first vice-rector of the Global Learning Division, described the need for global learning as "the need to learn how to accept, understand, and profit from cultural diversity" (Ploman, 1986, p. xxiii). Diverse people and points of view are needed to prevent ethnocentric solutions to problems that have varied, differential impacts (Soedjatmoko & Newland, 1987, p. 216).

Global learning was also developed to produce new knowledge about the well-being of the global community, not to recapitulate old schema, beliefs, and biases. The process of global learning, according to Soedjatmoko and Newland (1987) was conceived as an "open system" that "includes self-generated knowledge acquired through experience or observation, interaction, sharing of information, experimentation, and feedback in addition to instruction" (p. 221). Furthermore, Ploman (1986) asserted that prejudice reduction would result from perspective exchange and the cross-fertilization of ideas presented by people of all ages and socioeconomic levels. New complex conceptions of the world and new progressive solutions to global problems would be developed if global learning enabled people to connect diverse ideas horizontally, "across disciplines and professions . . . cultures, societies, and ideologies," and vertically, "across local, national, regional, and international levels" (Ploman, 1986, p. xix).

Definition of Global Learning

Imagine our surprise when we read this rich history of global learning, only to hear the voices of FIU's current faculty, staff, and students echoed in the words of its pioneers. Imagine our double surprise when we discovered an even deeper connection to global learning and to the UNU: The guest of honor at FIU's groundbreaking on January 25, 1971, was none other than United Nations Secretary General U Thant (see Figure 1.1).

Taking a cue from our own stakeholders and the history of the term, we at FIU define *global learning* as "the process of diverse people collaboratively analyzing and addressing complex problems that transcend borders" (Landorf & Doscher, 2015, p. 24). Global learning develops the knowledge, skills, and attitudes individuals need to become global citizens and engage in global problem-solving. Global learning strategies prompt groups of people to determine relationships among their diverse perspectives on problems and to formulate equitable, sustainable solutions for the world's interconnected human and natural communities.

Global learning isn't about the inputs and outputs traditionally associated with internationalization. Global learning is a process that prepares students for active global citizenship by involving them in collaborative global problem-solving as a central part of the college experience. Universality, or inclusion of the diverse perspectives and participation of all students, expands the efficacy of global learning. When global learning is limited to some, it limits the effectiveness of global problem-solving for everyone. Ploman (1986) stated this in concrete, measurable terms: Global learning must "foster participation in the learning and information sharing process, at all social levels, and at all ages" (p. xxii) because it is "the aggregate of individual decisions" (p. xxiii) that determine the success or failure of solutions to global problems.

Our goal in defining *global learning* is also to determine the essential attributes of the process of global learning. A number of contemporary researchers have explored the kinds of learning practices that promote the knowledge, skills, and attitudes of global citizenship (Bourn, 2014; Braskamp & Engberg, 2011; Gadsby & Bullivant, 2010; Gibson, Rimmington, & Landwehr-Brown, 2008; Hartmeyer, 2008). Their findings point to three practices in particular: engagement with diversity, collaborative learning, and a focus on complex problems that transcend borders. These characteristics define FIU's global learning courses and activities. In part two of this book, we provide examples of how these characteristics can be applied through multiple learning modalities inside and outside the classroom. For now, however, we elaborate on the meaning of these characteristics and the key roles they play in fostering global learning.

Figure 1.1. FIU groundbreaking.

Note. Attending the FIU groundbreaking ceremony were, from left to right, Ruben Askew, Florida governor; U Thant, United Nations secretary-general; Charles Perry, FIU president; and D. Burke Kibler III, chairman of the Florida Board of Regents. Photo courtesy of Special Collections and University Archives, Green Library, Florida International University.

Engagement With Diversity

Although the presence of a diverse student body may be a valuable source of diverse perspectives, diversity alone is not a sufficient condition for facilitating global learning. Global learning involves students' experience with, rather than their exposure to, difference. Engagement with diversity requires long-term, sustained participation in pedagogies of difference that involve individual and group reflection on pluralism (Chickering & Braskamp, 2009). Such pedagogies involve content generated from diverse disciplinary, theoretical, and sociocultural perspectives, and opportunities for intensive dialogue about this content among students with different backgrounds, beliefs, and cognitive attributes. This combination compels students to recognize the limits of a single approach to analyzing or addressing complex problems (Braskamp & Engberg, 2011; Gurin, Dey, Hurtado, & Gurin, 2002). Chapter 2 takes a much closer look at the meaning of diversity and the critical role it plays in effecting universal global learning and, in turn, inclusive excellence.

Collaborative Learning

Rooted in the idea that learning is social and that new knowledge is constructed through information exchange and discourse, collaborative learning encourages students to bring their diversity to the classroom for the benefit of others, particularly when challenged with complex tasks or questions (Barkely, Cross, & Howell Major, 2005; Bruffee, 1998; Gerlach, 1994; Smith & MacGregor, 1992). Whereas cooperative learning maintains the traditional structure of the classroom and is aimed at coordinating individual efforts to implement a predetermined solution, collaborative learning is largely unstructured and encourages critical reflection on knowledge and new ideas (Bruffee, 1995).

Collaborative learning for global problem-solving is guided by research-based principles. It begins with an examination of one's own beliefs, values, and assumptions, known as perspective consciousness, which is prompted by the cultural contrast or culture shock that often accompanies engagement with diversity (Hanvey, 1975). Such contrasts can be felt even when individuals remain immersed in their home or typical cultural context by applying pedagogies of difference or the use of long-distance communication technologies (Gibson et al., 2008). Allport's (1954) contact hypothesis provides direction concerning how to advance collaboration and reduce prejudicial, stereotyping, and discriminatory responses to cultural contrast (Pettigrew, 1998; Pettigrew & Tropp, 2006). Following Allport's lead, global learning courses and activities should present students with substantive, authentic global problems to explore—problems that affect all students but in different ways and require the varied expertise and perspectives of all participants. This promotes equal status and a level playing field, because complex problems such as these cannot be addressed by any single individual, perspective, or approach. Moreover, the entire institution should endorse collaborative global problem-solving to normalize engagement with diversity as part of the campus culture. Faculty and staff play a critical facilitating role in collaboration by helping groups reconcile differences in language, customs, behaviors, perspectives, and thinking patterns.

Complex Problems That Transcend Borders

If students are expected to graduate with the ability to collaboratively analyze and address complex, open-ended global problems such as climate change, poverty, population growth, and terrorism, then they must be tasked with doing so during their college experience. In school students are traditionally taught to draw boundaries around problems to better allow analysis and evaluation using discrete, linear processes (Downey et al., 2006). Global learning requires a shift away from a narrow focus on subject matter, "forged over a century ago, in an era that placed high value on broad understanding, reasoning, and abstract analysis" (AAC&U, 2007, p. 21). As a process, global learning's focus is the collaborative exploration of complex problems that defy neat categorization by discipline, culture, or geography. Because categorization curtails people's ability to contemplate complexity, global learning pedagogies must enable boundary breaking and enhance transdisciplinary understanding. Such pedagogies include mapping definitions of problems from differing sociocultural, spatial, and theoretical perspectives; ascertaining power relationships among alternative definitions of problems; and adapting understandings of problems to accommodate multiple perspectives and definitions (Downey et al., 2006). These methods open up students to a more holistic view of the causes of global problems and help them detect the equity and sustainability implications of potential solutions. More fundamentally, collaborative exploration of global problems with diverse others changes the relationship students have to their own education. Rather than seeing college as preparation for navigating and coping with the world's conditions in the future, students begin to see themselves as agents of change who can positively shape the present. This is the ultimate purpose of global learning for global citizenship.

Determining Global Learning Outcomes

In 2009 FIU changed the name of its Internationalizing the International University initiative to Global Learning for Global Citizenship to better match our stakeholders' vision. As part of the newly named initiative, all students are required to engage in multiple global learning experiences prior to graduation. Whether a student enters as a freshman with no credits; transfer, part-time, full-time, domestic, or international student; or low-income, first-generation, or historically underserved student, all FIU undergraduates participate in collaborative global problem-solving with diverse others throughout their undergraduate career. Faculty and staff also receive professional development to enable them to revise existing courses and activities and develop new ones to facilitate universal global learning.

Having developed an overlapping consensus to provide global learning to all, the steering committee was now faced with the challenge of delivering on that promise. A new global learning curriculum framework required each student to take at least two courses with a global learning designation and participate in integrated cocurricular activities prior to graduation (FIU, 2010). Global learning courses are vetted and approved through the Faculty Senate's standard curriculum review process, passing through committees at the department and college levels before advancing to the Global Learning

Curriculum Oversight Committee (GLCOC; FIU, 2010). The university needed to determine guidelines for global learning course approval, which mainly included common global learning SLOs.

SLOs describe the knowledge, skills, and dispositions students should develop as a result of having participated in specific learning experiences (Ewell, 2001). The steering committee again turned to stakeholders to find out what they thought global citizens should know, feel, and be able to do as a result of participating in global learning. As one might expect, faculty, staff, students, alumni, and community members valued a broad spectrum of SLOs, everything from tolerating difference and viewing the world from other perspectives to knowledge of current events, geography, and foreign languages. At the same time, a faculty learning community was convened to review the capacities researchers and employers valued in global citizens. Landorf and Doscher analyzed these results, along with those from stakeholders, to distinguish which outcomes FIU considered essential to global citizenship. The essential learning outcomes became our graduation-level SLOs. All FIU global learning courses and activities are designed to instill these capacities in all students.

Determining a common set of essential SLOs was perhaps the most difficult conversation at our institution. Faculty in departments who traditionally thought of themselves as owning international content, such as modern languages, political science, history, and geography, felt very strongly that the knowledge and skills associated with their fields were indispensable to global problem-solving. Faculty in the applied professions, for example, nursing, business, and engineering, held a slightly different view. Although these faculty members agreed that foundational world knowledge and communication skills are necessary, they felt these outcomes were not sufficient to enable collaborative global problem-solving. In their view, global learning should instill something beyond foundational capacities; rather, it should build applied critical thinking and cognitive flexibility (Spiro, Coulson, Feltovich, & Anderson, 1988). After comparing our stakeholders' responses to our definition of *global learning* and the results of our faculty learning community's literature review, FIU determined three essential graduation-level global learning SLOs for all its students: global awareness, global perspective, and global engagement.

Global Awareness

Complexity is the heart of this outcome, which we define as "knowledge of the interrelatedness of local, global, international, and intercultural issues, trends, and systems" (FIU, 2010, p. 54). The majority of stakeholders agreed with Nussbaum (2004) that global citizens can't solve problems on the basis of factual knowledge alone. Global citizens must understand prevailing world conditions and the interrelated dynamics that influence them so they can discern the multifaceted causes and effects of global problems. Adams and Carfagna (2006) likened global awareness to solving a connect-the-dot puzzle. They argued against focusing on individual facts or dots and instead attending to the space between them:

> As a society, we are flooded with information. It can be overwhelming, but it is critically important to find meaning. . . . Without understanding relationships and connections, we are forced only to react to isolated events. We can never make decisions or act in a way that anticipates or takes advantage of trends or events. We must each therefore develop the ability to connect the dots. (p. 2)

Contrary to what some might contend, global awareness is not the natural result of interaction with the Internet. Interconnected global knowledge networks expand our access to information about the world, but using these networks doesn't develop global awareness if students aren't able to connect what they learn from the Web with other media and their learning from their own and others' experiences. Global awareness requires students to be taught how to detect relationships among disparate, even conflicting, ideas, events, and disciplines. Students possessing global awareness should be able to articulate how various dynamics directly influence problems and how complex interactions among these dynamics lead to secondary effects and unintended consequences, locally and globally.

Global Perspective

First, let us clarify what we mean by *perspective*. When we use this term, we are not referring to customs and behaviors, the outward manifestations of perspective. We refer instead to people's "ordinarily unexamined assumptions, evaluations, explanations, conceptions of time, space, causality, etc." (Hanvey, 1975, p. 5). A person has to develop perspective consciousness—an understanding that he or she has a unique perspective not universally shared—before being able to understand that others have their own perspectives (Hanvey, 1975). This requires more than a passive intake of information through reading or lectures. Students achieve perspective consciousness through active questioning and reflection. To understand others' perspectives, students must attempt transpection, seeing "the world through the eyes of others" (Lumina Foundation, 2014, p. 17). Hanvey (1975) distinguished *transpection* from mere cultural knowledge, defining it as the ability to "put oneself . . . in the head of another person. . . . In transpection a person temporarily believes whatever the other person believes" (p. 12).

Individuals' ability to engage in transpection mediates the extent to which they can detect complexity. The world appears simple when viewed from a single point of view. In isolation, students may not be able to detect differences or inequalities resulting from problems they haven't experienced or studied. Students can form a global perspective when they exchange information with diverse others about how they and others perceive the world. FIU (2010) defines a *global perspective* as "the ability to conduct a multi-perspective analysis of local, global, international, and intercultural problems" (p. 54).

A global perspective involves the ability to discern the distinctive and common qualities between one's own viewpoint and those of others. This means that this learning outcome cannot be developed in isolation (Pascarella & Terenzini, 2005). Hanvey (1975) contended that a global perspective is formed through the interaction of diverse individual perspectives and is "determined by the specialized capacities, predispositions, and attitudes of the group's members" (p. 2). Global learning should prompt participants to move past opinion and delve into the deeper layers of perspective, looking for the ways hidden influences conflict or even intersect. When students are given opportunities to change their conception of the world based on these interconnections, they may begin to perceive a kind of unity in diversity. They may start to see how their own well-being is interdependent with that of others and that collective actions by diverse individuals are more effective in enhancing quality of life for all.

Global Engagement

The "willingness to engage in local, global, international, and intercultural problem solving" (FIU, 2010, p. 54) with diverse others, or as FIU calls it, global engagement, is the essential attitude that bridges the gap between one's global awareness and perspective and actual solution making (Landorf & Doscher, 2013b). It motivates the "action dimension" of global citizenship (Green, 2012, p. 2). Although not the equivalent of action, this attitude helps students organize and structure their responses to the world. As with any attitude, global engagement is composed of affective, behavioral, and cognitive components, all of which are shaped by experience (Eagly & Chaiken, 1993). This is why institutions can't afford to focus solely on knowledge and skill preparation for global citizenship; how can we know if global learning is having an impact on students' willingness to solve problems collaboratively if we don't give them opportunities to do so during their college career? Institutions require medical students to practice in real-world contexts before they graduate; why is it any different when preparing students to solve global problems like sea level rise, illiteracy, or poverty?

The process of global learning can lead students to a wide range of actions, from activism and volunteering to service-learning and even social entrepreneurship, that contribute to positive change in the problems they seek to solve. These efforts build students' self-confidence and self-efficacy as solution makers when faced with intractable global problems. Colleges and universities must help students "see themselves as not simply citizens of some local region or group, but also, and above all, as human beings bound to all other human beings by ties of recognition and concern" (Nussbaum, 2006, p. 389).

Defining *Global Learning*: Where Are You Now?

As promised, we're checking back in with you. What's the status of your thinking on the meaning of global learning? Reflecting on your responses to the questions we posed at the beginning of this chapter, what's changed? In light of our definition of *global learning*, how we differentiate it from internationalization and its relationship to the development of global citizens, what are your thoughts about the work you are already doing, or want to do, at your own institution? Perhaps, on one hand, you're feeling confident that some of your students are already experiencing global learning, and the task now is to take those strategies to scale. On the other hand, you may have just experienced a major paradigm shift and may be concerned about your ability to facilitate this shift for others. Let us assure you: No matter what you're feeling right now, you've come to the right place. The purpose of this book is to provide you with the tools you need to lead transformative organizational change. Whether you're feeling confident or concerned about your ability to implement universal global learning at your institution, our belief is that your knowledge of what global learning is and why it's important readies you to explore more deeply how to provide it to everyone. And so, in the next chapter, we fully address two questions we think we gave short shrift in this chapter: Should all universities engage students in global learning, and should all students engage in global learning? In chapter 2 we go beyond defining *global learning* to explore how it can enable institutions to reach one of the most challenging and important goals of higher education today: inclusive excellence.

2

UNIVERSAL GLOBAL LEARNING, DIVERSITY, AND THE PRACTICE OF INCLUSIVE EXCELLENCE

In all, we should be attuned especially to how decisions taken within and about institutional life advance or limit gains in the direction of what might be called democratic diversity, a pattern of inclusion that eliminates physical barriers, promotes human security, makes material conditions more equal, accords cultural regard, and is based on effectively equal civic membership. With artistry and rigor, we should aim at no less. (Katznelson, 2016, p. 191)

The goal of universal global learning is to produce and spread widely new knowledge and new solutions for complex global problems facing people and the planet. In this sense, universal global learning shares the same mission as higher education. But when global learning involves only some students, it limits global problem-solving for all. We contend, therefore, that all colleges and universities should engage all students in global learning. As the title of this book illustrates, we also believe that universal global learning serves another aspect of higher education's mission, which is the promotion of inclusive excellence for our increasingly diverse student populations.

What is *inclusive excellence*? We need to clarify what we mean by this term before we can discuss how universal global learning can lead to its fulfillment. Inclusive excellence is often described in very broad terms. For example, the AAC&U (n.d.) maintains that institutions make excellence inclusive when they "integrate diversity, equity, and educational quality efforts into their missions and institutional operations" (para. 1). Tienda (2013) depicts these efforts a bit more specifically as strategies and practices that "promote meaningful social and academic interactions among persons or groups who differ in their experiences, their views, and their traits" (p. 467). Many agree that inclusive excellence should result in educational equity "in which the nature of the cross-cultural experience of entering university does not particularly disadvantage particular students or particular categories of student" (Kalantzis & Cope, 2002, p. 30). We think it aids our discussion if we distill these descriptions into three necessary conditions for inclusive excellence. We assert that colleges and universities achieve inclusive excellence when the following occur:

1. Diverse students are brought to campus through equitable admissions practices.
2. All students are equally unhindered in their path toward quality educational opportunities and graduation.
3. Students' diversity is made indispensable to the achievement of the institution's mission to transmit and produce new knowledge.

In the discourse on inclusive excellence, diversity, equity, and quality are treated as closely related, but in practice, institutions generally address them in isolation. Clayton-Pederson and Caryn McTighe Musil bemoaned this fact in the following:

> Although we know meaningful engagement with diversity benefits students educationally, little has been done to create a comprehensive framework for excellence that incorporates diversity at its core. . . . And diversity is not typically a focus at any level in "quality improvement" efforts. As a result, education leaders routinely work on diversity initiatives in one committee on campus and work on strengthening the quality of the educational experience within another. This disconnect serves students—and all of education—poorly. (as cited in Milem, Chang, & Antonio, 2005, p. vii)

Twelve years later, the disconnect remains. We still hear clarion calls for a new framework that would hasten "broad-scale systemic innovation to advance educational practices that engage diversity and challenge inequities in order to make excellence inclusive" (McNair, 2016, p. 4). We maintain that universal global learning can be this framework. For educational leaders used to thinking about inclusive excellence solely in terms of supports aimed at historically underserved students, the connection to universal global learning may seem a stretch. We think we can bridge the gap if we take a deeper look at the element that universal global learning and inclusive excellence have in common—diversity.

We know we've been spending a lot of time defining terms, but clear definitions are important to advancing a shared vision for change toward which an array of individuals and groups may contribute. Therefore, in this chapter, we focus on the following questions:

- What does diversity mean in the context of higher education? What implications do different conceptualizations of diversity hold for students, educators, and society at large?
- What is the relationship between the different conceptualizations of diversity and how *inclusive excellence* is defined and measured?
- How can diversity enable educators to promote inclusive excellence through universal global learning?

A solid body of empirical evidence associates diversity with a wide range of civic and critical thinking outcomes indicative of quality higher education (Gurin, Dey, Hurtado, & Gurin, 2002). We won't review that literature here. Instead, we'll take you through three different ways of conceptualizing diversity, as demography, as curriculum, and as a cognitive tool set, and explore how each of these conceptualizations shapes how people may define and attempt to achieve *inclusive excellence*. You already know from chapter 1 that diversity is at the center of our definition of *global learning*. Our goal here is to describe how diversity, through universal global learning, can become an essential component of quality higher education and be used to promote a pattern of inclusion that supports all students' success as learners and citizens.

Diversity as Demography: Learning Among Others

When people talk about diversity in higher education they're usually referring to the student body's demographic composition, also known as the institution's structural diversity (Gurin, Dey, Gurin, & Hurtado, 2004; Pike & Kuh, 2006). Since the rise of the civil and equal rights movements of the 1960s, demographic diversity in the United States has primarily signified race and gender. In recent years, the nation has witnessed a steady increase in first-generation immigrants' share of the total population as well as efforts by other groups to achieve legal rights and social acceptance. In turn, Americans have become more sensitive to other categories of diversity, such as religion, ethnicity, socioeconomic status, sexual orientation, and gender identity. Regardless of the system used to categorize people, when *diversity* is defined in terms of demography, inclusive excellence consequently tends to become synonymous with representational parity in admission and graduation rates (Bauman et al., 2005; Clayton-Pederson, 2009; Haring-Smith, 2012).

Although colleges and universities, legislatures, courts, and the public may disagree on the best way to achieve representational parity, they have a shared interest in doing so, and this interest is rooted in important shared values. One of these is social justice, or the desire to right higher education's exclusionary wrongs of the past (Kahlenberg, 2015). Another is the wish to preserve social unity by reducing discrimination and promoting tolerance in response to the nation's increasing diversification (Prewitt, 2001). Some are motivated to protect Americans' right to equal access to education, enshrined in multiple statutes: Title VI of the Civil Rights Act of 1964, Title IX of the Education Amendments of 1972, Section 504 of the Rehabilitation Act of 1973, Title II of the Americans with Disabilities Act of 1990, and the Age Discrimination Act of 1975. Equal educational access and success are also linked to the public's interest in economic vitality. The earnings gap between college and non-college-educated workers is greater than ever before, and, despite a steady increase in degree attainment rates for all demographic groups since the 1960s, Black and Hispanic students are still far less likely to graduate from college (Patten, 2016; Pew Research Center, 2016).

The relationship among demographic diversity, a college education, and various social and civic outcomes is complex and interconnected. It is widely agreed that higher education plays a critical role in nurturing "the habits of heart and mind that Americans need to make diversity work in daily life" by ensuring that students "experience engagement across difference as a value and a public good" (Schneider, 1995, p. xvi). Institutions need structural diversity to fulfill this role. Preparing students for twenty-first-century democratic engagement in the absence of demographic diversity has been compared to trying to teach people how to swim without water (Humphreys, 2003). Representative structural diversity is necessary to provide a quality college education that advances social justice, social unity, economic security, and engaged citizenship. It stands to reason, therefore, that institutions must admit, retain, and graduate a diverse student body to achieve inclusive excellence.

Does Structural Diversity Alone Lead to Inclusive Excellence?

With the United States projected to be a majority non-White nation by 2045, representational parity will remain an issue of concern in higher education for the foreseeable future (Espinosa, Gaertner, & Orfield, 2015). Leaders, however, will be challenged in their efforts to achieve all three conditions of inclusive excellence if they focus solely on demography. Although educators must take responsibility for closing access and achievement gaps, attention to parity alone prompts disaggregating data and compartmentalizing students' needs according to neat categories of difference, which are more often guided by an institution's geographic, political, historical, and cultural context than by a compelling educational rationale (Asmar, 2005). The diversity we perceive in our environment is partly contingent on the complexity of the systems we use to classify people (Blaine, 2013; Page, 2007). Although educators need to group students according to standard categories of difference to uncover and address institutionalized biases, doing so risks masking meaningful identity traits that cut across those categories and may strongly influence individual students' success. A person's sense of identity is influenced by a complex mix of "family and social environment, historical or socio-political constructs, personal experience, context, and many other immeasurable factors" (Compton, Bentley, Ennis, & Rastogi, 2013, p. xi). Practices that obscure or ignore aspects of individuals' identity, however unintentionally, may obstruct students' psychological, social, and academic development and their persistence to graduation (Campbell, 2010).

What's more, students themselves are less and less likely to see themselves fitting into the neat identity categories we use to classify them (Pew Research Center, 2015). Students with intersecting identities, especially those with multiple minority group affiliations, have unique experiences of the campus environment that may be rendered invisible by our efforts to portray them in terms of traditional descriptive statistics (Purdie-Vaughns & Eibach, 2008). Even the act of dichotomizing the needs and characteristics of domestic versus international students seems restrictive and invalid when short- and long-term immigration dynamics have "transformed local communities into global communities" (Asmar, 2005, p. 292). Educational leaders are clearly caught in a difficult struggle to "balance the need to distill an overwhelming amount of social information with the need to have an accurate picture of our social world and the people in it" (Blaine, 2013, p. 36). But at a time when colleges and universities are supposed to be adopting policies, procedures, and pedagogies that reach "all of us and the many selves and cultures within us" (Inayatullah, 2000, p. 232), neither equity nor quality is necessarily advanced when we adhere to the same reductionist habits of mind that produced categorical discrimination in the first place (Amodio, 2014; Ho, Roberts, & Gelman, 2015; Maddox, 2006).

Then there is the question of quantity: How much structural diversity is enough to advance the educational benefits it's supposed to confer? U.S. Supreme Court Justice Antonin Scalia famously pressed this question in oral arguments for *Grutter v. Bollinger* (2003). The University of Michigan asserted in this landmark case that institutions reach a critical mass of diversity when the multiple perspectives existing in minority groups are present on campus, and all students have opportunities to interact with those groups and perspectives. In response to this assertion, Scalia asked Michigan's counsel, Maureen E. Mahoney, whether minority diversity couldn't also be achieved by suppressing numbers of majority students. In the following,

Scalia challenged the logic behind setting affirmative action policies in the absence of specific ratios or quotas, ruled unconstitutional in the court's *Regents of the University of California v. Bakke* (1978) decision:

> MS. MAHONEY: Your Honor it is not a question of not too many. It's that the law school has attempted to take race into account in a very moderate limited fashion, no more than necessary to achieve the goal of trying to have sufficient numbers of minorities that there can be an excellent educational experience for everyone.
>
> JUSTICE SCALIA: But—but without a quota? Just sufficient numbers, but that's not a quota?
>
> MS. MAHONEY: Your Honor it is not a quota.
>
> JUSTICE SCALIA: When you say sufficient numbers, you're—I mean that suggests to me that there is—there is some minimum. Now, you don't name it. But there has to be some minimum. But you say there isn't a minimum?
>
> MS. MAHONEY: Your Honor there isn't a minimum.
>
> JUSTICE SCALIA: Well, then you have to eliminate the word sufficient. ("Transcript of Arguments in Grutter v. Bollinger," 2003, para. 212–217)

Leaders who seek inclusive excellence through increased structural diversity find themselves stuck between a legal rock and a sociological hard place. Although quotas violate the 14th Amendment's Equal Protection Clause, research demonstrates that "insufficient representation can lead to perceptions of racial hostility and feelings of isolation among those students in the minority, eroding campus climate, limiting participation, and hampering the learning environment for all students" (Taylor, Milem, & Coleman, 2016, p. 8). Despite Scalia's rebuke, educators remain committed to maximizing structural diversity in order to advance social and civic goals and to increase opportunities for students to interact with diverse peers. Gurin and colleagues (2002) and others have found that informal interactional diversity is influential and has long-lasting impacts (Alwin, Cohen, & Newcomb, 1991; Astin, 1993; Newcomb, 1943; Newcomb, Koenig, Flacks, & Warwick, 1967). That's why some institutions have taken a granular approach to understanding the effects of structural diversity, measuring it in the communities students interact with rather than in the population as a whole. Rice University evaluates its diversity and inclusion goals in terms of the composition of its residence halls, the nexus of cocurricular activity, and the University of Texas at Austin studies whether diversity is present across thousands of individual class sections (Taylor et al., 2016).

Diversity interactions have been shown to advance a wide range of desired SLOs (Gurin et al., 2002; Gurin et al., 2004), but pairing structural diversity with diversity interactions as if the former begets the latter may be a faulty assumption (Lewis & Cantor, 2016; Tienda, 2013). Inclusion and interaction involve more than just admitting students to campus and making sure they are present in certain courses, communities, and activities. Inclusion and interaction are influenced by the degree to which individuals are "connected to, effective within, and isolated from crucial institutional domains" (Katznelson, 2016, p. 187). A student's sense of belonging and their willingness to interact with diverse others is mediated by factors acting on their freedom of mobility, expression, and engagement. These factors include students' sense of security moving within and between campus zones, their material well-being, the level at which they are held in cultural regard, and the extent to which they are able to participate in and meaningfully influence civic discourse and decision-making (Katznelson, 2016). The relationship between increased structural diversity and increases in retention and graduation rates is equally complex and difficult to prove causal. The few studies that have explored this connection have yielded mixed results. Findings vary across minority groups and different types of institutions, suggesting that other factors influence this relationship, if one exists at all (Jones, 2011).

Structural Diversity: A Necessary but Insufficient Condition of Inclusive Excellence

It's been 70 years since the Truman Commission on Higher Education warned that if some groups were systematically denied access to a college degree when that degree was simultaneously deemed a prerequisite for occupational and social mobility, then education would "become the means, not of eliminating race and class distinctions, but of deepening and solidifying them" (Zook, 1947, p. 36). Higher education leaders are responsible for providing all students with pathways to achieve a quality education and a college degree. By the same token, history demonstrates that simply outlawing discrimination neither guarantees graduation nor creates a more just and equitable society (Tienda, 2013). If higher education is to promote all three conditions of inclusive excellence and prepare all students to "create better solutions to the problems we need to solve" (Schneider, 2016, p. 4), then we must think of diversity as more than just demography. On its own, structural diversity does not lead to all three conditions of inclusive excellence. To achieve this goal, we must conceptualize diversity in a way that affects all students' success, not just that of the minority students we seek to include on campus, through more receptive recruitment and admissions practices (Bernstein, 2016).

Diversity as Curriculum: Learning About Others

In addition to thinking of diversity as demography, we can also regard it as an educational resource that enriches the campus climate and adds value to the learning environment (Taylor et al., 2016). Since 1992 the AAC&U has encouraged campus administrators to treat campus diversity less as a social problem to be solved and more as "an educational and civic asset necessary to create academic excellence and responsible democratic citizens" (Bernstein, 2016, p. 29). This asset-based approach underlies the concept of classroom diversity, which involves content learning about minority cultures and issues (Chang, 2002; Gurin et al., 2002). Structural diversity is the impetus for classroom diversity; a more demographically diverse student body needs a more expansive curriculum in terms of the perspectives, identities, and ideas it covers (Bernstein, 2016).

Educators concerned with classroom diversity believe that although social justice is advanced through structural diversity, social learning arises from conscious efforts to explore the "controversies that inevitably arise when students find themselves challenging one another's deeply held beliefs, values, knowledge systems, and comfort levels in classrooms and in lecture halls" (Bernstein, 2016, p. 31). Classroom diversity is generally promoted through gender studies, ethnic studies, and intercultural communications courses at home and abroad and through diversity-related programming in the cocurriculum. Students are often prompted to participate in these courses and activities through general education requirements and graduation certificates and honors programs. Content learning is the hallmark of classroom diversity. Guest speakers, personal narratives and research-based readings, films, case studies, and other media from various sociocultural, theoretical, and disciplinary perspectives provide students with the background knowledge they need to understand the nature and impact of human diversity (Gurin, Nagda, & Zúñiga, 2013).

Does Classroom Diversity Lead to Inclusive Excellence?

When we start to think about diversity as curriculum, the measure of inclusive excellence shifts from representational parity to student learning. Classroom diversity is often assessed for its impact on the critical thinking and civic outcomes that employers want and citizens need (Hart Research Associates, 2013, 2015; Schneider, 2016). These outcomes include active thinking and intellectual engagement, integrative complexity, cognitive openness, and attitudes favoring equal opportunity and racial tolerance (Antonio et al., 2004; Chang, 2002; Gottfredson et al., 2008; Gurin et al., 2002). Most studies find that classroom diversity positively influences these outcomes, but vagueness and variance in operational definitions make it difficult to draw valid, generalizable conclusions about which aspects of classroom diversity influence student learning (Engberg, 2004). Higher education researchers have considered any and all of the following as sufficient approaches to classroom diversity: full-length courses on diversity issues, one-time workshops or trainings on racial or cultural awareness, information or activities directed at understanding other racial/ethnic groups and interracial/interethnic relationships, and participation in discussions on racial issues (Bowman, 2013; Gottfredson et al., 2008; Gurin et al., 2002). Even courses involving community service have been deemed emblematic of classroom diversity (Laird, 2005). But what aspects of these courses and activities make a difference for students? Is it their content or how students engage with the content that really matters? What kinds of content and teaching strategies lead to desired learning outcomes? And to what extent does the classroom's structural diversity influence student learning?

Although the results are mixed, research provides reason to believe that something about classroom diversity positively influences civic and critical thinking outcomes. At the same time, diversity courses have been found to have less of an impact on students' diversity and perspective-taking outcomes than either meaningful interactions with diverse peers or reflective learning (O'Neill, 2012). Some researchers attribute this to the fact that classroom diversity is often a passive learning experience. Without sufficient structural diversity and faculty and student critiques of dominant narratives, classroom diversity can reinforce the view that racial and cultural identities are rigidly bound, or that unbridgeable differences exist between people more often than commonalities or intersectionalities (Bhabha, 1994; Young, 1994). In the extreme, passive diversity learning can perpetuate negative stereotyping, strengthen implicit bias, and be used as a justification for discrimination and differential treatment (Bernstein, 2016; Gurin et al., 2002).

An overemphasis on learning about others can also fuel a campus climate that inhibits inclusion. Students' sense of belonging is influenced by a delicate interplay between how they define themselves and how others define them (Read, Archer, & Leatherwood, 2003). If classroom diversity is the primary means educators use to promote inclusion, then several critical issues should be addressed. What kinds of diversity courses are being offered, and who is taking them? In recent years, an increasing number of institutions have approved new general education diversity requirements. The University of California, Los Angeles (UCLA), for example, mandated that beginning in fall 2017, all undergraduates entering UCLA College must take at least one course from a list of more than 200 that "substantially addresses racial, ethnic, gender, socioeconomic, sexual orientation, religious or other types of diversity" (Jaschik, 2015). A major impetus for the requirement was that students perceived a hostile campus climate toward minorities (Jaschik, 2013). But even in a majority-minority institution like UCLA, the new diversity requirement was met with debate. Many faculty members were uneasy with what they viewed as a conflict between the mandate's purpose and its implementation. These faculty expressed a concern, based on research (Espenshade & Radford, 2009), that students would tend to take courses about groups with which they were already familiar and comfortable rather than opting for exposure to divergent ideas and identities:

> With approximately 90 percent of our undergraduate students identifying with at least one diversity identity group, many students may take the diversity course most aligned with their identity, and are then less likely to learn about perspectives different than their own. This possibility is even greater since the report of the Diversity Initiative Implementation Committee has indicated that many courses focus on one identity group. Rather than exposing students to perspectives of other groups that differ from their own, the diversity course may give the students an opportunity to stay in their own identity group, a "ghettoization" effect. (Jaschik, 2015, para. 11)

Faculty criticism of diversity course choice raises another critical question: Do all students benefit equally from classroom diversity? Research indicates that students' status as minority or majority group members shapes their experience of classroom diversity. Meta-analyses consistently demonstrate that White students experience larger learning gains as a result of participating in diversity-related courses and programming than do their peers of color (Denson, 2009; Engberg, 2004; Tropp & Pettigrew, 2005). Under the auspices of diversity learning, minority students may feel they are expected to tune in to the dominant discourse about who they are, act as token representatives of this narrative, and shed their cultural norms and perspectives to adjust to those of the majority. This process has been shown to have significant negative impacts on outcomes related to psychological well-being and learning (Allen, 2016; Greenman & Xie, 2008; Read et al., 2003).

Finally, what message do diversity requirements send to students about who belongs on campus and who is being admitted despite their otherness? Some contend that classroom diversity only focuses on the study of identities that the majority may regard as counternormative, for example, non-Western, non-White, nonmale, or nonheterosexual. This may reinforce exotification or notions that certain identities are other. In response, many colleges and universities now offer courses and programs devoted to understanding the social construction and experience of Whiteness (Wang, 2015). Critical Whiteness studies is a growing interdisciplinary field "whose aim is to reveal the invisible structures that produce and reproduce white supremacy and privilege" (Applebaum, 2016, para. 2).

Given the inconsistent and differential impacts of classroom diversity, educators must consider whether it's possible to achieve the three conditions of inclusive excellence by virtue of admitting more minority students to campus and requiring all students to pass a diversity course or two. The implication of thinking about diversity as curriculum may be that identity is merely a commodity, easily discerned by its outward package and readily traded in exchange for acceptance, tolerance, or a valuable good such as a college degree. To some, this exchange is a one-way transaction. Instead of advancing a quality education and graduation for all, classroom diversity may merely facilitate the ease of minorities' assimilation into the dominant culture and the majority's comfort with that assimilation (Allen, 2016).

Classroom Diversity: A Necessary but Insufficient Component of Inclusive Excellence

As we have asserted, a more diverse student body does need a more diverse curriculum. Students need to learn about their own and others' histories, experiences, cultures, and identities to function as informed, engaged citizens. However, classroom diversity alone doesn't promote inclusion in school or society, and it doesn't automatically produce educational excellence. Multiple studies demonstrate that for learning about others to have the desired effects, it must be conducted in structurally diverse settings and through pedagogical strategies designed to facilitate knowledge transfer and production in diverse environments (Gurin et al., 2002; Milem et al., 2005; Shaw, 2005; Taylor et al., 2016). This conclusion is consistent with psychosocial and social constructivist theories of identity development and learning that have supported best practices in education for decades, yet they have been applied increasingly infrequently in the context of the ever-expanding accountability movement (Brooks & Brooks, 1999; Ravitch, 2016). According to these theories, students are supported in moving from automatic, reductive thinking about the world and others to reflective, critical thinking when teaching strategies require them to "confront the relativity or limitations of their points of view" (Gurin, 1999, para. 27). Sustained, prolonged, and meaningful engagement with diversity helps students learn that knowledge is constructed collaboratively, not individually, and that diversity influences the nature of claims made about the world, how these claims are received, and how conclusions, predictions, and solutions are reached (King & Kitchener, 1994; King & Shuford, 1996). Institution administrators seeking inclusive excellence must be just as committed to harnessing diversity to benefit all students' learning and problem-solving as they are to diversifying student demographics and the content of their courses and activities. This requires thinking about diversity in a different way. Here we turn our attention to that new way of thinking about diversity and the conditions that lead to new insights and innovation. We're ready to consider how thinking about diversity not only in terms of identity but also as a cognitive tool set can enable us to achieve all three conditions of inclusive excellence through universal global learning.

Diversity as a Cognitive Tool Set: Learning in Collaboration With Others

Before we present you with a different conceptualization of diversity, let's take a moment to review our main contentions thus far. To start, institutions must satisfy the following conditions to achieve inclusive excellence: (a) maximize diverse student representation through equitable admissions practices, (b) ensure that all students are equally unhindered in their access to quality educational opportunities and a college diploma, and (c) make students' diversity central to the achievement of their mission to transmit and produce new knowledge. Next, although structural and classroom diversity contribute to inclusive excellence, both can lead to unintended negative impacts on student success. Grouping students by traditional demographic categories and aligning passive content learning with those categories may obscure aspects of individual identity. This can diminish students' sense of belonging and their willingness to participate in the free exchange of ideas, both of which are hallmarks of inclusive excellence. In light of these two contentions, we're left with the following challenge: How can higher education leaders conceptualize student diversity in a way that incorporates structural and classroom diversity and also satisfies all three conditions of inclusive excellence? How can universal global learning help leaders achieve this goal?

To address this challenge, we turn to the work of economist Scott Page (2007, 2011), who conceptualized diversity as a cognitive tool set. Page explored why diverse groups produce more benefits when they take on complex tasks like problem-solving and making predictions than their homogenous peers. He observed that under certain conditions, diverse groups generate more ideas and solutions overall and that their conclusions are more accurate, efficient, resilient, robust, and innovative. Page found that these benefits are the result of interactions among the varied cognitive tools that diverse individuals bring to their joint complex task. Page (2007) named the following four interconnected tools people use to understand and shape the world around them:

1. Perspectives, the ways of representing situations and problems
2. Heuristics, the ways of generating solutions to problems
3. Interpretations, the ways of categorizing or partitioning perspectives
4. Predictive models, the ways of inferring cause and effect

People's cognitive tools are sometimes associated with their membership in a demographic category such as race or gender, but differences and similarities also exist within and across categories of identity. This is an important point, because it's the fulcrum we can use to pivot to a new way of thinking about inclusive excellence. Namely, when diversity is thought of in terms of a cognitive tool set, then inclusive excellence involves not only supporting the needs of historically underserved students and removing barriers to their inclusion and achievement but also creating more diversity in school and society to produce better responses to the complex problems we face. Colleges and universities achieve inclusive excellence by bringing demographically and cognitively diverse students to campus; assisting all students in identifying the tools they already possess; helping them develop new tools, thus creating more diversity; and engaging all students in collaborative efforts to use their diverse identity perspectives and cognitive tools to analyze and address complex problems.

But wait, you say, haven't I heard that last part somewhere before?

Indeed, you have. You're recalling our definition of *global learning* as the process of diverse people collaboratively analyzing and addressing complex problems that transcend borders. We hope you're starting to see why we've spent so much time defining the terms *global learning, inclusive excellence,* and *diversity.* We also hope you're beginning to see how thinking of diversity as a cognitive tool set enables institutions to use universal global learning to achieve inclusive excellence. To further illustrate this point, we describe the cognitive tool set in more detail in the next section. We then follow that description with a brief explanation of where diverse cognitive tools come from and a summary of how interactions among diverse tools can lead to complex problem-solving benefits. We conclude the chapter with some final thoughts on the relationship among diversity, universal global learning, and inclusive excellence.

The Cognitive Tool Set

Thinking about diversity in terms of students' varied and wide-ranging cognitive tool sets allows us to make an empirical argument in support of the essential relationship between diversity and educational quality. It allows us to refute Scalia's claim in *Grutter v. Bollinger* that if the University of Michigan really wanted to eliminate racial imbalances in admissions, all it had to do was lower its standards and give up its desire to have a flagship "super-duper" ("Transcript of Arguments in Grutter v. Bollinger," 2003, para. 174) law school. That's a false dichotomy. As we examine the following cognitive tools, you'll see that "diversity and super-duperness can go hand in hand" (Page, 2007, p. 17). A great law school, or any great organization engaged in knowledge production, for that matter, requires cognitive diversity. Given that diverse cognition can be associated with identity differences, super-duperness also requires structural diversity, "and moreover, super-duperness may *always* require identity diversity, long after discrimination ends" (Page, 2007, p. 17).

Perspectives

In chapter 1 we define *perspectives* as "ordinarily unexamined assumptions, evaluations, explanations, conceptions of time, space, causality, etc." (Hanvey, 1975, p. 5). Page (2007) expands on this definition, writing that perspectives are revealed through the language people use to represent their perceptions of the world around them: "The names that perspectives assign to objects capture underlying structure" (p. 25). Perspectives play a critical role in problem-solving because the way people view a problem's structure influences how they perceive its complexity or difficulty. Viewed from one perspective, a problem may appear unambiguous and easy to solve, but observed from another point of view the same problem may look like a bewildering mess. Although one person's perspective reveals logical next steps, another person can't make a move without making a cognitive leap. Perspectives can simplify, or they can complicate. The good news is that perspectives can be shared, and new perspectives can be built and adopted by others. Most breakthroughs "involve a person learning to see a problem or a situation differently," and diverse perspectives are "the seeds of innovation" (Page, 2007, p. 25).

Perhaps the most interesting thing about perspectives is that they don't necessarily have to be right, in the sense that they lead directly to the best answer, to contribute to the best solution. When people with diverse perspectives collaborate to understand and solve a complex problem, they employ their perspectives sequentially. Someone explains the situation in one way, and then other people attempt to improve that explanation to reveal previously unseen details. Take any two different perspectives, and parts of each can even be combined to create a whole new perspective. Page (2007) dubs this dynamic the *superadditivity* of diverse tools, a situation in which one plus one literally equals three. Superadditivity means that the whole of a cognitively diverse group of people, in terms of their ability to analyze and generate solutions to complex problems, is greater than the sum of its individual parts. Superadditivity also explains why diversity and super-duperness go hand in hand. Colleges and universities that engage their diverse students in collaborative problem-solving actually create more cognitive diversity, leading to the transfer and production of new knowledge, a condition of inclusive excellence.

Heuristics

Heuristics are the rules of thumb, practices, and processes people use to organize data and generate solutions to problems (Page, 2007). People choose which heuristics to apply based on their perspective on the problem and the tools that are readily available to them. Heuristics are derived from many sources, including academic disciplines, organizations, professions, and even customs and habits. No single heuristic works best for all people all the time, but some kinds of heuristics are better for complex problem-solving than others. The simplest heuristics are topological. They involve a search for solutions within the problem's existing structure. Approaches such as trying the opposite or rearranging the furniture fall into this category. Gradient heuristics are also simple in that they entail determining the most efficient path to a solution and merely moving in that direction. More sophisticated heuristics allow errors and involve simulations, testing, and brainstorming that help the group learn from their failures. In the same way that superadditivity allows even a suboptimal perspective to contribute to a good solution, bad solutions produced through error-allowing heuristics can help a group get out of a rut and steer it in the direction of a better idea. Population heuristics test the efficacy of multiple solutions all at the same time. When diverse groups apply multiple types of heuristics to a complex problem, they have the potential to outperform homogenous groups of the best problem solvers. This means that under certain conditions, diversity trumps ability (Page, 2007). If the problem the group wants to understand and solve is complex, if the perspectives and heuristics at hand are diverse and applicable to the problem, and if the group of problem solvers is large enough to contain at least one person who can lead to an improvement, then "a randomly selected collection of problem solvers outperforms a collection of the best individual problem solvers" (Page, 2007, p. 162). Once again, there's no need to sacrifice super-duperness for diversity.

Interpretations

Like heuristics, interpretations exist within perspectives. Perspectives tell people what information to pay attention to, whereas interpretations are how people map and categorize that information. Demographic categories, for instance, are interpretations. People create projection interpretations by ignoring certain data points for a particular purpose (e.g., grouping students according to race or gender to identify achievement gaps) or clumping interpretations by assembling data points to create groups with similar constituents (e.g., analyzing characteristics to identify at-risk or high-potential students' (Page, 2007). By using different heuristics, two people operating from the same perspective can generate different interpretations of data, but different interpretations can also arise from differences in perspective. Resolving diverse interpretations is always difficult, but it's particularly important to do so when the conflict concerns interpreting causal versus correlational relationships. Such interpretations influence our ability to construct models that will accurately predict future circumstances and the consequences of actions. People tend to interpret data in terms of their individual preferences or values (Page, 2007). When group members share values, they tend to interpret data in the same way. This can cause the group to ignore important information, confounding its ability to interpret cause and effect. If a group's collective purpose is to generate a solution that leads to desired consequences, the group needs to make accurate predictions, and these are predicated on diverse interpretations. This is yet another instance of excellence requiring diversity.

Predictive Models
Models are equations that factor in a situation's multiple attributes and dimensions and produce an output, often in the form of a prediction. Although heuristics help people to decide what to do, predictive models help them figure out what will happen. As Page (2007) has noted, "We apply predictive models nearly every time we think" (p. 93). From deciding whether to put on a sweater in the morning to determining how to vote, people rely on their interpretations of data to make predictions that will in turn lead to action. Interpretations are foundational to the predictions we make, but experiences, intuition, and biases inform predictions as well. People need accurate predictive models to make good decisions. In fact, to obtain good models, we often turn to experts. As we have seen—the 2016 U.S. presidential election is a perfect case in point—even experts' most sophisticated models can be wrong if they all rely on the same limited perspective or interpret data according to a single faulty heuristic (Page, 2007).

Luckily, diversity can still outperform ability. A collection of diverse predictive models can outperform those of homogenous experts if the diverse crowd factors in important attributes or values that have been ignored by those experts. It's not just the super-duperness of our law school, college, or university that depend on this being true, our nation's civic future hangs in the balance. Page (2007) has argued that "a society whose citizens possess fewer predictive models has fewer checks on bad ideas. An effective democracy, therefore, may depend as much on its citizens' having diverse predictive models as on their having accurate predictive models" (p. 347). Justice Scalia once stated that if people wanted to enact social change such as outlawing discrimination, they should engage in legislative action rather than depending on "nine superannuated judges who have been there too long, imposing these demands on society" (Massey, 2011, para. 3). He went on with, "Persuade your fellow citizens it's a good idea and pass a law. . . . That's what democracy is all about" (Massey, 2011, para. 3). Although he balked at diversity's compatibility with educational excellence, at a minimum perhaps Scalia would have agreed that diversity plays a critical role in keeping a healthy democracy in check.

Where Do Diverse Cognitive Tools Come From?

We have seen how diversity as a cognitive tool set is indispensable to the achievement of higher education's mission to transmit and produce new knowledge. If institutions are to bring students with diverse tools to campus and help them develop new ones, then we need to understand the sources of cognitive diversity. Page (2007) cites education itself as a direct cause of diverse tools. Students in architecture programs, for example, form different perspectives and heuristics than students in nursing programs. Experience also directly influences cognitive difference. Page (2007) provides the example of people who develop different tools when living in diverse environmental settings. Those who grow up near water acquire tools for fishing and weather forecasting that are of little use to people residing in the desert. Not all types of education and experiences act on cognition in the same way, though. As Page argues, "Memorizing long lists of unrelated facts is far less valuable than accumulating tools and understandings" (p. 303). And whereas serendipitous experiences can potentially drive powerful breakthroughs, they can also turn into lost opportunities if people do not reflect on their meaning.

Identity also influences cognitive diversity, albeit indirectly. Because we know that people who affiliate with similar identity categories think individually in very different ways, "we cannot equate individual tools or collections of tools with specific identities. We can expect, however, that identity differences lead to experiential differences that in turn create tool differences" (Page, 2007, p. 307). Individually and in combination, different aspects of identity—race, gender, culture, sexual preference, religion, physical abilities—can also "limit, steer, and even guide" the education we seek (Page, 2007, p. 306). Society plays a role here too; norms, policies, stereotypes, and biases associated with particular identity groups determine the educational and experiential opportunities made available to people, in turn affecting the kinds of tools they develop. To quote Page (2007) once more: "Just because someone slips and falls does not mean that she is clumsy. It could mean that her front porch is icy" (p. 307).

What Circumstances Make Diversity Beneficial?

Let's turn now to environments and methods that lead diverse groups to be successful. You'll find that these will map neatly onto the conditions of global learning discussed in chapter 1 and onto the teaching and learning strategies and even the organizational leadership approach we feature in the rest of the book.

Conditions

Under the right conditions, groups of diverse problem solvers outperform groups of the best problem solvers. The first condition is that the problem under consideration must be complex. Cognitive diversity has few benefits for routine physical or mental tasks; in fact, too much diversity can make such tasks unnecessarily difficult. Second, contributing perspectives and heuristics must be pertinent to the problem, even if only tangentially. As Page (2007) puts it, "All of the possible problem solvers must have some ability to solve the problem" (p. 159). Third, diverse cognitive tools must actually be present within the group. There must be at least one perspective or heuristic available, even if it's a minority, dissenting, or ultimately incorrect view, which can lead to superadditivity. Fourth, the population from which problem solvers are drawn must be large enough to cultivate cognitive diversity, and smaller groups of problem solvers mustn't be so small that they limit superadditivity. Page (2007) tells us that "there is no explicit size that these collections have to be for the result to hold" (p. 162). The number of diverse tools needed to understand and address a problem is relative to the problem's complexity. The harder the problem, the more diversity is needed. In other words, Maureen E. Mahoney had a justifiable argument when she stated in *Grutter v. Bollinger* that universities should aim for sufficient amounts of diversity without setting absolute racial quotas ("Transcript of Arguments in Grutter v. Bollinger," 2003). Page (2007) recommends that "organizations, firms, and universities that solve problems should seek out people with diverse experiences, training, and identities that translate into diverse perspectives and heuristics" (p. 173). Given the right problem and sufficient variety of tools, diversity can be more important than ability.

Nevertheless, just because a group contains diverse identities doesn't necessarily mean it will perform better. Sometimes, relative to the problem being studied, the relationship between structural diversity and cognitive diversity is weak. This undermines the second condition, that is, that cognitive diversity is meaningful and applicable to the problem. Other times identity-diverse groups have conflicting beliefs and values concerning what is to be accomplished, such as incompatible fundamental preferences (Page, 2007). Groups may have different instrumental preferences about how to accomplish a task, but if they're fundamentally at odds about goals and outcomes, then few if any progressive ideas or innovations will result. And then there are group dynamics; sometimes identity-diverse people just have a harder time communicating, trusting, and bonding with one another. Page (2007) said that for diverse groups to get along, members need their identities "validated and their contributions verified. If a person's involvement in a group does not require abandoning her self-view, the result is that the person contributes more and the person performs better" (p. 328). Furthermore, if the group's foundational belief is that identity diversity is beneficial, the group is more likely to rise to this expectation.

Strategies
Say all four conditions of diversity are in place, and you have a group that is willing and able to explore a complex problem. How do students' diverse tools interact to produce accurate, efficient, resilient, robust, and innovative solutions? How do students develop new tools in the process? The pursuit of new ideas and tools involves purposeful collaboration guided by a skilled faculty, staff, or peer facilitator. Facilitators guide students in the process of "exploitation (copying and learning from others) and exploration (searching for new representations and search algorithms)" (Page, 2007, p. 134). They can use a wide range of strategies to prompt students to exchange information, transfer ideas from one discipline to another, or rearrange data or ideas in new ways. Sometimes mistakes will happen during the process. If these blunders lead to new representations, heuristics, interpretations, or predictions, they can later be recognized as strokes of genius (Page, 2011). One need only think of what happened when Alexander Fleming's *Staphylococcus* bacteria was accidentally contaminated by C. J. La Touche's *Penicillium* mold from the floor below to realize the innovative potential of human error (Podolsky, 1997). Such happy accidents can't occur, however, unless educational leaders make conscious, concerted efforts to bring diverse problem solvers together in collaborative settings and support the conditions of their success.

Conclusion

Educational leaders "do not leave to chance that which they value" (Tienda, 2013, p. 471). Institutions that value inclusive excellence seek to balance social and civic goals with their instructional and research goals. *Student diversity*, which is at the nexus of these two pursuits, should be defined as the varied cognitive tools that members of different identity groups apply to complex knowledge exchange and production tasks (Page, 2007; Thomas & Ely, 1996). To provide inclusive excellence to our increasingly identity-diverse student bodies, all institutions should engage all students in collaborative efforts to analyze and address complex problems with their demographically and cognitively diverse peers, that is, global learning. Through universal global learning, colleges and universities leverage student diversity in the aggregate to achieve their mission and help students individually to become more diverse and thus more successful. According to Page (2007),

> People should acquire diverse sets of perspectives and heuristics so that they can make larger contributions. . . . With more tools, a person is more capable of being diverse, of amassing more interesting perspectives, heuristics, and combinations of perspectives and heuristics. Paradoxically, the best way to be diverse is to be able—to have lots of tools. (p. 173)

Institutions can't reap the benefits of diversity if they merely recruit it and tolerate it. Inclusive excellence requires educators to encourage the cultural contrast and cognitive dissonance that accompanies interactions of diverse identities and tool sets. It also requires them to assist students in finding connections among diverse ideas and resolving internal and group conflicts. Universal global learning is the process of accomplishing this feat. At the very least, using the admittedly imprecise methods available to them, colleges and universities must bring a representatively diverse student body to their campuses. Once students arrive, however, institutions must seek to undo the strict coupling of particular identity categories with student success. Students need to reflect on the many influences on their cognition, including their previous experiences, their training, and the intersecting aspects of their identities. Throughout their higher education, through the process of global learning, all students should have opportunities to decide which cognitive tools they want to strengthen, which they want to adjust, and which new ones they want to add to their set. Administrators at some institutions may wish to redefine student success in terms of the breadth of students' tool sets and their capacity to apply those tools to complex problem-solving in new settings. In this way, inclusive excellence will be measured by the extent to which institutions enable all their students to participate effectively in the process of global learning on campus and in the world's communities.

3

MAKING GLOBAL LEARNING
UNIVERSAL THROUGH
COLLECTIVE IMPACT

It's pretty darn hard to find a president or a provost who doesn't say, "We've got to be international." Now they say, "OK, I buy the message, but what do I do, where do I start?" (Hudzik as cited in Fischer, 2012, para. 25)

In the previous chapter we left you with a final thought: Inclusive excellence should be measured by the extent to which institutions enable all their students to participate effectively in the process of global learning. Although the undertaking is complex and difficult, we contend that universal global learning is possible through effective leadership. Effectiveness involves choosing the right tools to achieve the task. In our experience, global learning leaders tend to start off with bold ideas for institution-wide reform but end up implementing comparatively simple strategies that can be conveniently represented through numbers, such as increasing study abroad programs, area studies certificates, speaker series, or exchange agreements. Newly appointed faculty leaders, often highly experienced in their disciplinary fields but with little or no background in global learning or educational leadership, may rely only on partners in academic and student affairs departments traditionally considered international (e.g., politics and international relations, international student and scholar services, foreign languages, study abroad, etc.). These leaders express frustration when their seemingly commonsense efforts yield little evidence of transformative student learning or are actively undermined by faculty who perceive their departments as owning all things international. Departmental politics, territorialism, and the silo mentality are common leadership threats that easily erode narrow, simplified approaches to providing all students with collaborative global learning opportunities.

So you want to be an effective leader of universal global learning? Where should you start? When higher education leaders decide they want to internationalize their institution, they often find it hard to choose from among the many possible points of entry: mission statements, administrative structures, curricula, faculty policies and procedures, student mobility, and collaborations and partnerships (American Council on Education, 2012). Leaders who know they want to internationalize by providing global learning to all are faced with a formidable task—curriculum reform. Curriculum entails "(i) why; (ii) what; (iii) when; (iv) where; (v) how; and (vi) with whom" students learn (Braslavsky, 2003, p. 1). Reform involves making changes to the status quo concerning one or more of these aspects of the curriculum, an act former U.S. President and Princeton University President Woodrow Wilson once deemed more difficult than moving a graveyard (Rhodes, 1998). The decision to make global learning universal implies reform in its broadest sense: All six interconnected aspects of the curriculum must be addressed to involve all students in collaborative global problem-solving with diverse others. This complexity makes leading universal global learning curriculum reform an exceptionally challenging undertaking (Anderson, 1992; Snyder, 2013).

Does curriculum reform really have to be so complex? In truth, some aspects of curriculum change are comparatively simple. Take the process of adding a new course to a program, for example. Although aspects of this process can be political and time consuming, the task generally involves known procedures and relatively predictable outcomes. Other changes to the curriculum, like developing and launching a new major, are much more complicated. This kind of problem involves bureaucratic hurdles, interdepartmental politics, and human and financial resource requirements. Furthermore, there's no guarantee of success even if the department succeeds in initiating a new degree program; there's still the task of enrolling and graduating a sufficient number of students to sustain it. Complicated problems such as this are larger in scope and harder to solve than simple problems, but given enough time and effort, their multiple influences can be analyzed and addressed through replicable strategies. This isn't the case with complex endeavors like making global learning universal. Providing global learning to all involves the entire institution making fundamental changes to the way all students are educated, encompassing why, what, when, where, how, and with whom students learn. Indeed, making global learning universal can be as complex a problem as those that global learners seek to solve. With so many interconnected stakeholders to influence and so many factors influencing individuals' willingness and ability to effect reform, it's little wonder that so few leaders attempt the challenge of making global learning universal.

Instead of offering you a single simple tool to accomplish your complex leadership task, in this chapter we offer a robust alternative—an entire tool belt—in the form of the collective impact methodology (Kania & Kramer, 2011). Collective impact was originally developed to enable a diverse set of community stakeholders to coordinate distinct yet interconnected efforts to solve complex social problems. Collective impact can also be used to lead complex initiatives in multifaceted organizations such as colleges and universities. To help you diagnose your institution's unique needs, we begin by exploring in greater depth the challenges of leading curriculum reform. This will also help you see how collective impact can enable you to engage multiple stakeholders simultaneously in a wide range of different activities to meet those needs. With this context in mind, we then proceed to define the five conditions necessary to achieve a successful collective impact initiative. The remainder of the chapter takes a detailed look at one of these conditions: the common agenda. We contend that the common agenda is the first thing you need to set the stage for universal global learning. The other four conditions of collective impact—the backbone organization, mutually reinforcing activities, shared measurement systems, and continuous communication—are explored in succeeding chapters. As we examine each condition, we provide specific strategies and examples from our work that may be applicable to leading universal global learning at your home institution.

But first, let's consider whether you already have some of the conditions of collective impact in place. Many leaders find collective impact intuitive; when they learn about the methodology, they realize they've been doing parts of it all along. Although a successful collective impact initiative requires all five conditions of success to be implemented at once, it's good to begin your work by exploring which conditions may currently be in progress. Take a moment to consider the following questions, each of which is tied to one of the conditions of collective impact:

- Common agenda: Has your institution determined why it's providing global learning to all? Have you developed SLOs or program goals that support global learning for all? Were all stakeholder groups involved in developing these goals and outcomes? Can all stakeholders contribute to the achievement of global learning goals and outcomes?
- Backbone organization: Do you have an office or a team of personnel responsible for coordinating your global learning efforts? Does this coordinating body maintain relationships with all stakeholder groups associated with the initiative? Does it have the human, physical, financial, and technological resources it needs to serve as an effective node for your institution's global learning network?
- Mutually reinforcing activities: Do stakeholders coordinate or collaborate when developing and implementing global learning courses and activities? Are there structures in place that support

coordination and collaboration across supervisory or departmental reporting lines?

- Shared measurement systems: Do you have a plan for assessing the extent to which students are achieving global learning SLOs and evaluating the institution's universal global learning program goals? Do all stakeholder groups have access to assessment and evaluation results?
- Continuous communication: Do you have a process for informing stakeholders of assessment and evaluation results, global learning opportunities, exchanging expertise, and sharing success stories? Do you have a process for using assessment and evaluation results to generate new ideas for sustaining and improving global learning for all students?

If you answered yes to any of these questions, then you already have some components of collective impact in place and are well positioned to use the methodology for making global learning universal. If you couldn't affirm any of them, don't despair, collective impact is coming to the rescue.

Challenges of Leading Universal Global Learning Curriculum Reform

A curriculum is complex and site specific. More than merely what students learn, the curriculum encompasses the entirety of the student learning experience, including why students learn (the institution's educational mission and vision), what they learn (SLOs, content, assessments), when they learn (course and activity schedules), where they learn (face-to-face, hybrid, online, or study abroad modalities), how they learn (pedagogical strategies), and with whom they learn (student body and community demographics). Dynamic internal and external forces influence the extent to which changes can be made to any of these aspects. These forces may include state and federal regulations, resource availability and strategic planning priorities, accreditation policies, long-standing disciplinary traditions, faculty beliefs and expertise, and student preferences. Across institutions, these forces play out in ways that don't necessarily follow set or known patterns. The impacts of these forces may manifest themselves differentially across insititutions, departments, and individuals. The unique combination of factors influencing the curricula in each college or university makes it difficult to simply import successful global learning reform strategies employed elsewhere. What works at a small, private liberal arts college in the Northeast may be impractical or irrelevant at a large, public research university in the Southwest, and vice versa. Intensive institutional self-study is required prior to planning and implementing potential global learning reforms so that such changes reach all students and produce intended outcomes.

When faculty members make changes to the curriculum, the changes have cascading effects. As soon as faculty alter one aspect of the curriculum, such as intended learning outcomes, other aspects must be modified accordingly, such as teaching strategies, assessment methods, and content. Faculty need support in the form of professional development, mentorship, and recognition to adapt to new ways of teaching and learning. This is especially true for global learning, which involves curriculum design elements that often conflict with traditional educational strategies implemented in the department or institution. Furthermore, when curricular changes involve such things as technology, the timing or location of courses, community-based activities, or the way classroom space is used for group learning, faculty may also need to collaborate with the nonacademic units that typically govern these activities.

These effects may be moderated, or amplified, by other stakeholders. Faculty may be unaware of the supports and resources available to them, unfamiliar with policies controlling their use, or uncomfortable employing methods with which they have little prior knowledge of or experience. To complicate matters, faculty support units may be located in different reporting lines or divisions whose administrators may not know the others exist, much less how to coordinate their operations to support universal global learning. Although the curriculum is generally considered to be under the faculty's control, external governing or accreditation bodies may mandate requirements that are misaligned with faculty beliefs and practices concerning global learning. All these issues make it impossible for faculty to effect universal global learning in isolation. Instead, leaders must help faculty and other stakeholders collaborate to create effective change and avoid unintended negative consequences.

Various interrelated philosophical, sociocultural, and economic factors also influence the extent to which global learning curriculum reform efforts can succeed, including preconceptions about what students are capable of learning and achieving, beliefs about the purposes of higher education, and entrenched organizational power structures. Some of these influences are subtly manifested in things that aren't normally associated with the curriculum. A prime example is student demographics or with whom students learn. Diverse student perspectives and cognitive tool sets are fundamental to global learning. Public institutions in particular are charged with serving the diverse educational needs of their local and state communities. In many states, funding for higher education is tied to all students' graduation success. In our home state of Florida, for example, performance-based funding metrics favor institutions that increase their four-year graduation rates and financially penalize those that make comparatively less progress. On the face of things, these metrics appear to benefit historically underserved students by motivating institutions to better support their success. But there's an unintended negative consequence of this policy: Because first-generation and underserved minority students have traditionally demonstrated slower time to graduation, institutions are disincentivized from admitting these students in the first place. This is both unjust and counterproductive to inclusive excellence. Although demographic diversity alone results in neither global learning nor inclusive excellence, it is a necessary source of different perspectives on the world and of different cognitive attributes. Decreases in demographic diversity mitigate faculty members' ability to facilitate global learning and achieve the mission of higher education (Chickering & Braskamp, 2009; Clarke & Antonio, 2012; Gurin et al., 2002).

Finally, successful universal global learning curriculum reform must be systemic. As Anderson (1992) has found, "significant and lasting changes in educational practice rarely occur without a substantial number of important and interrelated actions being taken" (p. 865). Systemic change is best accomplished through high degrees of interaction and communication among stakeholders (Snyder, 2013). Collective impact was built for making systems-level change. It's a holistic methodology, designed to enable leaders to involve a broad array of stakeholders in program development, implementation, and evaluation in a single, unified model. It's also adaptable; although collective impact delineates the organizational attributes of successful change, it doesn't prescribe specific activities that must be taken to achieve intended goals and outcomes. Most important, *collective impact* is defined by the same attributes that characterize global learning: diversity, collaboration, and complex problems that transcend borders. Although you can't ignore the challenges and obstacles to curriculum reform discussed earlier, collective impact can help you understand and address these through explicit design, organization, and communication components. Let's look at the five components of collective impact and take a deep dive into one of them: the common agenda.

Collective Impact: The Right Tools to Lead Universal Global Learning

Collective impact is a leadership methodology that involves adaptive interaction, communication, and problem-solving strategies to address large-scale, complex issues (Kania & Kramer, 2011). It has been used to lead cross-sector efforts to address complex challenges ranging from reducing substance abuse among youths in rural Massachusetts to increasing economic prosperity and quality of life in greater Memphis, Tennessee (Horton, 2013). The collaborative processes of collective impact empower stakeholders to be directly involved in solving the problems that affect their lives. Collective impact develops ties that bridge social or organizational borders, creating a sense of community and a culture of synergy, which involves "breakthroughs in thinking and action that are produced when a collaborative process successfully combines the knowledge, skills, and resources of a group of diverse participants" (Lee & Estes, 2003, p. 250).

Returning to the questions we posed at the beginning of the chapter, the following five conditions exemplify a successful collective impact initiative:

1. Common agenda—a shared vision for change, including a common understanding of the problem and a joint approach to solutions through agreed-on activities
2. Backbone organization—a coordinating infrastructure with dedicated staff who plan, manage, and sustain the initiative using technology, communications, data collection and reporting, and logistical and administrative tools and procedures
3. Mutually reinforcing activities—coordinated, differentiated activities as part of an overarching strategic plan
4. Shared measurement systems—a short list of common measurements of success and methods to analyze and report data
5. Continuous communication—regular meetings that follow a structured agenda to review formative and summative data and make incremental changes to increase success

All five conditions of collective impact need to be in place to effect successful systemic change. For the purposes of global learning curriculum reform, our experience leads us to conclude that one condition is foundational to the others—the common agenda.

Common Agenda

You can use the following questions to guide the development of your common agenda for universal global learning: Why is our institution providing global learning to all? What SLOs do we want all students to achieve? What program goals will support global learning for all? Which stakeholder groups do we need to involve in developing these goals and SLOs? How can all stakeholders contribute to the achievement of global learning program goals and SLOs?

The common agenda will be your North Star. Although your diverse stakeholders—faculty, students, instructional technologists, registrars, residence hall advisers, and others—may contribute to the common agenda in different ways, all will steer their efforts in its direction. Your global learning common agenda will likely be expressed as statements of intended program goals and SLOs. But an effective common agenda should be more than just a list; it should articulate a shared intention for change, a joint approach to creating change, and a collective sense of responsibility for making change happen. To help you get a clearer picture of what we mean, Table 3.1 contains a couple of examples of common agendas concerning complex educational reform initiatives.

Setting a common agenda for a collective impact initiative isn't like setting an agenda for a meeting. The common agenda is the heart of a plan for solving a particular problem, in this case, how to provide global learning for all, not a schedule of activities to be accomplished. Because the items on the common agenda must address the unique needs and values of your institution's stakeholders, these items can't be imported from other initiatives or simply follow a predetermined format. Your global learning common agenda should emerge from institutional will and enjoy broad-based acceptance; therefore, a few high-level leaders shouldn't dictate priorities and activities to be implemented. The process you use to determine the common agenda will also determine its effectiveness. This process should be iterative, allowing

TABLE 3.1
Examples of Common Agendas for Educational Initiatives

Project	Common Agenda
Road Map Project, Seattle, WA	"The Road Map Project goal is to double the number of students in South King County and South Seattle who are on track to graduate from college or earn a career credential by 2020. We are committed to nothing less than closing the unacceptable achievement gaps for low-income students and children of color and increasing achievement for all students from cradle to college and career." (Community Center for Education Results, 2015, p. 1)
Treasure Valley Education Partnership, Boise, ID	"Treasure Valley Education Partnership's goal is to coordinate the area's resources and institutions to support youth along the education continuum and ensure at least 80 percent of Treasure Valley students go on to post-high school education by 2016 and beyond." (Treasure Valley Education Partnership, 2013, p. 4)

constant input and feedback from a wide range of people, especially those most affected by planned changes—students. Although the final result should be strong enough to stand the test of time, your global learning common agenda should be a working document, and its meaning should be reconsidered, revived, and revised if necessary over the long term.

Now that you have an idea of what a common agenda is, you're probably wondering how to go about setting one. Let's examine some practical questions involved in this process.

What Items Need To Be on the Common Agenda?

Every initiative has its own common agenda, but all common agendas include three types of items. First, your common agenda should include at least one high-level goal, a mission statement that articulates why universal global learning is needed at your institution. Second, you'll want to determine a concise list of subgoals that support this mission and signal how you'll know when universal global learning has been achieved. Third, your stakeholders should break down your vision for change into the key levers needed to move the agenda forward (FSG, 2014). High-level goals, subgoals, and key levers should be meaningful to the vast majority of stakeholders. They should also be complex, meaning that no single group or person could possibly accomplish them alone. In the case of FIU's Global Learning for Global Citizenship initiative, we determined that our common agenda would need to comprise the items shown in Table 3.2.

High-Level Goal

The purpose of FIU's Global Learning for Global Citizenship initiative is "to provide every FIU undergraduate with curricular and co-curricular opportunities to achieve the knowledge, skills and attitudes of global citizenship through global learning" (FIU, 2010, p. vi). This high-level goal emerged from 18 months of research on our stakeholders' vision of an FIU education (see chapter 1). This goal describes the change we want for our entire

TABLE 3.2
FIU's Common Agenda Items

Types of Common Agenda Items	*Common Agenda Items*
High-level goal	Purpose of global learning for global citizenship
Subgoals	Program goals, SLOs
Key levers	Actions to be implemented, theoretical framework, operational definitions

community, including those experiencing and those facilitating global learning opportunities. It's also complex and multifaceted; to achieve it, we need to engage all our undergraduate students in global learning from the time they enter until the time they graduate and beyond. This goal also calls for us to collaborate with a wide variety of faculty, staff, and community stakeholders. Most important, this high-level goal gives rise to measurable, observable subgoals that will support universal global learning and describe how we'll know when it's achieved.

Subgoals
Your subgoals are the SLOs that apply to all students and the program goals that apply to your whole institution. Global learning SLOs should articulate essential and significant knowledge, skills, and attitudes that students will be able to reliably demonstrate as a result of participating in global learning experiences. The SLOs should be student centered, delineating what students will know and be able to do, not what professors will teach. They should be stated in terms that are clear to students and faculty alike, and each outcome should be focused on a single cognitive or behavioral attribute. Finally, make sure your SLOs are observable or measurable. As part of our subgoals, FIU included three graduation-level global learning SLOs—global awareness, perspective, and engagement—described in detail in chapter 1.

As opposed to SLOs, program goals pertain to the efficiency and effectiveness of activities that support student learning. These should be broad and complex enough to encourage shared responsibility across the institution. FIU established four program goals. Our first goal addresses our two-course global learning requirement that calls for first-year students to take at least one global learning foundations course as part of the general education curriculum and at least one discipline-specific global learning course as part of their major program of study. Transfer and readmitted students who enter with fewer than 60 credits and haven't met general education requirements prior to entering also take a foundations and discipline-specific course; those who enter with 60 or more credits or have met general education requirements take two discipline-specific courses (Landorf & Doscher, 2013a). When this new condition of graduation was proposed, many stakeholders worried that universal global learning would require students to have additional credits. Time to graduation is slowed down when students must have additional credits beyond those required by the degree; in Florida, this costs the university performance funding, and students' tuition doubles. To address this issue, FIU created a program goal to offer enough global learning courses so that every student could take at least two without having to accrue excess credits.

Our second goal aims to integrate global learning beyond the classroom. Most of our students work 20 or more hours per week and commute to school, so stakeholders knew that universal participation in global learning cocurricular activities would be impossible if we required a separate, additional burden on our students' schedules. Instead, FIU set a goal for faculty and student affairs professionals to integrate an increasing number of global learning cocurricular activities into courses as required, elective, or extra credit opportunities. This sent an explicit message to students, faculty, and staff that learning inside and outside the classroom were both important and that they should mutually reinforce one another. Knowing that faculty and staff need support to develop and integrate global learning opportunities, FIU devoted a third goal—providing ongoing high-quality professional development. Our fourth goal was for students to demonstrate increasing proficiency in the global learning SLOs between the time they entered the university and the time they graduated. Administrators resolved that if we were truly providing meaningful global learning to all, this should be reflected in greater student learning across the board.

Subgoals—which will often take the form of SLOs and program goals—should be mutually supportive and should also fulfill the initiative's high-level goal. We recommend that you pare your subgoals to the leanest number possible. The more focused and highly interrelated your subgoals are, the easier it will be to keep a broad array of stakeholders concentrated on a common purpose.

Key Levers

To achieve your high-level goals and subgoals, you'll need to determine the activities necessary to effect change. As part of the initial plan for universal global learning, FIU administrators determined five main activities to advance the institution's common agenda (see Table 3.3). These were approving global learning foundations and discipline-specific courses, providing faculty and staff development, developing global learning in the cocurriculum, publicizing global learning, and gathering support for global learning. The theory undergirding Global Learning for Global Citizenship also acts as a key lever, providing consistency and coherence to diverse activities implemented throughout the university. Finally, research-based operational definitions of the key terms in the title of our initiative—*global learning* and *global citizenship*—are critical to advancing our common agenda. Common language enables stakeholders to exchange ideas and discuss challenges and achievements across organizational and disciplinary borders.

Your high-level goal, subgoals, and key levers should all be grounded in the values and feedback of diverse stakeholders, which begs the question in the following section.

TABLE 3.3

FIU's Global Learning for Global Citizenship Common Agenda

Types of Common Agenda Items	FIU's Common Agenda Items	FIU's Global Learning Common Agenda
High-level goal	Purpose of Global Learning for Global Citizenship	To provide every FIU undergraduate with curricular and cocurricular opportunities to achieve the knowledge, skills, and attitudes of global citizenship through global learning
Subgoals	Program goals	• FIU will provide a sufficient number of global learning courses to enable students to meet the global learning graduation requirement outlined in the Global Learning for Global Citizenship Curriculum Framework • FIU's faculty and student affairs professionals will integrate an increasing number of global learning cocurricular activities into the baccalaureate curriculum. • FIU's Office of Global Learning Initiatives will provide high-quality faculty and staff development workshops designed to advance interdisciplinary, problem-centered global learning. • FIU students will gain proficiency in the knowledge, skills, and attitudes of global citizenship over the course of their FIU education.
	SLOs	• Global awareness: Students will be able to demonstrate knowledge of the interrelatedness of local, global, international, and intercultural issues, trends, and systems. • Global perspective: Students will be able to demonstrate the ability to conduct a multiperspective analysis of local, global, international, and intercultural problems. • Global engagement: Students will be able to demonstrate willingness to engage in local, global, international, and intercultural problem-solving.

Key levers		
	Activities to be implemented Theoretical foundations	• Global learning course approval, faculty and staff development, cocurricular activities, publicity for global learning, support for global learning • Attributes of the process of global learning, global learning SLOs (Gibson et al., 2008; Hanvey, 1975)
	Definitions of terms	• *Global citizenship*: the willingness to apply one's global awareness and perspective to local, global, international, and intercultural problem-solving (FIU, 2010) • *Global learning*: the process of diverse people collaboratively analyzing and addressing complex problems that transcend borders (Landorf & Doscher, 2015)

Note. FIU = Florida International University.

Who Needs To Be Involved in Developing the Common Agenda?

Leaders need to engage a broad array of stakeholders in the development of the common agenda if they want to build enduring acceptance for universal global learning. This doesn't mean that hundreds of people should attend the first planning meeting. Think of the beginning stages of your initiative as tossing a pebble into a pond rather than casting a wide net. As the common agenda grows from aspiration to outline to a concrete plan of action, ever-widening circles of stakeholders will become involved as their interests in the initiative emerge.

You might consider convening a steering committee to begin developing your high-level goal. The optimal size for such a working group is no more than 20 (Parkinson, 1957). Although this number may seem generous, you should still be intentional and transparent when recruiting members. Conduct a survey of existing committees; are there any other groups on campus with overlapping purposes? Recruit members of these groups and consider whether it's better to ask a standing committee to take on the new task of goal setting or to create a new group with intentional links to other committees. Your next step should be to recruit student representatives, for they are the ultimate beneficiaries of universal global learning. If the goal is to serve students, then students must play an active role in developing the plan for providing universal global learning. Stakeholders must understand the actual needs of the people they intend to serve "rather than posing a hypothesis about what they might need. All successful innovations balance the requirements of desirability (what people need), feasibility (what technology can do), and viability (what is sustainable or profitable)" (Brown, 2011, para. 10).

In seeking student and nonstudent steering committee members, try to go beyond the usual suspects, those for whom leadership is part of their job description or who already overextend themselves in service to the institution. Focus on innovators and early adopters who have a natural passion for global learning and unique insights into the kind of supports faculty, staff, and students need to fulfill their ambitions. These people will provide a burst of energy and examples of what's possible on a larger scale. Involve instructors who are already implementing innovative global learning pedagogical strategies, especially in disciplines that aren't traditionally thought of as international or global. Locate students who actively pursue study, internship, service, or research opportunities that involve global problem-solving. Recruit alumni in fields related to global problem-solving and staff members and administrators with a demonstrated commitment to diversity and collaboration. Start breaking down traditional silos from the outset by making sure you have representatives from academic, student, and administrative affairs at the initial visioning table.

As the collective conception of change coalesces, the discussion should evolve from what's desirable to what's feasible. Expand your network to include people with the knowledge and expertise needed to design measurable subgoals and key levers. You'll need people who have the power to move the initiative forward by allocating human, physical, financial, and technological resources, but you'll also want to invite midlevel managers and entry-level staff. High-level administrators have the authority to determine whether activities are strategically and financially viable, but they may lack on-the-ground experience necessary to determine feasibility. Remember that high-level and midlevel leaders may not know whether certain activities lead to undesirable secondary impacts; organizational borders and silos often prevent people from understanding how their work influences that of others. A secondary benefit of designing a common agenda is helping stakeholders see organizational interconnections they did not know existed.

One of the biggest challenges of this work is determining when and how to interest laggards and those who actively oppose the initiative. We encourage you to pay attention to these people because the work you do to address their concerns can strengthen the power of your case for universal global learning. Draw a stakeholder map to keep track of your expanding network and compare it to your institution's organizational chart to identify decision makers and those directly and indirectly affected by the activities associated with subgoals and key levers. Note supporters, detractors, and those who might be threatened by change. Be purposeful in your outreach efforts to active and potential critics, bringing them on board at times when you and your colleagues are prepared to field their questions and attend to their feedback. It can be especially effective to ask for critics' advice about specific aspects of the initiative, but be sure to follow up by reporting how you've responded to their feedback and why you've taken the path you have. Often, fear is the source of resistance; continuous communication builds trust and support.

Membership in the steering committee may change over time, and that's just fine. As word spreads, a snowball effect will increase the number and variety of people who want to be involved. New members may volunteer to accomplish needed tasks, and veterans may elect to step down or serve in an advisory, executive, or ex officio capacity. As the number of interested participants grows, you'll need to implement new methods of incorporating their feedback into the common agenda.

How Is Input Sought and Used to Set the Common Agenda?

Think of the development of a common agenda as a giant qualitative research project led by your steering committee. To answer the research questions posed at the beginning of this section, the committee can collect data from faculty, staff, students, alumni, and community members and leaders in the field of global learning. It can look for common themes that lead to the development of robust goals and key levers. The committee may then continue to bring in new stakeholders and gather more information until it reaches consensus or saturation, the point at which new data no longer shed new light on the research questions (Glaser & Strauss, 1967). This is when the committee will know it has truly developed a common agenda.

You can get to saturation and build overlapping consensus at the same time through participatory dialogue (Parker, 2003) and democratic deliberation (Sen, 2009). Participatory dialogue "can take place in private conversations and in public arenas. It emphasizes the fact that the individuals involved in dialogue listen to each other, speak to each other, and in particular share the dialogue space with respect and consideration" (Hemmati, 2007, p. 65). Dialogue is the heart of the process of developing a common agenda. Participatory dialogue builds mutual recognition of diverse stakeholder beliefs, goals, resources, knowledge, expertise, constraints, and asymmetries related to the provision of universal global learning. Democratic deliberation involves coming to a decision through participatory dialogue, by talking "about shared problems and disagreement over what to do about them in the presence of different perspectives" (Parker, 2007, p. 26). Participatory dialogue and democratic deliberation are consistent with processes of global learning and collective impact. But in practical terms, how can leaders effectively involve hundreds, even thousands, of stakeholders in such collaborative decision-making conversations?

At FIU, we accomplished this by posing open-ended questions to a wide variety of stakeholder groups and then facilitating a respectful exchange of diverse views among and between these groups. We started off with students, our most important stakeholders. We administered a paper-and-pencil survey to undergraduate students, asking the following questions:

- What is the difference between *international* and *global?* Which term best describes education at FIU?
- What comes to mind when you hear the term *global citizen?*
- What do global citizens need to know and be able to do?
- How do people learn to be global citizens?

We organized the results into some central themes, and then we convened a series of interdepartmental faculty focus groups, beginning each session with the same questions we posed to students. After faculty provided their answers, we presented them with the student survey results. We asked faculty to reflect on the meaning of those results and compare them to their own views. In some cases, faculty views overlapped those of students. When they diverged, we asked faculty to probe deeper into the source of their differing perspectives. After analyzing faculty responses, we returned to student focus groups and asked them to engage in the same comparative self-reflection.

We continued this process over the course of 18 months, adding additional groups of students, faculty, staff, alumni, and community members. To gather participants, we asked for time on the agendas of every meeting we could find, including those of departments, colleges, the Faculty Senate, student government, student affairs, alumni groups, and community advisory boards. We also conducted one-on-one interviews with high-level administrators, members of the Board of Trustees, and donors who were unavailable for group events. The steering committee reflected on the findings monthly, and as themes emerged, we began developing subgoals and key levers that adhered to an overlapping consensus. The questions posed to stakeholders also became more specific as we sought to clarify and focus the common agenda: Should global learning courses be required or elective as part of the program of study? How can students be encouraged to participate in more cocurricular global learning activities? How can we incentivize professional development?

At the same time stakeholder discussions were being held, an interdisciplinary faculty learning community was assembled to conduct a global learning literature review. Its purpose was to determine relationships among stakeholders' views on global learning and the history, theory, and research behind the concept. Another interdisciplinary faculty group began field testing draft versions of the SLOs, experimenting with methods of communicating the outcomes to students, developing them through pedagogy and content, and assessing them through traditional and authentic strategies. All these data were brought back to the steering committee for analysis.

Using these multiple methods—participatory dialogue, the literature reviews, and action research of our faculty learning communities—the committee brought about university-wide democratic deliberation concerning how best to provide global learning to all our students. Each time we invited stakeholders to share their perspectives and consider the relationship between their perspectives and those of others, another contribution was made toward achieving acceptance and overlapping consensus. Ultimately, the committee was able to build broad-based support for universal global learning and synthesize diverse views into a common agenda, one meaningful to the vast majority of stakeholders and to which everyone could make valuable contributions.

So You've Got a Common Agenda—Now What?

It took 18 months to determine our common agenda for universal global learning, and although the process was mostly collegial, it was by no means pain free. Like all higher education institutions, ours is politically charged and challenged by communication obstacles. At virtually every turn, we encountered resistance inspired by perceived threats to academic freedom, disciplinary turf wars, fears of additional layers of bureaucracy, and suspicions of an underlying liberal political or social agenda. Our open process of participatory dialogue did give naysayers a megaphone to publicize their views, but it also facilitated a collective response to them. Democratic deliberation took the pressure off nominal leaders and empowered a broader number of stakeholders to serve as thought leaders for global learning. Over time, resistance subsided and was replaced by genuine efforts to take concrete steps toward realizing our vision and reaching our goals. The most pressing of these efforts was allocating the human, physical, financial, and technological resources needed to provide global learning to all.

4

RESOURCING UNIVERSAL
GLOBAL LEARNING

*Much ingenuity with a little money is vastly more profitable and amusing
than much money without ingenuity. (Bennett, 2012, p. 119)*

Let's start this chapter with some good news: When it comes to resources,
you may already have much of what you need to get your universal
global learning initiative off the ground. We want you to know this at
the outset because the mere mention of resources can strike crippling fear into
the hearts of even the most committed global learning supporters. Energetic
planning may grind to a halt during the resourcing phase; people sometimes
lose steam and simply give up when confronted with budgeting realities such
as scarcity and competing priorities. In fact, we wouldn't be surprised to learn
that you either skipped this chapter completely or reluctantly saved it for last.

We're aware that few, if any, new resources may be allocated to your initiative, so we aren't going to present you with a catalog of the latest and great-
est global learning goods and services available. This chapter won't help you
build a shopping list, but it should help you build acceptance and momentum. So rather than recommending quantities, we recommend the qualities
you should look for when assembling the human, physical, financial, and
information technology resources you need to implement universal global
learning. Our discussion is guided by the following critical questions:

- Given your common agenda, what resources does your institution
  need to provide global learning for all?
- Are needed resources already available? If so, who has access to these
  resources?
- If resources aren't currently available, how can you acquire them?

Before we dive in, though, we want to clarify our perspective a bit further with three principles. First, we ground resourcing needs and ideas in the
context of our definition of *global learning*. The process of global learning can

occur anywhere and at any time, and it doesn't necessarily require any specialized tools or materials. The need for resources is driven by decisions concerning how you want to facilitate global learning. For example, if you want students to be guided by one or more trained faculty members, then professional development necessitates resources. Do you want global learning to happen online or abroad? If so, these decisions carry costs. Resources are also needed if you want to inspire global learning through speaker series or marketing campaigns, or if you want to share the results of students' global learning through conferences or symposia. Unlike endeavors that have minimum facilities or equipment requirements such as athletics or the fine arts, global learning resource needs are dynamic and dependent on design decisions.

This leads us to our second principle: Faculty and staff should prioritize the most efficient and effective methods available to enable all students to engage in global learning. Economical choices are sometimes eschewed in favor of exotic ones. Administrators go to great lengths to recruit diverse participants for trips abroad but may spend little time exploring local or regional options for engaging students with other perspectives and cultures. To be clear: We're agnostic when it comes to learning modalities. Meaningful, sustained engagement with diversity can be facilitated on campus, online, or abroad. We don't favor any particular global learning strategy over another. We hold that the problem to be investigated, and the perspectives needed for that investigation, should drive curricular and cocurricular design choices and the incumbent need for resources.

By extension, we adhere to a third and final principle: Your initiative's quality is determined by the excellence of the global learning it generates, not by the number of bells and whistles it provides. Glamorous destinations, powerful videoconferencing software, elaborately equipped classrooms—if you've got these resources, by all means deploy them. But if you don't have them, don't worry. None of these assets are fundamentally necessary for facilitating high-quality global learning and, in certain circumstances, may even get in the way of meaningful collaboration. Go for depth and authenticity before you pursue modernization and innovation. Focus on global learning as a process, not a product. So with that in mind, let's explore what you should consider as you gather the human, physical, and information technology resources and the financial means necessary to make global learning happen for all your students.

Human Resources

People and the knowledge, skills, and energy they offer are the most critical resource you need to implement universal global learning. At FIU human resource investments in our backbone organization in particular have enabled us to move our common agenda forward. You'll recall from chapter 3 that the backbone organization is the coordinating infrastructure for a collective impact initiative. As FIU's initiative has expanded, support for human resources outside the backbone has expanded as well. This has helped us weave global learning deeper into the fabric of university operations. In this section, we present some general human resourcing principles for collective impact and describe how we used these to achieve universal global learning at FIU.

Backbone Organization

Backbone organizations are usually formed during the second stage of collective impact development, after a more loosely organized group of stakeholders, in FIU's case our steering committee, coalesces a shared vision for change and drafts a common agenda. As stakeholders begin to implement differentiated activities, the need for a harmonizing force becomes apparent. Someone must perform the duties necessary to keep things together and on track, such as guiding the initiative's overall strategic direction, facilitating dialogue among stakeholders, supervising data collection and analysis, organizing communications and outreach, and administering budgets and resources (Hanleybrown, Kania, & Kramer, 2012). The backbone is also essential for creating partnership synergy, the unique power of collaboration and of collective impact (Lasker, Weiss, & Miller, 2001; Lee & Estes, 2003). When the work of the whole is greater than the sum of its individual parts, you know you've got partnership synergy.

The backbone coordinates and catalyzes stakeholders' wide-ranging knowledge, skills, and activities by performing two distinct yet complementary functions: administration and leadership. Administration entails day-to-day execution of management tasks, whereas leadership involves instilling an ongoing sense of purpose and ownership among stakeholders. Owen and Lambert (1998) explained that although administration "is concerned with control and order, leadership is focused on movement, direction and change" (p. 57). Backbone organizations for universal global learning are certainly concerned with transformative change; stakeholders must reconsider and break away from long-held paradigms and bureaucratic conventions to provide relevant, collaborative problem-solving opportunities for all. At the same time, transformational change doesn't happen in an organizational vacuum. The backbone must support stakeholders' abilities to address the exigencies that determine the feasibility of change, that is, policies, procedures, laws, accountability processes, and evaluation requirements. Table 4.1 summarizes representative tasks associated with the administrative and leadership functions of the backbone organization.

The backbone's capacity to carry out its administrative and leadership functions is influenced by its position in the institution's broader organizational chart and the composition of its staff. Effective backbone organizations can take many forms. You should design a structure that meets your institution's needs rather than simply copying what another institution has done. Next we describe some options for situating and staffing your backbone as well as potential financial and functionary impacts of different backbone design decisions.

Situating the Backbone Organization

Should your backbone be a centralized office staffed by personnel dedicated full-time to implementing universal global learning, or should it be a decentralized structure composed of a core group of faculty and staff already responsible for operating key levers of your common agenda? Both options have their advantages and disadvantages. Benefits of centralization include

TABLE 4.1
**Tasks Associated With the Backbone Organization's
Administrative and Leadership Functions**

Backbone Organization Administrative Tasks	Backbone Organization Leadership Tasks
• Performing secretarial duties • Coordinating activity, meeting, and project schedules • Collecting and disbursing funds • Monitoring time lines and deliverables • Facilitating information exchange among stakeholders • Applying for and supervising grants • Maintaining data and records • Executing data analysis • Performing program evaluation • Providing orientation to new stakeholders	• Maintaining focus on the common agenda • Taking responsibility for the stakeholder partnership • Inspiring, motivating, and empowering stakeholders • Working to develop a common language • Facilitating dialogue among stakeholders • Fostering respect, trust, inclusiveness, and openness among stakeholders • Creating an environment wherein differences of opinion and perspective can be voiced • Resolving conflict among stakeholders • Combining stakeholders' perspectives, resources, and skills • Helping stakeholders look at things differently and creatively

reduced operating costs and increased decision-making power and flexibility. Centralized offices are easy for new and external stakeholders to locate, and executive leaders can easily hold them accountable for the quality of operations and outputs. On the downside, centralized offices may become insular and authoritative over time, stymieing communication, cooperation, and continuous improvement across the institution. To encourage broad-based acceptance and responsiveness, some backbones are decentralized. This is common in large institutions, especially those with multiple campuses where a single office simply can't span the organization's size and the spread of its stakeholders. Decentralized backbone organizations may be composed of individuals who spend all or part of their time contributing to the common agenda, and these individuals may be in different departments or divisions. But just as centralized offices can become silos, dispersed leaders may feel isolated and cut off if they're too loosely connected. Imbalances in involvement can provoke ill will that spreads throughout the initiative, disintegrating individual and collective progress. Distributed backbone organizations must establish explicit collaboration processes so that decentralization doesn't result in a decomposition of vision and momentum.

Whether centralized or decentralized, the backbone organization should act as the node in a network of stakeholders. This is somewhat contrary to the traditional hierarchical nature of most higher education institutions. Colleges and universities build vertically oriented organizational structures to support independence and creativity in disciplines and divisions. Vertical structures generally don't lend themselves to close engagement with a broad spectrum of students, and they also don't facilitate interdisciplinary or interdepartmental collaboration. People in vertical reporting lines can feel they have more in common with those doing similar work in other institutions than they do with colleagues in other parts of their own college or university. Left unchecked, vertical organization can encourage concern for narrow internal goals and purposes rather than those of the broader organization (Kuh, 1996). Competitive performance-based funding models exacerbate the insular effects of vertical organization by pitting parts of the institution against each other in the struggle to increase the bottom line. Can the backbone be situated in such a way to surmount obstacles to systems change?

Institutions create offices with a horizontal orientation when their functions are supposed to address the needs of all students. Examples of horizontally oriented offices include student health, dining, counseling, and recreation services. Horizontal structures are also formed to decrease redundancy and competition when the same function is supposed to be performed across multiple departments (e.g., advancement, communications, and alumni relations). In a horizontally oriented organizational structure, the backbone's personnel report to a central office with a single reporting line, but to build and maintain relationships across reporting lines, these personnel serve constituencies in different departments across the institution.

Centralized and decentralized organizations and horizontal and vertical orientations can be mixed and matched in different ways to address your institution's unique culture, assets, and challenges. To illustrate, let's look at FIU's backbone organization, the Office of Global Learning Initiatives (OGLI). The OGLI staff report to the university's chief academic leader, who serves as the provost and executive vice president, by way of the vice president for academic affairs, but the OGLI is not located in the vertical line of a college or school. The OGLI's mission is not solely academic; this centralized office is responsible for coordinating all the moving parts associated with global learning at FIU, from cocurricular activities and internal and external communications to coding global learning courses on student transcripts. Because the OGLI lacks the full range of expertise needed to address FIU's complex common agenda, it's horizontally oriented. The OGLI doesn't have direct authority or hard power (Nye, 2004) over any other offices, so its staff must collaborate with the staff of nearly every academic, administrative, and student affairs department in the university to accomplish the items on FIU's common agenda for universal global learning. Proximity to the provost gives the OGLI the gravitas it needs to gain access to high-level decision makers in these departments, but its lack of hard power requires it to build strong trusting working relationships with middle-level and entry-level staff members to get things done.

The OGLI's soft power (Nye, 2004) has been a determining factor in its ability to connect across reporting lines. As Keeling, Underhile, and Wall (2007) have observed, horizontal functioning is often achieved through "astute political savvy by inspired leaders and key influencers of opinion and through the force of strong human relations, rather than through policy-driven, mission-centered, or otherwise explicit expectations for transdivisional collaboration or systematic change" (p. 25). Shrewd backbone placement is no substitute for skilled administration and leadership. So once you've determined how to situate your backbone's structure, what personal and professional qualities should you look for in its staff? Where do you find personnel with the knowledge, skills, and dispositions necessary to lead and administer universal global learning?

Staffing the Backbone Organization

Effective leaders of collective impact initiatives are

- visionary, possessed of a clear conception of global learning, the common agenda, and universal global learning's relationship to the institution's mission, history, and strategic plan;
- results-oriented, able to motivate a wide variety of stakeholders beyond talk and toward concrete action for advancing universal global learning;
- collaborative, able to work well with stakeholders across departments and divisions and make everyone feel his or her contribution is important;
- focused but adaptive, prepared to cultivate a wide range of ideas for advancing global learning and able to discern those that hold the most potential for achieving the items on the common agenda;
- charismatic, influential communicators adept at passionately articulating the meaning and importance of universal global learning and spreading that passion to others;
- politic, possessing the political savvy and diplomatic skills needed to bridge divides caused by organizational, disciplinary, racial, cultural, and other differences; and
- humble, willing to act as a servant-leader, sharing power and focusing primarily on students' needs. (Turner, Merchant, Kania, & Martin, 2012)

We contend that in addition to these qualities, successful leaders of universal global learning initiatives share the following important trait: They exhibit the same global learning outcomes they wish to imbue in their students. These leaders are globally aware; they have an ability to see interrelationships among people, ideas, and disciplines that others don't necessarily detect. They're excellent networkers and matchmakers, viewing interrelationships as resources that fuel innovative learning, research, and engagement. They also have a global perspective; they are able to transcend their personal point of view to help other faculty and staff see how global learning can benefit themselves and their students. Finally, effective global learning leaders are globally engaged. Their entrepreneurial mind-set, sense of curiosity, tendency toward optimism, and comfort with risk support their ability to cocreate rich opportunities for bringing diverse people together to achieve global learning for all.

Sounds like a tall order, doesn't it? Well, we're about to add another set of requisites to the job description—knowledge and skills specific to universal global learning curriculum reform. Table 4.2 presents the areas of proficiencies we recommend for your backbone organization.

You don't have to look for all these proficiencies in one person. You can construct a backbone team that encompasses all the capabilities you need,

TABLE 4.2
Areas of Proficiency for Universal Global Learning Backbone Personnel

Areas of Proficiency	Description
Internationalization of higher education	Knowledge of the six interconnected areas for comprehensive internationalization (American Council on Education, 2012)
Global learning curriculum and pedagogy	An understanding of globalization and its impact on knowledge acquisition, production, and spread; expertise in collaborative problem-solving and cross-cultural communication pedagogy
Cocurricular programming and student advisement	Knowledge of student development, cross-cultural communication and diversity issues, student services, and methods for promoting integrative learning
Professional development	Ability to design and implement differentiated methods for helping faculty and staff acquire and expand their capacities to provide global learning to all
Student learning assessment	Knowledge of fundamental concepts in the measurement of student learning, including direct, indirect, criterion-based, and performance-based assessment strategies, and methods for using results to facilitate continuous improvement
Educational technology	Awareness of Web-based tools for collaborating, communicating, and acquiring and spreading knowledge across borders
Program evaluation	Expertise in methods for collecting, analyzing, and using information to determine the efficiency and effectiveness of projects, policies, and programs
Multiple disciplines	Knowledge of fundamental concepts in the pure and applied sciences, social sciences, and humanities; awareness of approaches to global learning in diverse disciplines

and you can expand your team as your initiative evolves. FIU turned to its School of Education and Human Development to find its director of OGLI, Hilary Landorf, whose deep knowledge of international and global education and specialization in curriculum design and instruction made her an ideal choice. Her previous administrative experience at FIU included serving as leader of its social studies and international and intercultural education programs, associate director of its global awareness program, and director of the Institute of International and Intercultural Education initiatives. She also had proven her financial acumen as treasurer of one of the largest international education organizations in the world, the Comparative and International Education Society. Before coming to FIU, Landorf had been the administrative director of the Multinational Institute of American Studies at New York University and had more than 20 years of experience as a teacher and administrator in K–20 educational settings throughout the world. For associate director, Landorf selected Stephanie Doscher, who came to her position with a background in educational leadership. As a K–12 teacher, Doscher had assumed numerous leadership roles in public and private schools undergoing organizational change. She was also a skilled consultant, having served as a teacher mentor, internal evaluator, and program reviewer for a range of secondary and tertiary institutions. Doscher offered robust expertise in strategic planning, curriculum design, professional development, student learning assessment, and program evaluation. A program assistant was brought on board soon after to manage scheduling, correspondence, and budgetary matters. Landorf and Doscher's complementary expertise enabled them to fulfill nearly all the office's administration and leadership responsibilities in its first couple of years. But as the complexity of the initiative and the density of its stakeholder network increased, their roles became more specialized, and the OGLI needed additional personnel.

The OGLI's next stage of growth saw the addition of a coordinator for cocurricular programming and advisement, Eric Feldman. A two-time FIU alumnus, Feldman's long résumé of undergraduate activities included serving as a peer adviser, writing for the student newspaper, and being an active member of a Greek organization. While a student ambassador, he worked with the Office of the President, alumni relations, and other partners to host visiting dignitaries and stage numerous university and community functions. Feldman first came to the OGLI as a graduate assistant in the School of Education and Human Development's higher education administration program, and he immediately became indispensable. His deep knowledge of the institution and his broad view of student development pathways rapidly accelerated faculty, staff, and students' abilities to identify global learning opportunities and construct integrative bridges between the global learning curriculum and cocurriculum. Feldman's work has expanded to include career advisement, which is discussed in more detail in chapter 7.

Part-time personnel address a variety of other OGLI needs. A student from FIU's College of Engineering handles data management and integration, including the design and maintenance of OGLI records and databases. An economics graduate assistant performs statistical analysis for student learning assessment and program evaluation studies. To execute qualitative research, the OGLI engages a doctoral student from the School of Education and Human Development's international and intercultural education program. A .25 full-time equivalent external relations account representative, supported by a cost share with the School of Education and Human Development, has assisted with communications and Web design. Finally, a variety of students in the school's higher education administration program have completed semester-long practicums in the OGLI, implementing special projects such as designing new outreach, mentorship, and leadership development strategies for global learning student clubs and organizations.

Taken together, staff members housed in the centralized, horizontally oriented OGLI possess the competencies necessary to perform many of the tasks associated with the office's leadership and administrative functions. Still, they can't do everything. Distributed personnel such as committee members, appointed departmental representatives, and full-time global learning specialists have enabled expansions in FIU's global learning initiative that OGLI staff couldn't have imagined or implemented solely on their own.

Distributed Global Learning Personnel

Broad-based committees have been vital to the evolution of global learning at FIU. The steering committee that coalesced FIU's common vision was known as the Development Team, and its members, appointed by the provost, included students, faculty, staff, high-level administrators, alumni, and community members. Having accomplished its goal of creating a blueprint for change, including establishing the OGLI, the committee was decommissioned in 2009. Several of its members went on to serve on the Design Team, which was created to help implement the Development Team's recommendations and support the OGLI. This committee was composed primarily of midlevel staff with close understandings of FIU's governance structures and institutional processes, policies, and resources. The Design Team's responsibilities included providing enrollment and course scheduling data, conducting feasibility assessments, setting up operational functions such as digital degree audits, and serving as the initiative's public relations ambassadors. When the global learning graduation requirement was successfully launched in fall 2010, the Implementation Team was formed to help monitor operations, analyze student learning assessment and program evaluation results, and recommend continuous improvements. This committee included people who had previously served on the Development and Design Teams as well as executive leaders with bird's-eye views of the university and the systems in which it operates. Implementation Team members were influential champions who perceived the initiative's importance to FIU's mission and to the field of higher education. They also possessed valuable leading-edge knowledge of broader dynamics influencing the work, including state funding and institutional strategy changes. These powerful executive advocates had the decision-making authority needed to quickly address threats and opportunities facing the fledgling global learning project, ensuring the initiative's survival in its hectic early years.

Beyond the committees, administrators of various units have also taken the initiative to appoint representatives to lead the expansion of global learning in their areas. FIU's Division of Student Affairs appointed the director of the Center for Leadership and Service as its liaison to the OGLI. The director has collaborated on a variety of projects including providing professional development to faculty and student affairs staff, collecting program evaluation data from the division, and codeveloping a global living-learning community in partnership with the OGLI and the Departments of Housing and Residential Life. Academic departments with a high number of global learning–designated courses have tasked faculty or staff with responsibilities such as leading course revision, orienting new instructors, and collecting and analyzing course assessment results. Faculty members serving as raters for FIU's student learning assessments have also greatly enhanced communication between the OGLI and various academic departments (for more on assessment and evaluation, see chapter 9).

One of FIU's most exciting human resource developments occurred in fall 2014 when administrators in the Division of Libraries decided to hire a dedicated global learning librarian. This strategic investment offered convincing evidence that the university had truly embraced global learning. FIU's libraries had long been involved in our initiative; a librarian served on the Faculty Senate Global Learning Curriculum Oversight Committee and was part of the team that developed one of FIU's first global learning courses, How We Know What We Know. The libraries division had also invited the OGLI to collaborate on a grant-funded study exploring the influence of instructional collaborations between global learning and library faculty on students' information literacy and global learning SLOs. The OGLI regularly approached the Division of Libraries with requests from global learning faculty for librarians to assist with instruction, student advisement, and resource location and acquisition, but it was an incredible surprise to learn that the libraries division faculty and staff had voted to create a brand new full-time position to serve these needs. Among her many duties, FIU's global learning librarian develops online library research guides for courses, acts as an embedded librarian, provides professional development for subject matter liaisons, and leads global learning collection development.

People such as backbone staff, committee members, and distributed personnel may be your most indispensable global learning resource, but they can't work without the basic tools of their professions and the spaces to operate these tools. What kinds of physical and information technology resources might you need to implement universal global learning?

Physical Resources

As we've said about resources in general, we advocate aligning your decisions with your common agenda. Thus, at FIU, it was important to us for the OGLI to be located in a central location so that students would find us even if they weren't looking for us, and in turn we could readily initiate collaborations with students, faculty, and staff. We were thrilled when we secured space in the Steven J. and Dorothea Green Library, which is literally in the center of FIU's main Modesto A. Maidique Campus. Anne Prestamo (2017), dean of libraries, calls Green Library "the physical and metaphorical heart" (para. 1) of the campus. In 2016 the OGLI moved to Primera Casa, FIU's main administrative building, to accommodate the addition of the Office of the Executive Director of the Comparative and International Education Society under the OGLI umbrella.

Classroom space is another essential physical resource, and we strongly encourage you to think about it while planning your initiative. In an ideal global learning classroom, groups of students can work together easily. We're lucky that FIU's director of space management is knowledgeable about interactive pedagogies and is a strong supporter of active learning, especially team-based learning. Early in the development of the global learning initiative, she was determined to have a number of buildings then under design and construction contain active learning classrooms. These were intentionally designed to be flexible, connected, and collaborative to encourage interactive, student-centered learning experiences (Brooks, 2011). With the director's backing, four active learning classrooms were built at FIU in 2009 and 2010, and more have been added since. Global learning courses are regularly assigned these spaces.

Information Technology Resources

Increasingly, information technology is essential to making global learning universal. By information technology we mean the tools, processes, and methodologies used to collect, process, store, secure, and exchange electronic data ("Information Technology," 2017). Today information technology is used not only to capture, sort, collate, and summarize data but also to analyze and disseminate data necessary to evaluate and continuously improve the extent to which you provide global learning to all. Information technology also facilitates global learning by helping students, faculty, and community members communicate and collaborate across borders of time and space.

Using Information Technology to Evaluate Global Learning

Carrying out our common agenda at FIU depends on the efficient and effective use of information technology. If you recall from chapter 3, our four program goals call for us to provide enough global learning courses to enable all students to meet their two-course global learning graduation requirement, integrate an increasing number of cocurricular activities into the undergraduate curriculum, deliver high-quality faculty and staff global learning workshops, and ensure that students gain proficiency in the global learning SLOs. Without technology, we couldn't accomplish the evaluation and improvement of these goals. Our systems track every student in nearly every aspect of global learning, whether taking a global learning course, completing one of our institution-level student learning assessments, enrolling in our graduation honors programs, or even attending discussions or international internship advisement sessions. We use information technology to keep account of global learning course offerings and enrollment statistics. We also use our systems' data analysis and reporting tools to track short-term and long-term trends in student learning assessment and program evaluation results to uncover issues that require improvement.

We're continually working to keep up with advances in technology to improve our systems' functionality and efficiency. As with any initiative, some of our efforts have been more successful than others. There isn't one turnkey system for universal global learning. The following four recommendations are based on what we've learned in our information technology journey; these are successes we've had, the challenges we've found, and ways we've learned from experience.

Make Information Technology Part of Your Planning Process

Too often the technology needs of complex change initiatives like universal global learning are an afterthought, developed and implemented only after stakeholders are buried in data on their own computers and realize the severe limitations of relying solely on electronic tools such as Microsoft Excel spreadsheets. Rather than putting off technology needs until after you've begun to collect data, we strongly urge you to include it in the planning stages of your initiative. The same critical questions we started this chapter with apply to information technology planning. To begin, figure out the resources you need to complete the items on your common agenda. Once you know what technology resources you need, take an inventory of all the assets available at your institution, determine who has access to these resources, the level of expertise needed to use them, and how much they cost for you to use. Of course, you'll want to involve your technology and data management departments in the initial planning discussions. In your audit you may also find other academic or student affairs departments that are using resources similar to those you need, and you should involve these units in planning as well. For example, we learned from the College of Business staff that FIU already had deeply discounted institution-wide licenses for the customer relationship management and data visualization software the OGLI wanted to use. Brainstorming the architecture of these systems with College of Business staff was an invaluable exercise for us.

Work With Information Technology Experts

Knowing what you don't know is an important skill in planning any initiative. We knew from the get-go that we'd need technology but that the OGLI didn't have the in-house expertise necessary to choose or set up these systems. We turned to experts in FIU's Office of Analysis and Information Management to help us design a system for integrating student enrollment and global learning assessment data. We enlisted an outside consultant to help us with a system for recording faculty and staff participation in professional development activities. She helped us set up our system and taught us how to use it. She also customized modules to track students' participation in cocurricular activities and their progress toward our global learning graduation honors.

Track Everything

We also encourage you set up your system to track as many variables as you can think of at the outset, and be prepared to track more as they emerge. We say this from experience; it's so much easier to collect data and not use them than to try to add data midstream. Here's a concrete example: We set up our professional development tracking module to collect, collate, summarize, and analyze the following data for each participant: title, position, college or school, contact information, type of workshop attended, dates of attendance, global learning courses or activity being developed or revised, and dates of semesters teaching global learning courses. We inserted a notes field to record additional data we hadn't initially anticipated we'd need, and this turned out to be information about stipend payments. Luckily, our consultant could create a new field and backfill this information, but it was cumbersome and expensive.

Integrate Information Technology Systems Whenever Possible

Our last recommendation is to integrate information technology systems whenever you can. As stated previously, we house our global learning course and assessment data in one system and our professional development and student cocurricular activity participation data in another. This has worked for us in terms of tracking, analyzing, and communicating progress toward our four program goals. However, there are instances when we'd like to analyze relationships among data in these separate systems. Because these systems don't talk to each other, these comparisons are difficult. The best systems are those that integrate information and enable users to retrieve and share it easily.

Using Information Technology to Conduct Global Learning

Technology can facilitate communication and collaboration across borders, whether in Web-assisted, hybrid, or fully online courses. Some global learning pedagogies, such as Collaborative Online International Learning (COIL) and the X-Culture Project, are specifically designed for international student partnerships and can only be conducted through the use of communication technology (Connell, 2014). In COIL and X-Culture, students talk with each other and work on a common project, primarily asynchronously. They can use any software platform they wish to exchange and store information, whether it is Google Docs, Google Hangouts, Dropbox, Facebook, Slack, Prezi, Skype, or any other. If institutions have site licenses for platforms like Adobe Connect, VoiceThread, Blue Jeans, or Join.me, faculty can use these to facilitate guided interactions. Students in far-flung locations can now use technology to participate in activities that previously would have been possible only in face-to-face contexts. SearchTeam allows students to review research together and organize their findings. Mind42 is a brainstorming and mind-mapping tool. Skitch, CoSketch, and Padlet are all multiuser whiteboards that allow partners to visualize ideas and add annotations, links, videos, images, and other media to make ideas come alive using few words. The universe of online collaborative learning tools is constantly expanding. We recommend including an educational technology specialist as part of your curriculum and professional development planning team. Don't confine global learning to physical spaces; make sure you reach all students by enabling it to occur in virtual spaces as well.

Financial Resources

We started this chapter saying that you may already have much of what you need to get your universal global learning initiative off the ground. But what if this isn't the case? How will you secure funds for the human, physical, and information technology resources you need, much less for the stipends and fees associated with other items on your wish list, such as the following:

- Course development
- Professional memberships
- Conference travel
- Faculty and student research
- Internships, service-learning, and study abroad
- Consultants
- Workshops
- Branding and communications

You already know that financial resources are hard to come by. State support for public colleges and universities is dwindling (Pew Charitable Trusts, 2015). Dollars are also scarce in private nonprofit institutions where declining enrollments are driving tuition discounts to an all-time high (Woodhouse, 2015). Your chief financial officer is likely struggling just as you are to expand revenue streams and identify alternative funding sources for important programs (Seltzer, 2016). In addition to cutting costs and increasing efficiencies, chief financial officers are pursuing entrepreneurial approaches to raising the bottom line, "asking questions and delving into enterprises that may be quite unfamiliar and new" (Pelletier, 2012, p. 3). You can do this, too, if you know the right questions to ask and which enterprises might be available to you. Drawing on our own work and that of creative colleagues, we now outline some avenues you might want to explore in your quest for new financial resources.

Internal Funds

Sometimes referred to as education and general expenditure (E&G) funds, internal funding comes from state appropriations or tuition revenues. Annual E&G allocations support operations aligned with the institution's mission and strategic priorities. If your initiative receives an annual E&G budget, it's a sign that universal global learning is valued and that you have the support of high-level leaders.

Our operating budget for Global Learning for Global Citizenship comes almost entirely from E&G funds. Also known as hard money, internal E&G funds are generally prized because they're seen as more dependable and less demanding than external soft money sources, such as grants and auxiliary enterprises, which carry significant bureaucratic burdens and must be constantly sought (Thelin, 2011). But according to Harvey Charles, dean for international education and vice provost for global strategy at University of Albany, hard money has its downside too. Charles has served as senior internationalization officer at public and private institutions across all regions of the United States and cautioned in an interview that E&G appropriations are subject to the whims of state legislative and administrative preferences and so may be cut with little warning (H. Charles, personal communication, May 22, 2016). Charles told us that when he accepted a prior position at Northern Arizona University, he was leery of soft money. He said he was quickly disabused of that notion in 2008 when just after taking his position, the Arizona legislature slashed higher education budgets by $141.5 million (H. Charles, personal communication, May 22, 2016). Because Charles's budget was mostly derived from non–E&G funds, the budget cuts had far less impact on his unit than on others. Although Charles agreed that a fair budget allocation from central administration is an important symbol of administrative support for universal global learning, he recommended diversifying budgets through soft money sources such as tuition capture to shield programs from the vicissitudes of E&G cuts.

Tuition Capture

While serving as Northern Arizona University's senior internationalization officer, Charles's Center for International Education was funded primarily from a captured percentage of every international student's tuition. The center housed numerous offices, and its responsibilities were manifold: international student admissions and recruitment, international student and scholar services, education abroad, faculty research and professional development abroad, and the Global Learning Initiative for internationalizing Northern Arizona University's curriculum and cocurriculum. Charles described the tuition capture model as a "win-win-win-win proposition" for everyone (H. Charles, personal communication, May 22, 2016). The university won because it could increase the diversity of its student body and receive out-of-state tuition rates from international students. It was a win for the center because the model gave it a vested interest in recruiting and retaining as many international students as possible. International students won because their needs were attended to and supported by motivated, well-resourced staff members. Finally, domestic students won because tuition capture funds supported improved opportunities for them to participate in global learning with diverse others on campus and abroad.

Student Fees

Texas offers an alternative to tuition capture—student fees. In 1987 University of Texas at Austin students decided to financially support their classmates' participation in international exchange and study through a $1 mandatory fee for all those enrolling in the university. Since then, the Texas legislature has mandated that all public campuses may charge a maximum $4 fee for such purposes (University of Texas at Austin International Office, 2012). Other states have followed suit (Redden, 2009; University of Illinois at Urbana-Champaign, 2017). According to staff at University of Texas at Austin, this student-led, student-focused approach is proof that anything is possible in terms of resourcing global learning. It yields a continuous stream of hundreds of thousands of dollars per year without requiring additional fund-raising efforts on the part of staff (NAFSA: Association of International Educators, 2017). Nevertheless, with private giving to colleges and universities on an annual upward trend since 2010 (Koenig, 2016), philanthropy does represent another avenue for diversifying revenue streams.

Private Philanthropy

Philanthropic gifts can come in a variety of forms. The Voluntary Support of Education survey of the Council for Aid to Education (n.d.), the most comprehensive accounting of such funding available, analyzes income from the following sources:

- Gifts and grants to the institution for current operations and capital purposes
- Gifts and grants to affiliated foundations and organizations created to raise funds for the institution
- Securities, real estate, equipment, property, or other noncash gifts
- Deferred gifts, cash surrender value of life insurance contracts, insurance premiums paid by donors, and cash payments returned as contributions from salaried staff

In terms of global learning, what do private philanthropists want to fund? According to Martin Shell, vice president for development at Stanford University, U.S. institutions "attract significant private support in part because donors appreciate their efforts to tackle major global challenges" (Koenig, 2016, para. 12). Case in point, in 2015 the Mellon Foundation allocated about $28 million to support international, interdisciplinary collaborations of humanistic scholars and artists seeking to answer grand challenge questions, such as postconflict reconciliation, environmental justice, religious coexistence, freedom of speech, the pursuit of happiness, the preservation of history, and cultivation of aesthetic beauty (Andrew W. Mellon Foundation, 2015). According to Mariët Westermann (2012), Mellon's executive vice president for programs and research, foundations increasingly want to fund innovative, sustainable models for collaborative research and learning across borders rather than individual scholars engaging in research and study abroad. Westermann cites the following three reasons foundations prefer collaborations that emphasize exchange and reciprocity:

1. They attract energetic, motivated scholars who find value in working with unfamiliar perspectives and gaining access to new modes of thought and inquiry. The most forward-looking research questions and results emerge from these scholars.
2. They prepare faculty to teach for the new global century. These faculty will bring new knowledge to their fields and provide observable evidence of the utility of global learning for understanding our complex world.
3. They make funds go farther. When U.S. foundations work in partnership with funding agencies abroad to support international collaborative work, this expands the impact of U.S. dollars and rebuts the charge that foundations are merely exporting tax-exempt charity to support work in other countries.

Westermann (2012) also draws attention to the need to support faculty in decentering their curricula and research from Western content and perspectives. Institutions can seek private professional development grants and donations to help faculty acquire the language, subject matter, and intercultural communication expertise they need to make their research and teaching more comparative and collaborative in nature.

Public Grants

Federal and state government agencies also fund global learning. The U.S. government has long supported the internationalization of higher education for economic, diplomatic, and national security reasons, investing about $230 million every year in the Fulbright Program alone. Perhaps the nation's most popular and well-known international education program, Fulbright's broad menu of grants is funded by an annual appropriation by the U.S. Congress to the U.S. Department of State's Bureau of Educational and Cultural Affairs. This agency maintains other initiatives that can support global learning at home and abroad for students, scholars, teachers, professionals, and citizen groups. These include the International Visitor Leadership, Disabilities in Exchange, and Sports Diplomacy programs (for more information, see eca .state.gov/programs-initiatives). The Department of Education's Office of Postsecondary Education houses the International and Foreign Language Education office, which administers grant and fellowship programs for foreign language instruction, area and international studies instruction and research, and professional and curriculum development (for more information, see www2.ed.gov/about/offices/list/ope/iegps/index.html). The National Institutes of Health, National Science Foundation, U.S. Institute of Peace, and other agencies also facilitate a variety of international education, research, and training activities. You can visit www.grants.gov to search for all U.S. government–funded grants.

Many state governments want to make their economies more globally competitive and are doing so in part through the internationalization of public higher education. The authors of a multimethod study found that although state governments differ widely in the extent to which they engage with the higher education sector, support for internationalization generally falls under one or more of the following pillars: an international higher education policy agenda, strategic planning and goal setting, international exchanges and study abroad, and collaborative and innovative research programs (Lane, Owens, & Ziegler, 2014). States have historically limited the use of taxpayer funds for out-of-state activities, and some states downplay international activities for fear of political repercussions. In their quest to transform economies, governors and legislatures are beginning to support internationalization to raise awareness of their region and attract trade and direct foreign investment. States are also coordinating study abroad, foreign language offerings, and international student recruitment among campuses. Washington and Michigan have even created collaborative public and private research and training programs to develop their states' economic, health, and environmental development sectors. Based on their research, Lane and Owens (2014) advise global learning leaders to build state support for their work by determining whether their state has

- resolved to support international education,
- incorporated international dimensions in its higher education strategic plan,
- sponsored a student exchange or study abroad relationship with other countries, and
- developed a network of excellence and innovation in global research.

Self-Supporting Instructional Programs
Harvey Charles told us that a distinguishing characteristic among adequately funded global learning initiatives is the presence of an intensive English program in the institution (H. Charles, personal communication, May 22, 2016). Such programs are generally self-supporting in that they receive neither state subsidies nor tuition capture funds. Self-supporting programs are

also generally mission focused in that they provide the public with services that fulfill demonstrated higher education and workforce needs. Charles described to us a particularly innovative program at his institution: a global online language training certificate. Supported in part by a private funder, a pilot study was launched to determine the feasibility of offering training in multiple languages to tens of thousands of displaced people. Charles's institution captured part of the program's tuition revenue and used it to increase global learning opportunities for domestic and international students and faculty (H. Charles, personal communication, May 22, 2016).

Conclusion

By now you've probably surmised that it takes leadership to build acceptance and momentum for universal global learning through the resourcing process. And so we want to leave you with three key leadership insights we gained from Harvey Charles. First, secure your high-level administrators' trust. Charles cautioned that presidents and chief academic officers need assurances that resources will be used to support universal global learning as a strategic endeavor. Second, Charles advised making special efforts with chief financial officers. These individuals are extremely influential leaders who seldom know much about global learning. Chief financial officers need to be informed of the value and draw of global learning for current and potential students and the revenue-related differences between third party and institution sponsors of study abroad and bilateral exchange programs. Innovative and effective global learning efforts can actually be moneymaking enterprises, drawing the attention of interested funders (Carleton College, 2013; Georgia Tech University, 2012; Washington and Lee University, 2013). Third, Charles recommended looking for opportunities to help deans and chairs fill their own global learning resourcing gaps. Charles found that when he could provide support for such things as faculty members' international research or conference attendance, deans and chairs lowered their resistance to proposals for new global learning initiatives (H. Charles, personal communication, May 22, 2016). We couldn't agree more. Trust, information sharing, and mutual reinforcement are key to resourcing universal global learning.

PART TWO

WHAT GLOBAL LEARNING LOOKS LIKE: MUTUALLY REINFORCING ACTIVITIES

5

GLOBAL LEARNING PROFESSIONAL DEVELOPMENT

Global learning has improved my approach to teaching in all of my classes. In both content and pedagogy my courses have become more sophisticated.

My thoughts on global learning are improved and expanded. Global learning involves good teaching and course design and is a process.

We should improve ourselves to accommodate our students' needs better, to improve our global learning teaching and their global learning experiences. This workshop was really valuable for moving forward on this goal. (Participant comments, Global Learning Course Design and Instruction Workshop, January 8, 2015)

I f we want to provide global learning to all students, we must provide professional development to all global learning educators. Student learning is predicated on faculty and staff learning. How can we expect educators to facilitate global learning if they don't really know what it is or how to do it (Clifford, 2009; Leask & Beelen, 2010; Stohl, 2007)? As global learning leaders, we must give the same attention to our faculty's and staff's growth and development as we do to our students'. This involves establishing a common language for educators to talk about universal global learning and common opportunities for them to critically reflect on their own global awareness, perspective, and engagement. We must also help educators connect the dots between self-reflection and instruction, empowering them to determine diverse ways to facilitate global learning for others. Most important, as global learning leaders, we need to know which concepts and pedagogical strategies make it from the workshop into the syllabus and the conditions that determine whether these strategies succeed or fail. This information will help us improve the quality of the professional development we offer and in turn improve the quality of students' global learning.

As you read in chapter 3, FIU's common agenda calls for our backbone organization, the OGLI, to provide high-quality professional development to advance global learning across the university's curriculum and cocurriculum (FIU, 2010). For us, high quality means news you can use, or in other words, relevant global learning tools and concepts that can be customized and efficiently and effectively employed in different courses and activities. Such professional development is vital to unleashing the synergies that arise from a collective impact initiative's mutually reinforcing activities. Breakthroughs in thought and behavior and exponential growth in the initiative's impact are generated when stakeholders coordinate separate but complementary contributions to the common agenda. To advance global learning through mutual reinforcement, our professional development offerings are open to all: administrators, staff, graduate and undergraduate faculty, faculty teaching dual-enrollment courses in high schools, graduate assistants, and even leaders of student organizations. From in-person and online workshops to brown-bag lunches, reading groups, day-long symposia, and multiday conferences, FIU global learning professional development opportunities enable participants to design and implement a wide range of strategies on and off campus. With few exceptions and in keeping with the idea that mutual reinforcement involves cooperation across reporting lines, professional development is also interdisciplinary and interdepartmental.

Over the years our experiences with educators in our own institution and others have taught us a lot about how to provide meaningful, even transformative, global learning professional development for all. Next we explore the following questions we grapple with on a daily basis:

- How do you get people to attend global learning professional development?
- What should global learning professional development entail?
- How do you get participants to apply what they've learned?

Other components of your global learning professional development plan (i.e., evaluation and continuous improvement of its quality and effectiveness) are addressed in chapters 9 and 10.

How Do You Get People to Attend?

Between summer 2009 and this book's publication, FIU's OGLI has staged more than 110 different professional development events ranging from one hour to six weeks in length involving more than 1,500 participants. These numbers indicate our program's broad reach, but they don't reveal the lengths we've gone to in addressing our diverse stakeholders' unique circumstances. You see, that's our first rule of thumb for professional development: Provide people with what they need, not just what you want them to know. You will enhance the likelihood that people will enroll in your workshops and eventually apply the tools you present if you can make convincing, data-based arguments on why professional development will be useful.

Before you start shopping around for potential workshop topics and presenters, investigate the challenges people face as they attempt to integrate global learning into courses and activities. For example, nearly half (45%) of all respondents to a survey of undergraduate faculty reported that they felt unprepared to address diversity-related conflicts in class (Eagan et al., 2014). Is this an issue on your campus? Sometimes survey results can be deceiving; from their limited points of view, faculty and staff may not perceive deficits in their practice. Comprehensive needs assessment should incorporate data from multiple perspectives, especially those of students. Focus groups, program reviews, standardized and authentic learning assessments, and observations can all provide information that may help you uncover gaps in students' global learning that could be filled at least in part through professional development support.

To tap into students' views, determine whether your institution already administers instruments such as the Culturally Engaging Campus Environments survey (National Institute for Transformation & Equity, 2017) or the National Survey of Student Engagement (NSSE) (2015). These and other similar instruments have implications for professional development. For instance, NSSE (2015) has made available a Global Learning Topical Module that asks students to report the extent to which their courses have encouraged them to "understand the viewpoints, values, or customs of different world cultures, nationalities, and religions" (para. 3), how often they've "discussed international or global topics and issues with others" (para. 4), and how well they've been prepared to understand how their "actions affect global communities" (para. 6). If results aren't what you'd hoped, the reason might be that faculty and staff want to involve students in global learning, they just don't know how to do so effectively. When advertising and marketing professional development, be transparent in your intended purpose and learning outcomes. Even if educators are unable to identify or admit their own frustrations, they may be drawn to offerings that will reduce those expressed by their students.

Along with providing persuasive reasons why professional development will improve student learning, you'll want to clear impediments to faculty and staff participation. Enrollment processes, scheduling, instructional modalities, and follow-up methods can all be customized to address people's needs. Instruments such as the Questionnaire on Internationalization of the Curriculum, the Blockers and Enablers survey (Leask, 2015), and assessments provided as part of the American Council on Education's (2017)

Internationalization Toolkit can probe the conditions influencing stakeholders' willingness and ability to participate in professional development.

One participatory obstacle you will never be able to remove completely, though, is people's discomfort with change. Many prefer the safety of the old to the uncertainty of the new, even if their current situation is ineffectual or uncomfortable (Matthews, 2017). It's important to realize that for most of your faculty, staff, and students, global learning differs significantly from the educational approaches they've grown accustomed to. When you ask people to adopt or adapt to new global learning methods, you're asking them to change how they teach and learn. In effect, you're asking them to innovate. An innovation is "an idea, practice, or object that is perceived as new" (Rogers, 2003, p. 12). Global learning will turn off some of your stakeholders just because it's an innovation. Others will be attracted to it for the very same reason. Differences in the ways people adapt to change, adopt new tools and approaches, and communicate these activities to others will definitely complicate your ability to immediately engage large numbers of faculty and staff in global learning professional development. But if you design a menu of opportunities that accommodates these differences, you may be pleasantly surprised how fast you can get people to sign up for professional development and spread global learning innovations throughout your institution.

Diffusing Global Learning: Different Approaches for Different Folks

Rogers (2003) divided people who embrace new technologies at different rates into separate categories: innovators, early adopters, early majority, late majority, and laggards. Your institution is composed of people from each of these categories. If you know a bit about what makes people in each category tick, you can structure and pace professional development in ways that will bring increasingly broad and diverse circles of stakeholders on board. Offer a high-quality product people need and can use successfully, and word will get out. And you know the saying: Word of mouth is the best publicity.

Innovators and Early Adopters

Some of your faculty and staff will be natural innovators, interested in global learning because it's novel. Innovators are willing to take risks. They're energized by change and are quick to try out the latest things when they feel they have the freedom to do so. Innovators are highly connected to other innovators, and frequent discourse about new ideas is the norm in these circles.

Early adopters are also connected to innovators, but their communications are a bit more discreet. Early adopters are often considered opinion leaders because they occupy central positions in the institution and make moves that are visible and strategic. Innovators and early adopters are can-do types who like to focus on the potential benefits of change rather than its challenges. You'll find innovators and early adopters among junior, senior, full-time, and part-time faculty and staff. Regardless of their status, these people are willing to devote vast amounts of time and energy to perfecting untested strategies because life on the cutting edge is internally rewarding to them. Their efforts shouldn't go entirely uncompensated, however. Innovators and early adopters provide the institution with extremely valuable feedback concerning the efficacy of new professional development and teaching strategies. Meaningful recognition can come in a variety of forms, such as stipends, course releases, fellowships, additional resources, awards, or commendations.

FIU provides innovators and early adopters with options for extended global learning professional development, which can last a full day or as long as a full semester, to allow ample time for digging into the nitty-gritty details of new methods. Participants also get opportunities to practice or apply what they've learned, as their success stories will get the global learning ball rolling for others. One example is the OGLI's summer institute for faculty developing interdisciplinary, team-taught global learning foundations courses in the general education curriculum. Participants are chosen through a juried application process and receive stipends of about $2,000 each for full participation in the four- to six-week institute and submission of a new course to the Faculty Senate. The OGLI also brings nationally recognized experts to campus to conduct one- and two-day symposia for those who want to implement complex global learning strategies such as team-based learning (TBL) and COIL. These faculty receive free implementation resources, such as Immediate Feedback Assessment Technique forms (Einstein Educational Enterprises, n.d.) for TBL and instructional designer support for COIL courses. Semester-long faculty learning communities are convened to reinforce the work of those pioneering new global learning outcomes, assessments, pedagogies, and content, with members receiving letters documenting participation for their professional files.

Early and Late Majority

Early majority adopters tend to occupy less central positions in the organization than innovators and early adopters. They need a little more time to get on board with something new, often electing to participate only after they can personally relate to someone else's success story. Young faculty, graduate teaching assistants, and some staff may be in this category because they have a strong need for tools to overcome the challenges faced by novice educators. They may not be able to participate in professional development as readily as they would wish, however, because early-career professionals often require a supervisor's or chair's support to be involved in anything beyond their primary duties. Tenure-track faculty members especially have trouble diverting time from their research responsibilities, driving these would-be early majority adopters toward the late majority. Late adopters approach innovation with skepticism. Busy midcareer faculty and part-time adjuncts are often in this category because they're in less frequent contact with others in the institution and have access to fewer resources. Late adopters are a tough sell, but as their name suggests, they can eventually be brought around.

At FIU positive reviews from innovators and early adopters led to an initial burst of interest in global learning. Deans and department chairs supported faculty professional development because every academic program needed new global learning courses to accommodate students' graduation requirement. Student affairs directors encouraged staff to participate because they perceived a valuable opportunity to collaborate with faculty in the development of integrative cocurricular programming. To meet the high demand presented by the early majority and to alleviate the time pressures they experienced, the OGLI developed a two-day Global Learning Course and Activity Design and Instruction Workshop and provided a stipend of $500 for full attendance and submission of a course proposal to the Faculty Senate Global Learning Curriculum Oversight Committee (GLCOC). The first day of these workshops, conducted one week before the second day, explored the meaning of global learning, global learning course and activity design, and powerful global learning strategies that could be implemented almost immediately with minimum preparation. During the week separating Days 1 and 2, participants drafted three potential global learning course or activity outcomes that were aligned with the graduation-level SLOs. Day 2 involved the collaborative refinement of these outcomes along with the development of associated assessments, teaching strategies, and content.

FIU's late majority is composed largely of adjuncts, new hires, graduate assistants, and others teaching sections of courses that already have a global learning designation. Members of this group take a shortened Global Learning Course Design and Instruction Workshop, lasting one day, that enables them to plan assessments, teaching strategies, content, and cocurricular activities addressing their course's GLCOC-approved global learning outcomes. The late majority is also brought into the fold through our annual Global Learning Conference, which is a gathering of all FIU's global learning supporters and instructors and celebrates our growing institutional knowledge and expertise. To create a family reunion feel, attendees enjoy breakfast, lunch, and an end-of-conference reception in a room lined with 18-inch-by-36-inch posters highlighting significant milestones in the initiative's development. The following are examples of items featured on conference agendas:

- Global Learning Blasts, similar in format to TED Talks, which are 10- to 12-minute hands-on demonstrations of powerful global learning strategies by faculty and staff
- Lectures on current global issues by *New York Times* editors and journalists
- Keynote addresses by internationally renowned global learning scholars such as Graham Pike and Toni Fuss Kirkwood-Tucker
- Panel discussions featuring global learning students and alumni
- Presentations of research conducted by global learning faculty fellows and their student mentees

The conference is carefully planned to enable people to attend all or part of the day-and-a-half event. All presentations are filmed, and videos are freely accessible on the OGLI website (goglobal.fiu.edu/resources/gl-instructional-strategies).

Laggards

Last we have the stragglers, the slackers, the dawdlers, the naysayers. No matter what you call them, if you focus on laggards too much, they may assume the power necessary to slow or stop the progress of your entire initiative. If you ignore them, the very same thing can happen. Who are these people, and what is the right approach to take with them?

Typically laggards are your recalcitrant senior faculty, those with the biggest investment in traditions of the past. But laggards may also include anyone with a particularly strong aversion to change or who happens to occupy an exceptionally remote position in the organization. Laggards tend to maintain contact with only the people closest to them, cutting them off from healthy flows of new information. If a laggard is in either a formal or informal position of power in the institution, his or her resistance can prevent large numbers of colleagues and students from participating in global learning. For this reason, laggards cannot be ignored. Even if they elect not to play in the sandbox, they must be influenced to get out of the way of others' progress.

The key to reaching laggards is to meet them where they are. In some cases, laggards are physically remote. Distance faculty teaching online seldom if ever set foot on campus, so FIU provides these instructors with an asynchronous online version of the Global Learning Course Design and Instruction Workshop. This option also gives innovators and early adopters a chance to take a refresher course and allows campus-based cynics the freedom to explore global learning in the privacy of their own homes or offices, at their own pace, without losing face with their fellow laggards.

Laggards can also purposefully distance themselves from others through constant negativity. Their disparagement may be rooted in a desire to not be perceived as followers. We've found that you can break down laggards' emotionally charged prejudices by providing them with low-stakes opportunities to mix with more congenial colleagues. Book groups, for example, invite critics to voice their reservations in a scholarly context. Try using titles that explore aspects integral to global learning, like diversity, problem-solving, and collaboration, but don't refer to global learning per se. Examples of such works include those from Banaji and Greenwald (2013); Post, Ward, Longo, and Saltmarsh (2016); and Barkley, Cross, and Major (2014). Brief brown-bag workshops taught by fellow faculty can also introduce laggards to strategies that cut across disciplinary boundaries and don't necessarily carry the offending nomenclature. FIU colleagues have presented concise lunchtime sessions on methods for facilitating diverse teams, researching complex problems with big data sets, conducting culturally responsive instruction, and assessing performance tasks with rubrics.

Finally, laggards may protest global learning on the grounds that it threatens academic freedom or the foundations of the discipline. In these special cases you may want to conduct department-specific workshops, but we recommend these only when absolutely necessary. Participants in homogenous professional development events lose out on the benefits of meeting others in a critical interdisciplinary space, particularly the insights into their own field that emerge when "different disciplines contest each other's theoretical frameworks, perspectives and practices" (Rowland, 2006, p. 79). Homogenous workshops also deny participants opportunities to discover overlaps between their work and that of their colleagues in other departments and to feel part of a broader institutional network. However, discipline-specific workshops do provide the safety some laggards need to consider new ways of thinking. Faculty in the social sciences, in particular, may be reluctant to engage in interdisciplinary global learning professional development because they perceive themselves as already being global. In the privacy of their own department, these faculty may feel more comfortable admitting their disciplines' Western-focused, sage-on-the-stage tendencies, opening the door for them to contemplate pedagogical innovations that align with global learning and their professional expertise but that don't violate disciplinary standards or principles of inquiry (Leask, 2013).

Laggards are a challenge to bring on board, but they also present opportunities to have a truly transformative impact on faculty beliefs concerning global learning. The funny thing about laggards is that when they do finally embrace global learning, they sometimes do so with the same gusto as innovators and early adopters. It's incredibly gratifying when a particularly reluctant attendee, perhaps an intimidating emeritus faculty member, stops you at the end of the workshop with a comment such as, "I thought I knew everything about teaching, but you taught me something new today." We've been honored to hear such comments, and we want you to hear them, too. So now, having explored the types of professional development that can diffuse global learning throughout your institution, it's time to think about what it should entail. What types of content will enable educators to provide global learning to all students? What kinds of professional development experiences will lead educators to their own powerful global learning aha moments?

What Should Professional Development Entail?

Effective professional development for universal global learning must be transformative. As Burkholder (2016) reminds us,

> For better or for worse (and it's usually for worse) most of us started out teaching the way we'd been taught ourselves—and many of us still do. Only when we realize that these approaches can't achieve our desired learning goals do we stare into the instructional abyss to contemplate the fundamental riddles of education (para. 5).

Global learning educators need to understand how their own learning experiences have shaped their assumptions about teaching and how these assumptions affect their instructional decisions and students' success. When faculty and staff realize their traditional educational methods don't necessarily lead to the global learning outcomes they intend for themselves and others, they're experiencing what Mezirow (1978) refers to as a *disorienting dilemma*, which

> cannot be resolved by simply acquiring more information, enhancing problem solving skills or adding to one's competencies. Resolution of these dilemmas and transforming our meaning perspectives require that we

become critically aware of the fact that we are caught in our own history and are re-living it and of the cultural and psychological assumptions which structure the way we see ourselves and others. (p. 109)

Once we become aware of a conflict between our actions and ideals, the only way to end this conflict is to take new actions and to adopt new behaviors that conform to our new meaning perspectives. Mezirow (1991) said that learners become aware of the need for action through reflection, the "process of critically assessing the content, process, or premise(s) of our efforts" (p. 104). You can precipitate transformative changes in your stake-holders' beliefs about global learning by engaging them in critical reflection on its underlying design premise, its nature as an educational process, and various content-based approaches to global learning. If you follow up critical reflection by presenting educators with global learning tools they can use to put their new beliefs into practice, you can also influence changes in teaching behaviors that will affect all students.

Backward Curriculum Design

Ask faculty to tell you the first thing they do when planning a new course, and they'll likely respond, "Choose the textbook." Ask what they do next and you'll probably hear, "Decide what content to cover and schedule readings and lectures." The last task on their list is often their least favorite: "Work up quizzes, tests, or papers." This traditional, instructor-focused approach to curriculum design can be summarized as, Tell them what you're going to tell them (syllabus), tell them (lecture), and have them tell you what you told them (assessment). Although this approach is valid and appropriate in contexts that require rote recall of established facts and concepts, it's anti-thetical to global learning. Global learning is a learner-focused process that involves the production of new knowledge about the world and its inhabitants rather than a recapitulation of the old. This calls for educators to change the first question they ask themselves when designing a new course from What do I want to cover? to What do students need to know and be able to do? which is actually the first step in backward curriculum design (Wiggins & McTighe, 2005), a transformative alternative to traditional methods. In back-ward curriculum design, after educators determine the knowledge and skills they want students to achieve, they ask, How will I know my students have achieved these outcomes? Backward curriculum design prompts instructors to formulate a clear vision of student success at the outset rather than as an afterthought. This converts assessment from being just another accountability hoop to jump through into a tool for ensuring all students are learning. The last step in backward curriculum design follows naturally from this new way of thinking about assessment: What kinds of content and learning experiences will prepare students to demonstrate desired learning outcomes? In backward curriculum design, content and teaching strategies are a means to the end of student learning rather than ends in themselves.

Backward curriculum design can help you respond to faculty who protest global learning on the grounds that it edges out content coverage. It provokes reconsideration of the premise that all students need to become subject matter specialists by prompting faculty to take a "step back from our fields of expertise, which we know so well and hold so dear, and approach the learning process as novices" (Burkholder, 2016, para. 4). After spending so many years carving out their own special sphere of subject matter expertise, faculty forget what it's like to be a beginner in the field, lacking background knowledge yet open to a wide range of disciplinary ideas and interdisciplinary connections. When faculty view their course from the novice perspective, it helps them "make tough decisions about what content is really needed for our students to achieve their learning goals" (Burkholder, 2016, para. 5). The change from focusing on what they need to cover to what students need to experience also helps faculty make room in the syllabus for active learning and authentic assessment strategies either in addition to or in place of traditional lectures and tests (Fink, 2003; Maki, 2010; Mueller, 2014; O'Brien, Millis, & Cohen, 2008).

In terms of curriculum design, if the goal is to determine which students can recall the most information an educator has presented to them, then traditional lecture-based instruction and accountability assessment may be the best way to go. But if the goal is for graduates to be able to apply their global awareness, perspective, and engagement to real-world problem-solving, then we must provide students with opportunities to practice these activities and receive feedback for continuous improvement while they're still in school (Wiggins, 1989). Active learning and authentic assessment strategies provide all students with valid opportunities to fail, a necessary component of learning. When faculty give all students multiple productive opportunities to fail and correct their failures, they're maximizing all students' capacities to learn (Cavagnaro & Fasihuddin, 2016). Once faculty perceive the mismatch between failure-resistant, instructor-focused methods and the meaning and purpose of global learning, then backward curriculum design provides the structure educators need to weave student-focused learning outcomes, authentic assessments, collaborative global learning strategies, and diverse content and readings into their syllabi. Our Global Learning Course Design and Instruction Workshops cover all four of these topics. In chapter 9 we describe in more detail how we help faculty develop global learning course outcomes and student learning assessments for those outcomes. Here we'll describe how our workshops help faculty develop appropriate global learning strategies and content.

Active, Collaborative Learning Strategies

At first, most faculty and staff will think of global learning as either study abroad or as readings and lectures about other countries and cultures. The professional development you offer must transform these limited perceptions into richer, more relevant understandings of global learning as a process. This requires educators to practice the same active, collaborative problem-solving strategies you want them to use for their students. Leonard (1968) said that lectures are the "best way to get information from teacher's notebook to student's notebook without touching the student's mind" (p. 2). The same holds true for professional development: If you want to change how faculty and staff think about and apply global learning, you must help them feel the transformative impact it has on global awareness, perspective, and engagement.

When we design global learning professional development, we adhere to a twist on the old writing teacher adage of show, don't tell; we show, then tell. Avoid the temptation to start a session by defining operational terms and concepts through detailed PowerPoint presentations. Instead, involve participants in experiences that exemplify the ideas you wish to convey, then inspire them to internalize meaning through guided reflection. To illustrate how this works, we describe how we kick off our Global Learning Course Design and Instruction workshops.

At FIU we want all stakeholders to be able to articulate the meaning of global learning and how the process leads to the development of global learning course and activity outcomes and eventually our graduation-level SLOs. Because we organize our workshops according to backward curriculum design, this exploration of what we want students to know and be able to do is the very first item on our agenda. Following brief introductions, we launch right into an active global learning strategy that places participants in a collaborative exploration of a complex global issue such as sea-level rise, immigration, or the spread of infectious diseases. Participants can easily employ the strategies themselves in virtually any discipline or modality, such as

- consequence maps, which are graphic organizers that help students visualize the effects of a real or hypothetical event, problem, or trend and help students envisage complexity and interrelatedness (Baker, 2008), and
- role-playing, which are opportunities for students to take on the perspectives of a stakeholder in a real or hypothetical case study by

increasing student engagement with content, encouraging empathy and transpection, and allowing students to apply their learning in a collaborative setting (Golich, Boyer, Franko, & Lamy, 2000).

Role-playing is particularly effective in heightening participants' understanding of diversity as a foundational component of global learning. Role-playing stimulates transpection by moving participants out of their own perspectives as educators and subject matter specialists and into that of a character from another part of the world and another walk of life. We assign roles according to the nature of the problem to be explored, making sure the characters possess varying amounts of economic, political, and social power. Role-playing also creates equal status among participants by removing the power of privileged knowledge. When everyone in the group is taking on perspectives that are unfamiliar and differ from their own, no one in the room is an expert. This heightens awareness of how little we as individuals know about the world and how much we need others to help us understand it.

When the strategy is complete, participants reinhabit their own perspectives and reflect. We ask them to describe what happened and to consider what they learned about the problem, themselves, and others. We also ask them to think imaginatively about how such a strategy could be applied to their own course or activity, including how they would prepare students to participate in and reflect on the experience. During this discussion, participants share a wide variety of key messages. Some report a greater understanding of local and global interconnectedness and a new awareness of the need for powerless perspectives, whereas others express a heightened sense of the value of collaboration. At this point, having shown what global learning is all about, it's time to tell them. We unveil formal definitions of *global learning*, *global citizenship*, and *graduation-level global learning SLOs*. This is the true transformative aha moment when participants realize that the words they're reading aren't expressing abstract concepts. Instead, the language is describing the real, replicable learning that they've just experienced and the meaningful, observable knowledge and skills that result. Inspired and energized by the power of global learning and its implications for practice, educators are primed and ready to investigate new tools for infusing global learning in the curriculum and cocurriculum.

An entire body of literature is devoted to active, collaborative strategies that can be used for global learning in a variety of disciplines, modalities, and settings. Conferences and trainings can provide access to more ideas. A simple Google search for active and collaborative strategies will turn up resources compiled by faculty, college and university professional development centers, as well as international bodies such as Oxfam Education and Britain's Global Learning Programme. You'll find ideas in the K–12 literature as well. Don't ignore these just because they're used in primary and secondary education. A whole world of active, collaborative learning is out there for faculty and staff to discover, but the following are a few of our favorite resources to get you started: Barkley, Cross, and Major (2014); Michaelsen, Knight, and Fink (2004); Howell, Harris, and Zakrajsek (2015); and Golich and colleagues (2000).

Discipline-Based Approaches to Global Learning Content

One of the most common misconceptions about global learning is that it can't be done in certain disciplines. Some faculty contend that because their field is technical, students don't need to know about different cultures and countries. Others claim that their field is inherently global because people all over the world study the same foundational ideas and theories. Both assertions are faulty. Global learning is not a characteristic of disciplines; rather, it characterizes how disciplinary knowledge is understood and employed. All fields lend themselves to global learning because it's a process that results in the creation of new knowledge, which is the purpose of scholarship in every discipline. At this point in the book, you probably already grasp these concepts. The question is, how do you get your colleagues across the institution to transform their views concerning the relationship between global learning and disciplinary content?

Faculty may have a difficult time conceptualizing how the topics studied in their courses can lead to the development of students' global awareness, perspective, and engagement. These faculty may grasp the concepts behind global learning and backward curriculum design, but when it comes to applying them to their courses, they're stymied by their content-focused curriculum design habits. Even faculty who can compose clear, focused, meaningful, and measurable global learning course outcomes experience difficulty identifying readings, films, and other informational resources to support those outcomes. We've heard almost every protest in the book to changing their reading lists, such as,

- "My course is already global because math transcends borders—everyone in the world does calculus and algebra the same way."
- "I don't need to include non-Western readings in my syllabus because the topics we study—justice, human rights, the morality of war—are all global."
- "I've decided to add a chapter on kabuki to my Theater Studies reading list—is that enough?"

At the outset of our initiative, the OGLI found that the GLCOC regularly kicked global learning course proposals back to faculty for revision because of conflicts between course outcomes and the content assigned. How can you expect students to analyze problems from multiple perspectives if you only expose them to readings from a single textbook with a single author? committee members asked. This conflict also surfaced in the misalignment of proposed assessments and teaching strategies. In our role as curriculum design coaches, we were really at a loss about how to remedy the situation. We weren't subject matter experts; we couldn't make knowledgeable content recommendations. We tried sending faculty to library liaisons for assistance, but this didn't seem to make much difference. The essential problem was that some faculty still approached global learning as an add-on rather than a holistic course revision. The committee's resistance continued, and our frustrations mounted.

All this changed one day when we had our own transformative professional development moment. For the first time, Doscher and Landorf understood what was meant by a comment frequently uttered by one of FIU's most innovative global learning faculty members, Ligia Collado-Vides, a marine biologist: "Ooh! That's a good global learning problem!" We realized this was Ligia's way into global learning; global problems were her on-ramp to global learning course revision. Ligia began to think about her course in terms of complex global problems to be collaboratively analyzed and addressed rather than as a series of topics for individual students to master. Once she started thinking this way, she was able to commence her backward curriculum design journey (What do students need to know and be able to do to understand and solve these problems together? What kinds of content and learning experiences will prepare them to understand and solve the problems? How will I know they have understood and solved the problems?).

Ligia was a participant in one of our first faculty learning communities. In one of her reflections, she described the difficulties she faced while trying to infuse global learning into her advanced laboratory biology course on marine reserves.

> The first challenge is time. I already have a very heavy and compact schedule in which I need to teach all the principles in each of my courses, therefore [the] time we need to incorporate the principles of global learning such as concepts of self-awareness and engagement needs to be allocated within my finite time for teaching. The idea here is how to incorporate methods that will transform students' awareness from persons isolated from nature to beings that belong to nature and are responsible for the consequences of their actions towards nature.

My second challenge is to find a way to bring international concepts and all the other objectives such as teamwork and the use of technology into a science class. This has been a challenge as I have been practicing science with a rigid scientific method, rather than confronting human realities.

I need to understand fully what it means to teach a global course in the context of science. How far can I discuss global issues, that we have a tendency to see as human issues, and keep the discussion focused on nature?

When Ligia began to think of her course in terms of the problems marine biologists face in the protection of reserves, some interesting things happened. Most importantly, her mind opened to the possibility of having students apply their content knowledge to real-world decision-forcing case studies. This led her to think creatively about authentic ways she could engage students in exploring these cases. Surprisingly, she found that she could expose students to even more content by having them conduct additional research and experimentation to better understand and address the problems in the cases. Ligia was impressed by the ways students' research-based dialogues produced new knowledge and enhanced the quality of their scholarly analysis. Chapter 6 includes a description of town hall meetings, one of the global strategies Ligia now uses to get students to grapple with real-world cases. While a member of the faculty learning community, Ligia reflected on the transformation she experienced after experimenting with this new approach to content:

I have been challenged to think about my class in a different sphere, beyond covering the topics of the class. In this way I think this experience has made me a more human teacher, if you will. I have found that by the exercise of trying to connect with the student to make them think about international issues I am learning to listen to them. I have also managed to get a better and more systematic way to evaluate students' projects, and altogether I feel that this is a better course in terms of bringing to the class discussions connected to society.

We now regularly support faculty across disciplines in their efforts to identify good global learning problems to examine in their courses. Although these examinations often incite learners to draw on knowledge they've gained from other disciplines, we're cognizant that faculty want their students to view problems primarily through a particular disciplinary lens. Researchers have examined differences in the ways groups of disciplines approach knowledge acquisition and production (Becher & Trowler, 2001), as well as differences in the ways these groups approach internationalization of their curricula (Agnew, 2013; Green & Whitsed, 2013; Jones & Killick, 2013; Leask, 2013;

Leask, 2015). Table 5.1 is a tool we have developed from this research to help faculty think about the attributes of their disciplines and the kinds of approaches to global learning that might be appropriate for their courses. We use this tool to prompt reflection and brainstorming and encourage faculty to think of disciplinary groups, attributes, and approaches as a flexible continuum (Agnew, 2013).

How Do You Get Participants To Apply What They've Learned?

When it comes down to it, there's no substitute for personal support when helping faculty and staff achieve their visions for global learning in courses and activities. People need a guide on the side. If there is a secret to our success in diffusing global learning throughout FIU, it is the time and energy the OGLI has spent coaching faculty and staff through the entire process of adopting and adapting to global learning innovations. We've formed strong relationships with our stakeholders, letting them know through our actions and communications that the OGLI's mission is to support the global learning goals of all faculty, staff, and students and not the other way around. As leaders at a public university, we face monumental accountability measures. We're subject to constant pressure to prove the value of our initiative in terms of the institution's bottom line. We work hard not to transfer this stress to our faculty and staff, who already feel as if their every move is being measured. As the initiative's backbone organization, the OGLI strives to counteract the demotivating force of accountability by ensuring that all global learning educators feel that their every global learning need counts. We make ourselves available to assist with every aspect of activity and course development, from drafting global learning course outcomes and developing rubrics to locating guest speakers and requesting room assignments. No issue is too trivial. What may seem inconsequential to us as administrators may be critically important to faculty and staff. We have witnessed again and again how assistance with even the smallest of details has made the biggest impact on people's willingness to take on greater curricular and cocurricular challenges. There's really no other way around it; in the majority of instances, the quality of your professional development's impact is determined by the quality of the follow-up support you provide.

Part Three of this book explores how the OGLI uses two components of collective impact—shared measurement and continuous communication and improvement—to stay in touch with all our stakeholders, support their practice, and uncover the stories of global learning's transformative effects on faculty, staff, and students. But before we launch into the technical details

TABLE 5.1

Discipline-Based Approaches to Global Learning Course Design

Disciplinary Group	Attributes	Approaches to Global Learning
Hard—pure (pure math and sciences)	Discipline is borderless Universal language Transcends cultural context Value free, impersonal Relevance of scientific process (data) Standardized curricula English as global language and homogenization	International and intercultural case studies Interpretation of results via cultural, economic, political lenses Marginalization of non-English speakers, non–Western ideas Mobility of ideas International issues around data collection, measurement, storage, publication, sharing, utility, and ownership Intercultural communication and collaboration strategies Interrelationship of local and global, homogenization and diversification
Hard—applied (Technologies)	Competitive, purposive, functional Economic imperative Technology and product driven International faculty or little technology transfer Relevance of language ability	International design, manufacturing, testing, packaging, marketing, and usage practices and regulations International content Intercultural communication and collaboration
Soft—pure (Humanities)	Inherently international Inherently interdisciplinary Highly interpretive Empathy Value of human experience Relevance of local culture Moral imperative	Social construction of knowledge Critical self-reflection Empathic understanding of others' lived experiences Interdisciplinary approaches to problem-solving Knowledge of diverse cultural beliefs, values, and practices Experiential learning Intercultural communication and collaboration skills Application of knowledge in service to others
Soft—applied (Social sciences)	Value of reflexive practice Relevance of local culture Challenges beliefs, values, assumptions Value of human experience Application of learning Multiple ways of knowing	Critical self-reflection and reflective practice Empathic understanding of others' lived experiences Interdisciplinary approaches to problem-solving Knowledge of diverse cultural beliefs, values, and practices Experiential learning Intercultural communication and collaboration skills Perspective taking

Note. Adapted from Agnew (2013).

of how we support and share these stories, we think you should read some of them for yourselves. We especially want you to see how different global learning opportunities in the curriculum, cocurriculum, and the K–12 pipeline mutually reinforce one another and how they have an impact on student success. It's time for us to listen to our own advice and stop telling you about what universal global learning looks like. It's time for us to show you.

6

GLOBAL LEARNING COURSES
AT HOME AND ABROAD

Real teaching happens within a wild triangle of relations—among teacher, students, subject—and the points of the triangle shift continually. What shall I teach amid all that I should teach? How can I grasp it myself so that my grasping might enable theirs? What are they thinking and feeling—toward me, toward each other, toward the thing that I am trying to teach? How near should I come, how far off should I stay? How much clutch? How much gas? (McDonald, 1992, p. 1)

W hether on campus, online, or abroad, the classroom is where the curriculum comes to life. In chapter 3, we defined *curriculum* as the means and materials that enable students to achieve intended learning outcomes. We noted that a curriculum is composed of six interconnected dimensions, and each dimension is shaped by dynamic internal and external forces. Just as a curriculum is multidimensional and constantly changing, individual courses in the curriculum are developed and taught in intersecting and shifting spheres as well. We like McDonald's (1992) characterization of what happens in the classroom as a "wild triangle of relations" (p. 1). We think this metaphor is particularly apt for global learning courses, which are designed to encompass the evolving perspectives of teachers and students, the elasticity of course content, and the dynamic dimensions influencing the learning process. In this chapter, we show you how a variety of FIU educators facilitate global learning in the shifting points of the wild triangle.

This chapter contains five case studies of exemplary global learning courses. We intentionally chose courses offered through different modalities—face-to-face, online, and study abroad—to show that the process of global learning can occur in various formats. We developed these cases from class observations and discussions with the faculty who teach the courses. We enter each case through a single global learning strategy directed at one or more global learning course outcomes aligned with FIU's graduation-level SLOs: global awareness, global perspective, or global engagement. We provide examples of unique assessment and pedagogical strategies. We also share a case in which conditions weren't conducive to global learning, and then we discuss how the OGLI addressed this situation. Above all, these cases demonstrate how faculty who engage students in global learning can assist them in moving beyond merely learning about differences toward learning and working with differences, resulting in the production of new knowledge, higher quality work products, and true inclusive excellence (Wong & Branham, 2016).

Multiple Perspectives on Marine Reserves

FIU marine biology professor Ligia Collado-Vides gives her class the question of the day: "Should a cruise ship company be allowed to make a day stop on Vieques, a tiny island-municipality of Puerto Rico in the northeastern Caribbean?" The answer to this question is determined in a simulation of a town hall meeting, attended by students who play the roles of a variety of stakeholders with interests in the outcome. The first stakeholder who comes forward, a student playing a cruise company representative, says,

> Happy Cruise Lines would like to use this island as a day stop on our four-night cruises out of Miami. We are prepared to make an agreement with government officials of the island on the cost and regulations of this endeavor.

Next, a student playing a marine scientist weighs in:

> A ship coming in that close to the island will have a negative impact on the area's natural habitat, even if the cruise line tries not to be invasive. Pollution is also a big concern. Many areas of the Caribbean are facing pollution issues because international regulations on cruise liners aren't strong enough to protect the environment.

"We worry the ship will scare away the fish," says a student in the role of a local fisherman. "Our livelihoods depend on fishing!"

A student playing a priest speaks on behalf of the community, expressing concern that tourists' contact with local children will result in the diminishment of cultural norms and traditions. "At the same time," he adds, "residents are excited about the job prospects tourism will bring to the island."

This town hall deliberation is one of several role-playing activities conducted in Marine Protected Areas, a discipline-specific global learning course in FIU's Department of Biological Sciences. It's an example of how active learning in a science, technology, engineering, or math course can simultaneously increase scientific knowledge and encourage a global perspective.

The global perspective course learning outcome for Marine Protected Areas calls for students to be able to develop a multifaceted argument for a site's preservation based on its biological value, cultural value, social benefit, and human capacity to manage it. To see how this outcome is achieved, let's look at the details.

Collado-Vides conducts two town hall meetings as part of her course's lab section, which she has revised to include bench experiments and experiential activities such as site visits and field research. One meeting deals with an issue occurring abroad, such as the Caribbean cruise liner case; the other concerns a current local issue, such as David Beckham's proposal to fill in part of the state-designated Biscayne Bay Aquifer Preserve to build a soccer stadium (Mazzei, 2014). Collado-Vides conducts deliberations at local and international levels so students can develop "the ability to compare themselves with the world" (L. Collado-Vides, personal communication, September 11, 2015). She intends for students to be able to demonstrate their global perspective by constructing an analysis of the diverse ways people around the world experience and solve common problems in marine reserve protection.

Students prepare for the deliberations by reading texts and peer-reviewed journal articles on methods for designing and managing reserves. They also learn about biological and sociological concerns affecting reserves through lectures, films, articles, and other resources. Collado-Vides has students conduct their initial analysis of each case in groups of five to eight, asking them to reflect on the question at hand and to critically examine their personal views concerning the issues involved. After that, Collado-Vides assigns her students different characters to play in the town hall meeting and gives them a week to conduct background research to inform their portrayals. On the day of the meeting, the students rehearse their roles in groups. When Collado-Vides senses they are ready, she opens up the deliberation to the class as a whole.

The meeting engages students in democratic deliberation (Sen, 2009). They argue from their characters' perspectives, listen to others, and look for solutions based on an overlapping consensus (Rawls, 1987). At the end of the semester, having participated in two role-playing activities, each group also composes a summative case analysis. The groups present their findings and proposed solutions to the class and are assessed for their command of technical knowledge and the extent to which they demonstrate a global perspective on marine reserve protection.

Why does Collado-Vides go through the trouble of conducting case study analysis through role-playing? The answer lies in how Collado-Vides views global learning, which she described to us as "a way of living" (L. Collado-Vides, personal communication, September 11, 2015). Perceiving global learning as a practice, Collado-Vides said that it cannot occur without active learning (L. Collado-Vides, personal communication, September 11, 2015). She maintained that global learners must reflect on the factors that influence their own perspectives and recognize that the world is shaped by interactions among multiple unique perspectives. Global learners must accept personal responsibility to discover others' perspectives and make decisions that are sensitive to the diverse ways people understand and experience the world. As Collado-Vides asserted, "Accepting that responsibility is global learning. . . . If we don't accept that we will never get to change our habits" (L. Collado-Vides, personal communication, September 11, 2015). After seeing the difference in her students' perspectives in Marine Protected Areas, she now includes global learning in all her biology courses.

What's in a Zip Code? Discovering the Social Determinants of Health

Students cluster around classroom tables in groups of four or five, examining Google maps of specific addresses in a Miami-Dade County zip code.

"How many fast food restaurants are there within a 1.5 mile radius?" asks one student, jotting down figures in her notebook. Another student locates parks and bike lanes in the area, and her teammate determines the price of metformin, a drug used to treat Type 2 diabetes, at the closest pharmacy. At another table, a student researches the addresses in the zip code on Miami Matters (miamidadematters.org), a database that provides quality-of-life measures, recommended targets, and comparative statistics for other communities. On the Community Data page, the student scrolls over each icon on the page—Demographics, Disparity Dashboard, SocioNeeds Index—and clicks on Community Dashboard. There he finds information on a wide range of indicators, from residents' average life expectancy to voter turnout rates.

This activity begins one of the units in Challenges in Healthcare, a year-long global learning foundations course in FIU's interdisciplinary Honors College. Aimed at students interested in medical professions, the course is taught by Barbra Roller, assistant dean for student affairs and assistant professor of cellular biology and pharmacology in FIU's Herbert Wertheim College of Medicine. Roller focuses the first semester of the course on the life of the physician, exploring requisite knowledge, skills, and attributes. In the second semester, students delve into the physician's interaction with patients, communities, and health care systems. The course is strongly informed by the centerpiece of the college's curriculum, Green Family Foundation Neighborhood Health Education Learning Program (NeighborhoodHELP). The only program of its kind in the country, NeighborhoodHELP engages students in service-learning, providing them with experiences in "population-based medicine with a focus on the ethical foundations of medicine, the social determinants of health, and culturally competent primary care, while simultaneously meeting the needs of local communities and households" (Herbert Wertheim College of Medicine, 2017). NeighborhoodHELP sends interdisciplinary teams of medical, social work, nursing, public health, business, and law students into disadvantaged communities where they establish a long-term relationship with one or two families and track, monitor, and advocate for the health of these families throughout the students' four years of medical education. Teams collect baseline and follow-up data, identify health concerns, and work with households to implement and refine care plans in collaboration with the families' health care providers.

Challenges in Healthcare meets twice a week. One session features a guest lecture by a faculty member from the medical college on a particular topic (e.g., the history of medicine, healthy lifestyles for medical students, complementary and alternative medicine, global health issues), and the second session involves a related active learning strategy. In researching the social determinants of health in one of Miami's underserved neighborhoods, students draw from their own disciplinary knowledge and their diverse experiences living in South Florida and other parts of the world. Roller gives students real street addresses and asks them to use Google Earth and other resources to discover factors influencing community members' well-being. Teams synthesize their findings and present them to the class, including a proposed new policy to address a neighborhood health disparity.

In this course, Roller not only challenges students to imagine solutions to real-world dilemmas, similar to Collado-Vides's Marine Protected Areas, but also tasks them with identifying the wicked or unscripted problems that need to be addressed (Cavagnaro & Fasihuddin, 2016; Schneider, 2015). A *wicked problem* has "innumerable causes, is tough to describe, and doesn't have a right answer" (Cavagnaro & Fasihuddin, 2016, p. 8). Such problems are extremely complex and multifaceted, their origins "reflective of the wildly unpredictable environments—physical, social, economic, and geographic—in which people live, as well as the social history of race, class, gender, and place baked into community, personal identity, behavior, and worldview" (Gibson, Smyth, Nayowirth, & Zaff, 2013). Wicked problems such as health disparities require global awareness to at least describe the challenges people face, much less formulate solutions. In this course, global awareness is knowledge of interrelated global dynamics (sociocultural, political, economic, etc.) that shape health care delivery in diverse cultural contexts. The causes of health disparities are so multifarious and hard to decipher that each explanation suggests another avenue for intervention. Students discover that every "problem can be a symptom of another problem. It's like a game of whack-a-mole: Try to address one problem, and another one pops up somewhere else" (Gibson et al., 2013, para. 10). With so much variability in the ways health disparities can be understood and with such an array of possibilities for coping with them, how does Roller validly gauge the extent to which students have developed global awareness? How is it possible to grade answers to questions when students are determining the answers and the questions at the same time?

Roller begins her assessment of global awareness with an initial appraisal of students' background knowledge. At the start of the semester, Roller asks students to anonymously report their perceived knowledge of course topics on a 4-point Likert scale. She often finds that students report little or no prior knowledge of course topics at the outset but report high levels of familiarity by the end of the course. Although such gains are developmentally important, they alone aren't valid assessments of students' understanding of the interrelatedness of those topics. Roller looks for direct evidence of students' global awareness of health disparities in the artifacts produced through activities such as research reports on the social determinants of health in an underserved Miami neighborhood. She also looks for clues in students' personal reflections and records of cocurricular involvement.

Roller has students compose brief reflections after each guest lecture. Comments from these reflections, such as "I now understand the impacts of law and politics in the field of medicine" and "The concept of social determinants has allowed me to understand why there can be a source of racism in healthcare" provide her with insight into students' ability to draw connections between sessions. End-of-course reflections also support the importance of depth, rather than breadth, of coverage to encourage transference and making connections among multiple disciplines. The following are comments from two of her students:

> The course was the first to introduce me to the idea of "social determinants of health." This is a theme that has appeared in other classes I have been taking this semester like in human genetics and sociology. Having been exposed to it in this class prepared me in the other classes.

> I have already developed a pretty strong foundation in my understanding of sociocultural issues through many of the humanities courses I've taken, but they have never related these topics to medicine, so that was something very new for me. The presentations we had regarding this material really helped me see not only what issues were out there, but also how I could use my passion, for both medicine and socio-cultural issues, to address these problems in the future.

Like Collado-Vides, Roller wants students to use their technical knowledge to identify ways they can mitigate a problem's local and global effects. To that end, she purposefully provides students with pathways to convert their understanding into activism. Students Fernando Alvarez and Mideny Bell volunteered with the Pipeline Program after hearing about it from guest lecturer Cheryl Holder, associate professor of family medicine at the college. Pipeline matches medical, nursing, and undergraduate students with Miami-Dade County households to mentor and tutor underserved youth in math and science, with the goal of preparing these young people for careers in health and medicine.

Alvarez and Bell reported that working with Pipeline helped them transform the global awareness they formed in class into empowerment to effect positive change. As Alvarez recounted his involvement to us in an interview, his excitement was palpable: "Without our help students say they would fail" (F. Alvarez, personal communication, March 3, 2016). Bell described how volunteering helped him see that his own well-being was deeply interconnected with that of others: "It's been a very positive experience that has taught me about being less selfish. I realized that this is about small sacrifices of my time to help someone else grow and thrive" (M. Bell, personal communication, March 15, 2016).

Immigration Policies in the United States and the Slow Debate

Immigration represents one of the wickedest problems in the United States. Like all wicked problems, it's complex, and people's opinions about it and consequent actions are based on deep-rooted assumptions and values. Immigration in the United States is unstable and shifting, making a coherent response almost impossible. In addition, it's a social problem involving many different individuals and agencies across local, regional, and national borders and social divides.

In Introduction to Urban and Regional Studies, a discipline-specific global learning course in FIU's public administration department, students study two pivotal eras in U.S. immigration history—from 1870 to 1930 and the current era—to achieve the following global learning course outcomes:

- Global awareness: Students will be able to demonstrate knowledge of the motivations, sources, extent, and timing of immigration to the United States over the past two centuries.
- Global perspective: Students will be able to articulate the perspectives of the actors involved in immigration debates, including immigrants,

native-born Americans, politicians, and businesses, and explain how those perspectives interacted to influence policy decisions.

- Global engagement: Students will be able to propose solutions to the contemporary debate over immigration reform that take into account the full range of perspectives involved in the issue (Revell, 2017).

Achievement of these outcomes hinges on the instructor's careful scaffolding of students' knowledge of immigration in the United States. Keith Revell, associate professor of public administration, facilitates students' learning of the complexities of this wicked problem by structuring a series of developmentally appropriate course activities, including team-based responses to knowledge-based quizzes, videos, individual reflections, and multifaceted debates. In this last activity, which Revell calls a slow debate (K. Revell, personal communication, June 1, 2016), we can see how careful structuring of background knowledge facilitates student participation and success in a global learning course.

You may be familiar with the structured academic controversy method of discussion. Developed by education researchers David Johnson and Roger Johnson (1988), this method prompts students to explore a complex problem through primary or secondary documents representing contrasting viewpoints, then guides students to present those contrasting positions and discuss them to reach a consensus. Revell's slow debate method is similar to structured academic controversy in that it is an exploration of a complex problem in a step-by-step process that includes (a) background readings on the history and various perspectives on the problem, (b) the presentation of each perspective on the problem, (c) deliberation on the main points of each perspective, and (d) reflections on the debate's big questions as they relate to the meaning of diversity and community in the United States. Revell told us that he prefers this method over traditional debates in which students represent only one perspective, and "each side tends to dig in, listen poorly, and reiterate points already made." The purpose of the slow debate, said Revell, is "to get students to deepen their understanding of the perspectives that shape public policy in the U.S." To reach this goal, "They have to step back and see all the perspectives, and the consequences of the conflicts among them" (K. Revell, personal communication, June 1, 2016).

Revell also conducts this course using TBL, a collaborative method that enables instructors to simultaneously facilitate multiple active learning teams even in classes with large enrollments. TBL stresses the importance of out-of-class preparation, shifting class time from the traditional lecture and note-taking format and toward the application of knowledge and skills to real-world problem-solving (Michaelsen & Sweet, 2008). With TBL, students work in permanent teams for the semester, learning from one another and experiencing firsthand the necessity of considering multiple perspectives to solve complex problems.

In Revell's unit on immigration he facilitates two slow debates. The subject of the first slow debate is the legitimacy of the Immigration Act of 1924, a law that severely limited the number of immigrants allowed entry into the United States through a national origins quota. This is a closed-case debate, in that a decision has already been reached, so the debate focuses on understanding differing perspectives and not on posing alternative solutions to a historical problem. The second slow debate is on the legitimacy of the Support Our Law Enforcement and Safe Neighborhoods Act (2010). This Arizona law added new requirements, crimes, and penalties related to the enforcement of immigration laws in the state. It's an open-case debate in which students proceed from understanding and articulating various perspectives on the law to posing possible future solutions to dealing with its consequences. The second slow debate builds on the knowledge students have gained in the first debate and, in addition to fostering problem finding and problem framing skills, allows students to hone their creative thinking skills (Cavagnaro & Fasihuddin, 2016).

To prepare for the first slow debate, Revell provides students with background information on the history of immigration in the United States from 1850 to 1990, including graphs and charts on the demographics of the immigrants in the country, reasons for the major waves of U.S. immigration that occurred in this time period, and some of the effects of these immigration waves on U.S. cities. Students then read selected articles on the Immigration Act of 1924 and current U.S. immigration policies, and watch *Go Back to Mexico* (Fanning, 1994), a documentary that explores issues concerning undocumented immigrants who live in California.

Next, students take a short multiple-choice quiz on the readings, or a readiness assurance test (RAT), in TBL parlance. They take the RAT individually (iRAT) and then as a team (tRAT) to come to a consensus on responses. Students receive immediate feedback on the tRAT and can write an evidence-based appeal if they think they can make a logical and valid argument in favor of a response they got wrong. The purposes of the iRAT and tRAT include helping students prepare for problem-solving activities by gaining necessary background knowledge, generating shared understanding, and establishing positive group norms.

Final preparation for the slow debate consists of students' out-of-classroom reading of primary source texts that represent four different perspectives from the era when the Immigration Act of 1924 was passed: an immigrant, an industrialist in search of cheap labor, a nativist concerned about American cultural decline, and a politician writing the legislation. Students also answer questions on each of the perspectives, ranging from content-based questions (Who is Peter Mossini, where is he from, and when did he come to the United States?) to those that require analysis and interpretation (Who will the immigration law exclude, and who will it include?) (K. Revell, personal communication, June 1, 2016). Through the readings and the question responses, students prepare themselves to articulate all the perspectives to be covered in the debate.

On the day of the slow debate, students sit with their team members and take turns responding to questions. Revell leads the debate, asking the questions and calling on all the students. To start the debate, Revell asks each team, "What are the main elements (at least three) of each character's message or point of view regarding immigration?" All the teams write down their answers, and they announce their responses one at a time. Revell then asks each team, "What are the most convincing things each character could say to make his or her case?" and this time each team is called on to announce the answer from one particular perspective. Revell proceeds by asking a team that takes the role of one of the perspectives to respond to a team arguing for another perspective with the question, "How would X respond to Y?" Revell continues this pattern of questioning until all the teams have had the opportunity to respond to at least one other perspective. Revell concludes this first slow debate by asking each team to reflect on the debate's implications for American values and issues such as assmilation, diversity, and community (K. Revell, personal communication, June 1, 2016).

In the second slow debate on the legitimacy of the Support Our Law Enforcement and Safe Neighborhoods Act of 2010, Revell follows a similar procedure. Students prepare by reading primary source documents that represent different perspectives on the law from Arizona's former governor, Jan Brewer; a Mexican immigrant advocate; the director of the U.S. Immigration Policy Program Migration Policy Institute; the Heritage Foundation, an American conservative think tank; and an article from the *New York Times* that puts the law in a global context. Next, students take an iRAT and a tRAT on the facts and analyses of various positions on this law. After that, students prepare to represent each of the positions by doing their own research. Revell adds to this slow debate a final step in which students give policy recommendations for local, state, and federal governments to address multiple immigration issues in the United States. By having his students attempt to articulate solutions to the wicked problem of immigration in this debate, students use the knowledge they gained about the history of immigration in the earlier debate and the analysis skills they attained in considering multiple perspectives on the current immigration crisis. Revell is able to build his students' knowledge and analytic skills in each debate and from one debate to the next by carefully scaffolding their global learning (K. Revell, personal communication, June 1, 2016).

For Revell the best result of this debate isn't when teams provide a solution to the problem of immigration in the United States but when they recognize the complexity of the issue and the enormous difficulty of finding a solution that satisfies everyone. Success, Revell told us, is when he sees that "the scales have fallen from their eyes and the situation seems impossibly complex" (K. Revell, personal communication, August 27, 2015). What do Revell's students do in this situation? "They become excited with the process, which they express as one that is legitimate, democratic, and fair. If they do pose solutions, they are policy recommendations that take into account all the perspectives possible" (K. Revell, personal communication, August 27, 2015). To us, this is powerful global learning.

Does Modality Matter? Success in Global Learning Online

During the spring and fall semesters of 2012, undergraduates Andrew Hofmeyer and Florencia Dominguez each took sections of Women, Culture, and Economic Development, a global learning foundations course in FIU's general education curriculum. Both students were profoundly affected by the course, taught by Irma Alonso, professor emerita of economics. Dominguez (2014) said the course opened the door to her dream career by inspiring her to find solutions to problems related to human trafficking. A documentary screened in class, *Shackled Women: Abuses of a Patriarchal World* (Purdue, 1999) made her aware of

> the atrocities many women are suffering even today just because of their gender, the scarce value they hold as persons in different parts of the world, and the little it seems the rest of us is concerned in addressing these issues. (Dominguez, 2014, para. 3)

Dominguez decided to focus her class project on human trafficking, leading her to a job with the International Rescue Committee:

> While working on my assignment, I met [the International Rescue Committee's] Anti-Human Trafficking program manager, Ms. Regina Bernadin. . . . I was so motivated that when a position opened in the [group's] Anti-Human Trafficking department, I jumped at the opportunity. Today, I work as a full-time caseworker in that department and Ms. Bernadin is now my boss. (para. 4)

Meanwhile, Hofmeyer enrolled in Alonso's course because he was interested in the ways economic policies influence individuals and nations. Growing up in apartheid South Africa, he witnessed firsthand "how economics is intertwined with freedom, health, and personal happiness and the great effect determined individuals can have in changing lives for the better" (Hofmeyer, 2014). Describing the course, Hofmeyer (2014) said,

> Dr. Alonso taught us the academic principles behind global economic development, but also encouraged us to learn about international issues and to use our diverse, multicultural backgrounds to think of solutions. It was through an assignment that had this intention . . . that I learned of the Grameen Bank initiated by the Nobel Laureate Dr. Mohammad Yunus. Now a formal institution, Grameen Bank lends small sums of money to women in rural Bangladesh with the goal of having them start local businesses that inspire entrepreneurship and facilitate economic growth to break the cycle of poverty. (para. 3)

Hofmeyer was inspired to apply for an internship at Grameen Bank and was accepted. Within a few days of his arrival, he was attending Grameen-sponsored community meetings along with interns from other parts of the world and getting to know the women who used their loans to transform their own lives and those of their families. Toward the end of his internship, Hofmeyer even met his idol, Mohammad Yunus. Reflecting on Alonso's impact on his life, Hofmeyer (2014) said, "Through this course I learned how powerful it can be to combine our varying experiences—as parts of different cultures, family types, genders, and groups—to unite and use our differences to solve global problems together" (para. 6).

The global engagement course learning outcome for Women, Culture, and Economic Development calls for students to be able to "become engaged in solving local, global, international and intercultural problems, as they affect women worldwide" (Alonso, 2017). These students' reflections demonstrate that Alonso's teaching strategies successfully achieved this outcome.

But here's the most astounding part of this story: Alonso never met in person the students who were taking her course. This course is conducted fully online using a learning management system.

Semester after semester, students write to Alonso to report the transformative impact her course has had on the way they understand themselves and the power of their engagement with others. Diversity courses related to social justice, women's and gender studies, or diverse cultures and perspectives have been found to have a medium to large effect on students' openness to diversity, their enjoyment of being challenged by different perspectives, and their political and social involvement (O'Neill, 2012). But how does Alonso facilitate such meaningful exchanges of perspective among people who have never met one another? Alonso told us about the structured approach she developed to encourage collaboration online (I. Alonso, personal communication, September 15, 2015). In the first class, she and her students break the ice by introducing themselves to one another on the learning management system's discussion board, sharing information about their lives, their reasons for taking the course, their learning styles, and responding to each other's posts. Within the first week, students use the introductions to find a partner to work with and a country to analyze in depth throughout the semester. The pairs then spend four weeks learning foundational concepts underlying the course's theoretical framework, which is the human capabilities approach (Nussbaum, 2000; Sen, 1999). Students also compare and contrast variables related to common measures of economic development, such as gross domestic product, gross national income, and the human development indexes.

The second section of the course is divided into four 2-week units addressing major issues related to economic development: education, health, employment, marriage, divorce, family planning, and domestic violence. In the first week of each unit, students use 15 guiding questions to research their chosen country's policies and practices and the impact of those policies and practices on residents, particularly women. At the end of that week, pairs publish their research paper on the discussion board. The unit's second week involves comparative analysis, dialogue, and building solutions. Students read all their peers' research and view videos, then compose an evidence-based essay identifying which country other than the one they've studied they would rather live in as a woman, taking into consideration that unit's issue. They also discuss online how they would work to improve the condition of women in their own country. Next, students choose two other pairs to talk to online. The pairs compare and contrast conditions in their countries, ask each other critical questions, and suggest alternative policies and practices they've gleaned from readings and experience.

As with all global learning foundations courses in FIU's general education curriculum, students are required to participate in a cocurricular activity related to the course's content or theme. In the course's final two weeks, while studying for the final exam, students reflect on their chosen activity in small groups in the management system's group forum. They also read an essay on the pros and cons of globalization (Appiah, 2006b). The course's culminating assignment requires responses to two essential questions: Up to what point is it cultural imperialism for people in one country to defend women's rights in another country, and is it a violation of the convention of cultural diversity to promote the protection of women's human rights worldwide?

When interviewed about her course, Alonso said she communicates more often and in more meaningful ways with her students online than she is able to in a face-to-face format. For her, online education and collaboration go hand in hand (I. Alonso, personal communication, September 15, 2015). Alonso is atypical in her opinions; most faculty express more fear than excitement about teaching online, particularly if they have tenure, 20 or more years of experience, or teach in the social sciences or in large institutions (Allen, Seaman, Lederman, & Jaschik, 2012). A passionate and skilled online instructor, Alonso is a veteran of more than 47 years in higher education who started working at FIU in 1977 and continues to teach even after officially retiring in 2008. As she tells it, that retirement lasted exactly one month. Her love of teaching, and for Women, Culture, and Economic Development in particular, drew her back to the classroom through an online portal. She was mentored and supported by multiple instructional designers, who provide ongoing help for Alonso and other faculty with building and modifying online courses. In 2011 Alonso completed the training and revisions necessary to achieve Quality Matters certification for her course (FIU Online, n.d.-b). She was also the first of FIU's 13 winners of the Blackboard Exemplary Course Award, contributing to FIU's status as public university with the most awards in the program (FIU Online, n.d.-a). As a result of her training, Alonso fully uses the collaborative features of Blackboard Learn and Adobe Connect to chat live with her students and provide them with virtual office hours (I. Alonso, personal communication, September 15, 2015).

McDonald (1992) was referring to faculty like Alonso when he wrote that real teaching is prompted by the question, "How can I grasp it myself so that my grasping might enable theirs?" (p. 1). Alonso told us that before she revised her course for the global learning designation, she taught it from a philosophical and theoretical point of view using a collection of scholarly essays (Nussbaum & Glover, 2001) and that this approach just didn't click with students. She revised the course after reading a data-based study by Neft and Levine (1998) and working more frequently with the United Nations Human Development Index (Anand & Sen, 1994). She wondered, "How can I put these three things together in a single course?" (I. Alonso, personal communication, September 15, 2015). Alonso takes her students on the same developmental journey she took, first contending with philosophical and cultural perspectives on the status of women around the world and then analyzing data to compare these constructs to the real-world conditions women face. Most important, she asks all her students the essential question of global citizenship, the same question that, according to McDonald (1992), teachers grapple with on a daily basis: "How near should I come, how far off should I stay" (p. 1)? In her online global learning course, Alonso proves you can be very far off indeed and still have a great deal of impact on others' lives.

Frustrated in Florence, Problem-Solving in Paris

The 11 undergraduate students who participated in the study abroad section of the discipline-specific global learning course Inclusive Recreation Services knew from the syllabus that it would involve simulations replicating the experience of physical and sensory disability and that these would be carried out in the storied cities of Florence and Paris. The students were up to the challenge, or so they thought.

After two weeks of in-class preparation in Miami, a 12-hour flight to Florence, and an afternoon checking out wheelchair-accessible routes in the city, the students were eager to embark on their first simulation. The assignment seemed straightforward: Get 4 students in wheelchairs from the Hotel Albergo to the basilica of San Miniato al Monte. After consulting a map, they decided to take an estimated 26-minute walk to their destination, one of Italy's most beautiful churches set atop one of the highest points in the city. They began in good spirits, and despite heavy pedestrian traffic around the Uffizi Gallery, they were able to navigate the students in wheelchairs without incident. It was slow going on the walkway that crossed the Arno River, though, and the students had to abandon their original plan when they saw that the path to the basilica included 411 steps. After a few turns on the paved road, they arrived at their first panoramic view of Florence. The 7 able-bodied students excitedly ran to the edge of the overlook to take photos. Suddenly, they realized something was wrong. Stuck in the road below, their disabled peers were unable to enjoy the same view. Faced with this dilemma, they came up with a solution. They ran back to the wheelchair-bound students, grabbed the students' cameras, and returned to the overlook to take pictures for them (A. McKenney, personal communication, August 8, 2015).

The course's instructor, Alexis McKenney, formerly an associate professor of recreational therapy in FIU's School of Education and Human Development and currently professor of instruction in rehabilitation science at Temple University, allowed the incident to play out without interceding. Although the disabled students hadn't protested that they were unable to see the view for themselves, when the entire group reached the basilica, McKenney found them all sitting quietly together in a room on the ground floor. The able-bodied students didn't want to leave to see the rest of the basilica because that meant walking up steps and leaving their wheelchair-bound classmates behind. Instead, they preferred to enjoy what they could as a group. As McKenney (2015) noted, "The first truly empathetic moment had occurred" (p. 16).

This moment, the beginnings of a global perspective on travel and disability, is an example of the Latin phrase, *experientia docet* (experience teaches). Global learning occurred in this study abroad course not because students were able to observe Italians' problems with disability in situ but because they themselves felt what Italians feel *in toto,* collectively and with all five of their senses. Each student had a first-person experience of the lack of accommodations for the disabled and, in negotiating the meaning of their experiences, were compelled to confront the implications of these disparities for the group.

During this two-week study abroad course, McKenney's students encountered dozens of situations in which they had to make individual and group decisions regarding accommodations for their disabled peers. They also met with outright hostility: passersby who called them stupid, a bus driver who refused to lower an access ramp, and a café owner who refused to seat them. As McKenney told us later, "I don't really have to set up a problem. We just have to go out there and there will be problems" (A. McKenney, personal communication, August 8, 2015). After the students faced each challenge, McKenney guided them in reflecting on their decisions, reactions, and feelings. "The debriefing process after each of these activities is absolutely crucial," McKenney said, "especially at the end of activities such as being blindfolded on the train, when invariably students become angry and scared and cannot easily express these emotions on their own" (A. McKenney, personal communication, August 8, 2015). McKenney was referring to a side trip from Paris to the Château de Versailles by way of the train system serving Paris and its suburbs. McKenney split up the students into pairs, with one student in each pair making the trip blindfolded. "The students who were blindfolded felt a total loss of control and were completely dependent on their partner," McKenney said, whereas the sighted students had to exert high levels of patience, alertness, and verbal engagement with their partners (A. McKenney, personal communication, August 8, 2015). Reflection on these dynamics is a necessity because simulations such as these can produce frustration and anger, leading participants to wrongly conclude that disabled people are less capable of living independently (McKenney, 2015).

Additionally, students need to understand how legislation, economics, and personal and societal attitudes interact to shape the context of disabled people's travel experiences in the United States and abroad so they don't develop ethnocentric attitudes that lead to denial, defense, or minimization of the problems in their own country. Prior to departure, McKenney has students study various disabling conditions, provisions of the Americans with Disabilities Act (1990), and principles of universal design. They conduct accessibility surveys of campus recreation areas and participate in one wheelchair simulation. While in Florence, students explore Italian disability legislation and use the Americans with Disabilities Act checklist to evaluate accessibility at various sites, including a museum, a church, and a train station. The class compares and contrasts findings from their surveys at home and abroad, discussing ways to adapt all kinds of recreation spaces and experiences for people of diverse ages and genders and of various physical, mental, sensory, and cognitive abilities. By the end of the course, students see the challenges people face while traveling disabled or while traveling with disabled people as a truly global problem: it is complex, affects diverse people in different ways, and requires solutions that transcend borders. In the words of one student,

> This trip allowed me to examine personal, societal, and global attitudes toward people with disabilities. It added clarity to my understanding of how leisure and disability transcends culturally and geographically. . . . The experience from this trip has inspired me to ensure that inclusion will be the basis of my professional objective regardless of the position, the setting, or the population. (McKenney, 2015, pp. 21–22)

Taking the mission of the course to heart, FIU administrators have established the Accessing the World Scholarship to support disabled students' study, internship, and service activities abroad.

Challenges of Implementing Global Learning

Contrary to the impression you may have from the preceding cases, infusing a course with global learning is seldom an easy thing to do. Although the majority of courses can involve global learning, we know it requires a great deal of hard work on the part of faculty members to understand the process of global learning, risk trying new methods, and gain colleagues' support for these efforts. Sometimes, despite an instructor's best attempts, McDonald's (1992) "wild triangle of relations" (p. 1) among a course's content, the beliefs of others who teach it, and the departmental context of the course is enough to slam the brakes on global learning. The following case of two FIU courses that received the global learning designation and whose instructors later had it removed illustrates the challenges that can arise and how with patience and creative leadership these challenges can be converted into new opportunities for students and faculty alike.

The courses Political Ideologies and Development of International Relations Thought are taught in the politics and international relations (PIR) department of FIU's School of International and Public Affairs. Political Ideologies is part of FIU's general education curriculum and is an elective for political science majors. Development of International Relations Thought is required for all international relations majors. Both courses were submitted to the GLCOC and were approved for the global learning designation during academic year 2011–2012. Notably, this was also the year the political science and international relations departments merged to become PIR. In an interview, the late Rebecca Salokar, PIR's former department chair, winced when she recalled the details involved in the merger and the tension that cut through the faculty. "This was a challenging time for us. . . . The decision to globalize these courses was not thoroughly considered, and the actual infusion of the global learning elements into these courses was rushed" (R. Salokar, personal communication, September 29, 2015). It wasn't long before the department voted to request the GLCOC remove the global learning designation from the courses in academic year 2013–2014.

What happened? Both courses seemed then and now like natural fits for global learning. As described in the course catalog, Political Ideologies involves analysis of modern political ideologies since the French Revolution, including liberalism, conservatism, and socialism, as well as the relationship between ideology and totalitarianism (FIU, 2015b). One can imagine any number of active, collaborative strategies that would help students understand the interrelated forces that shape political ideologies, view them via various historical or sociocultural perspectives, and determine methods for addressing issues arising from the enforcement of ideology. The course Development of International Relations Thought requires students to examine the religio-philosophical, socioeconomic, and political ideas and systems associated with international relations. Students also study "historical occurrences and patterns of social change and their interaction with the dynamics of international relations" (FIU, 2015a, p. 567).

There are a number of reasons global learning wasn't effectively integrated into these courses. First, the faculty members who submitted the proposals for these courses chose to make global learning revisions on their own without having participated in a professional development workshop or conferring with other faculty teaching the course. On paper, the proposals appeared to the GLCOC to contain the necessary components: global learning course outcomes, traditional and authentic assessments, active learning strategies, and diverse content and readings. But within a year, it was apparent that course sections were being taught with Western-only content and that the active learning and authentic assessment strategies included in the proposals weren't being applied.

The lack of fidelity to global learning came to light in early 2013 when new faculty assigned to teach these courses began attending global learning professional development workshops. For the most part, these were junior faculty new to the university. They expressed a great deal of enthusiasm for the global learning approach; in one memorable moment, a new assistant professor with a dual appointment in religious studies and PIR realized that to teach Development of International Relations Thought he needed to include non-Western theories. "That means that I will have to *learn* those theories," he commented, homework that he was more than willing to do. However, when he and others discussed these global learning revisions with senior faculty, they encountered considerable resistance. Department leaders felt that the courses' traditional content was fundamental to students' program of study and shouldn't be changed.

Factors outside the department also contributed to what occurred. Academic year 2011–2012 was only the second year of life for the GLCOC. The majority of the committee's five members had neither developed nor taught global learning courses themselves, limiting the collective knowledge of what was possible to achieve in terms of revision. Members were still negotiating the meaning of the global learning SLOs, and they disagreed about the extent to which global learning should be apparent in the syllabus: Was a single unit enough, or did global learning need to be threaded throughout? With limited course-level student learning assessment data available to inform their expectations, the committee approved some proposals with little insight into their potential for success and few, if any, recommended revisions.

Academic year 2011–2012 was also the second year of implementation for the global learning graduation requirement, and departments were under intense pressure to make global learning courses available to their students. The early majority busily submitted proposals; the GLCOC approved 45 courses during that year alone. This pressure led the GLCOC's chair at the time, a junior PIR faculty member who had only been at the university for one year, to vouch for the global learning present in Political Ideologies and Development of International Relations Thought, even though he didn't teach either of the courses.

With the knowledge that PIR students needed global learning courses to fulfill their graduation requirement, the department voted to remove these courses' designations and immediately discussed which courses would be appropriate for global learning. Committed faculty stepped up to revise and teach the new courses, and this is when the door opened to an entirely new global learning opportunity. The PIR faculty working on the department's new courses asked if their graduate teaching assistants could also attend global learning course instruction workshops. When Rebecca Salokar heard about this request, she asked the OGLI if it would be willing to provide global learning professional development to all PIR graduate assistants as part of her required semester-long graduate teaching seminar. Since 2014 global learning has been part of all PIR graduate assistant training. As a result, global learning strategies are making their way into a multitude of PIR courses, regardless of whether these courses are designated as global learning.

Conclusion

In presenting these cases, we hope to demonstrate that effective global learning is a deliberate process. We want you to know there is no ideal classroom for global learning; motivated, creative, and skilled faculty can fashion the conditions of global learning in almost any context. However, our descriptions have fallen short. These cases only tell part of the story of these faculty. They detail the bold, inventive strategies these faculty have used to structure global learning, but they've shed precious little light on their personal characteristics as global learning pedagogues. We've hinted at a few of these characteristics, such as Collado-Vides's willingness to express her own passion for the environment and to ignite that of her students, McKenney's comfort with the unknown, Roller's and Revell's openness to divergent ideas and controversial topics, and Alonso's commitment to curricular innovation and lifelong learning. But to get a complete picture, you'd have to observe them in action, as we've had the privilege of doing. In some cases, these faculty discovered and honed these attitudes through the experience of teaching a global learning course. In others, they built their course's global learning activities around what they knew to be their unique strengths. In any case, global learning opens the door—or opens it up a bit wider—for faculty to bring their hearts and souls into the classroom, along with their minds and bodies. As you work with faculty to infuse global learning into their courses, it's important to remember not only what McDonald (1992) said about the fraught nature of teaching in the "wild triangle of relations" (p. 1) but also what he doesn't say about it. For it is faculty members who have the power to tame the triangle, softening its edges and shaping it into a form that includes every class member in the circle of global learning.

7

GLOBAL LEARNING IN THE COCURRICULUM

Fostering students' abilities to integrate learning—across courses, over time, and between campus and community life—is one of the most important goals and challenges of higher education.
(AAC&U & Carnegie Foundation for the Advancement of Teaching, 2004, p. 1)

One of the hallmarks of the Global Learning for Global Citizenship initiative at FIU is its integrative approach to learning, which is a deliberate process that enables students to make connections among ideas, issues, and experiences and to synthesize and transfer their learning to new and increasingly complex situations. Integrative learning involves making connections between courses in one discipline, among different disciplines, between academic knowledge and practice, and between the curriculum and cocurriculum (Huber, Hutchins, & Gale, 2005). It often occurs when students address real-world problems that are broad, difficult to describe, and "offer multiple solutions and benefit from multiple perspectives" (AAC&U & The Carnegie Foundation for the Advancement of Teaching, 2004, p. 1). Sound familiar? Integrative learning and global learning depend on students' engagement in complex problem-solving inside and outside the classroom. The cocurriculum plays an essential role in integrative and global learning, providing students with formal and informal opportunities to connect new and existing knowledge, skills, and experiences and apply them to local, national, or global issues. In this chapter, we refer to the intersection between integrative learning and global learning as *integrative global learning*.

From the beginning, the cocurriculum was integral to Global Learning for Global Citizenship. As you may recall from chapter 1, one of our four program goals calls for increasing the number of cocurricular global learning activities available to undergraduate students. One of our three graduation-level global learning SLOs, global engagement, encourages students to be involved in the cocurriculum. All global learning foundations courses in FIU's general education curriculum require students to participate in at least one cocurricular activity during the semester. We included these components in our plan to ensure a long-term focus on global learning in the cocurriculum. We knew from the literature and the experience of FIU leaders like Rosa Jones, former vice president of student affairs and undergraduate education, that collaborative partnerships between student affairs staff and faculty would be essential to make global learning integrative (Frost et al., 2010; Guarasci, 2001; Ozaki & Hornak, 2014). But we also knew from these same sources that the divide between student affairs and academic affairs was a deep one. "Many faculty probably didn't think that their courses could be enhanced by the co-curriculum just because they didn't know what existed," Jones said. "And on the cocurricular side, many staff felt that their contributions would probably be undervalued" (R. Jones, personal communication, April 19, 2016).

To resolve these differences in perspective, we opened all professional development workshops to faculty and student affairs staff alike. For a few years, these workshops were led by OGLI staff and Beverly Dalrymple, retired executive director of the Center for Leadership and Service. In the following, Dalrymple offered her perception of these combined workshops:

> I saw it happening—that at first faculty and staff might struggle with the global learning activities, with understanding each other's perspectives, but as they lived through the process, they started to understand how global learning presents other ways of analyzing issues and a way to get to understand one another's perspective. The natural collaborations that formed between faculty and student affairs staff through the global learning process were amazing. (B. Dalrymple, personal communication, April 22, 2016)

Our commitment to increasing faculty and staff collaboration was in large part because of Jones's strong belief that the initiative should provide opportunities to enrich and expand dialogue between the divisions' staff and faculty. Students themselves also built bridges between academic and student affairs. The president of the Student Government Association, a member of the steering committee that developed the vision and common agenda for global learning at FIU, expressed vocal support for the cocurriculum. Students' enthusiasm and in-class reflections about their global learning cocurricular experiences galvanized the faculty. "Students had an important role in helping faculty see the value that cocurricular activities brought to learning and in helping faculty be a lot more open about how they could engage students in these activities" (R. Jones, personal communication, April 19, 2016).

In the following pages, we walk you through several signature aspects of FIU's global learning cocurriculum. Some are programs we think of as integrative global learning habitats, environments that provide students with prolonged global learning engagement and opportunities to make connections among their activities, their course work, their personal lives, and the wider world around them.

Habitats for Integrative Global Learning

Habitats of integrative learning are "stable, dedicated structures (learning communities, capstones, and so forth) that have connection-making as a central, shaping goal" (Hutchins, 2005, p. 12). Integrative global learning habitats open the door for students to put the pieces of their global learning together, to connect their classwork with their personal experiences and their experiences in the broader campus, community, and world, all for the purpose of developing their global awareness, perspective, and engagement.

FIU offers hundreds of cocurricular activities with global, international, and intercultural aspects to its students each year, and in this way FIU is no different from many campuses across the country. We won't bore you by enumerating these activities here. Instead, we describe how we developed integrative habitats that provide our students with multiple entryways to collaboration with diverse others and multiple environments where they can plant deep global learning roots and thrive as global citizens. We provide a glimpse into one such habitat in chapter 6, global learning foundations courses like Challenges in Healthcare and Women, Culture, and Economic Development. Another habitat is the Excellence in Global Learning Medallion, a graduation honor open to all undergraduates in all academic programs. The Global Learning Medallion is nonselective and allows students to develop personalized integrative pathways across the curriculum and cocurriculum. The Peace Corps Prep program is a formal partnership with the national Peace Corps. This more selective habitat is attractive for students interested in international development. The Global Living Learning Community, a collaboration among Housing and Residence Life, the Center for Leadership and Service, International Student and Scholar Services, the Office of Study Abroad, and the OGLI, is a habitat that allows students to integrate global learning into their daily lives. Habitats aren't the only venues for promoting integration, though. GlobeMed is a student organization that prompts participants to connect course work in science, technology, engineering, and math fields with local and international health care development work. Recurring events like the Tuesday Times Roundtable discussion series attract a wide spectrum of student, faculty, staff, and community member participants. These regularly scheduled activities offer glimpses into further global learning opportunities and encourage students to make integrative global learning a signature aspect of their college education.

Global Learning Habitats in Action

Now it's time to show you what integrative global learning habitats look like in practice. By viewing them through students' eyes, you'll see how they learn to make connections and stand in others' shoes. We also describe these programs' requirements and features we think essential to providing opportunities that meet your students' diverse interests, schedules, and career preparation needs.

Global Learning Medallion

FIU's Global Learning Medallion is awarded to "students who have completed an extensive curriculum and co-curriculum designed to enhance global awareness, global perspective, and an attitude of global engagement" (FIU Global Learning, 2017a, para. 1). Specifically, students must complete the following to earn the medallion:

- Accrue 20 activity points by attending globally focused campus events and participating in globally focused clubs or other long-term global learning activities
- Earn at least a grade of C in four global learning courses
- Complete a global learning capstone that may consist of one or more of the following: a semester-long study abroad, additional foreign language study, a semester-long internship, or research on a globally focused topic
- Possess a minimum of a 3.0 grade point average at the time of graduation
- Create an ePortfolio that includes a multimedia reflection on global learning experiences

The OGLI hosts a special graduation ceremony to confer medallions and showcase all students' ePortfolios. Family, friends, mentors, students still working toward the Global Learning Medallion, and the OGLI's programming partners are invited, and refreshments are provided.

Students proposed the idea for the Global Learning Medallion. In spring 2013 a team in a master's-level advertising and public relations course took on the OGLI as a client. They evaluated the OGLI's mission and conducted a strengths, weaknesses, opportunities, and threats analysis of the OGLI's work. Data were collected via interviews with OGLI staff and students, reviews of key primary and secondary resources, and observations of global learning events and courses. The team's major finding was that undergraduates wanted a tangible way to share their global learning achievements with peers and potential employers. Based on this finding, the team proposed the creation of the medallion and provided a draft budget, communications plan, and an implementation schedule. The OGLI used these recommendations to develop the medallion during the 2013–2014 academic year and implemented it in fall 2014.

The medallion is a portal to everything FIU offers in global learning, from courses to volunteer opportunities, internships, and more. Students accrue points by attending globally focused campus events that are aligned with their personal interests and career goals. The medallion also incentivizes leadership. Volunteering earns students one activity point, and being part of an organization's executive board merits five points. We find that students' participation in global learning activities is greatly increased merely by enrolling in the program, even if they don't complete it.

Although career guidance isn't an explicit goal of the Global Learning Medallion, participants are exposed to different kinds of jobs and opportunities to lead organizations. For her capstone project, Andrea Jo, an international business major, participated in nonprofit humanitarian work. Jo said that serving as an executive member of FIU's United Nations Children's Fund campus initiative for two years opened her eyes to new opportunities:

> I started college with a vision of what I would do with a degree from FIU and I'm graduating this summer with a completely different idea of what I want my life to be and what this degree actually means to me. This change of vision has come about by participating in activities that include cultural responsibility, social responsibility, and global awareness. Now I see what I can do with economics and the kind of organizations I can be part of. (A. Jo, personal communication, July 21, 2016)

The OGLI's Eric Feldman, who leads the Global Learning Medallion and Peace Corps Prep programs, notifies students about events, talks with them about their goals and interests, and connects them to internships that involve hands-on real-world problem-solving. Lillie Garvin's Global Learning Medallion capstone was an internship with the Alliance for Global Justice, which works toward economic equity and social change by supporting local grassroots organizations (Alliance for Global Justice, 2013). In an interview with FIU News, Garvin described her favorite part of working with the alliance: working on viral mapping of the Zika virus. This project involved reviewing data on the virus's movement, analyzing affected areas, and identifying the ideal conditions for its spread. Garvin said that during her internship she needed to interact with people from many different cultures. Explaining how this connected to her academic work, she said, "I had taken a course on intercultural communication that I really put into practice. It taught me how to be culturally sensitive and how to interact with those who do not come from the same place as I do" (Garvin, 2016, para. 7). She also said the internship helped her develop a new love of public health and that her overall confidence increased with every new task she completed.

The Global Learning Medallion culminates with an ePortfolio in which students highlight and critically reflect on their own global learning. The ePortfolio consists of artifacts from all five-point activities, a written reflection of selected experiences and activities, work samples from global learning courses, and evidence of the capstone project (FIU Global Learning, 2017b). The ePortfolio also includes a stand-alone page in which students describe changes in their global awareness, perspective, and engagement. Students use the Web-based platform of their choice and take great care in curating their artifacts and written reflections.

Some students use their ePortfolio as a digital résumé. Others use it as a personal record for themselves or to share with friends and family. Completing the ePortfolio was extremely meaningful for Bianca Gutierrez, who said, "I was able to look back and say this impacted me this way and that impacted me that way . . . completing the ePortfolio brought everything full circle" (B. Gutierrez, personal communication, July 19, 2016).

Student reflections demonstrate how attending even a single lecture or event can be transformative. Although these experiences may be brief, they contribute to students' ability to empathize with others and analyze issues from different perspectives. Carla Santamaria (2015), a transfer student who earned a Global Learning Medallion, reflected how attending a Take Back the Night event affected her:

> Take Back the Night is a yearly event which promotes awareness of sexual assault by encouraging community members to speak out against abuse, emphasizes the importance of mutual consent, and empowers victims to speak up about their abuse. At Take Back the Night, there were survivors of sexual assault who spoke about their experience, not to elicit sympathy, but to empower other survivors to not let their assault define them. There were also multiple on-campus organizations whose missions it is to inform the community on what does and does not constitute consent, so as to create a culture in which sexual assault is less likely to happen. All in all, Take Back the Night was one of the most powerful events I've ever attended on campus. I was honored to have been a part of it. (para. 2)

Another Global Learning Medallion student, Borja Hazza (n.d.), participated in more than 40 different one-time events, including panel discussions on globalization, lectures on cyber security, student roundtable discussions on the withdrawal of Great Britain from the European Union, and more, saying,

> I realized how much of our opinions are often based on where we reside, and the access to information we possess. FIU has consistently amazed me with the high profile industry, political and academia experts that are available to us on a weekly basis; participatory events have been one of the great joys of my time as a student, greatly improving my global perspective and awareness. Some of the events I've attended by myself but many of them I've attended with school friends and my younger sister, allowing me to grow my communication and interpersonal interaction skills as we continued the conversation far after the event was over. (para. 5)

Choosing and collating artifacts for the ePortfolio requires students to describe their development as global citizens, the meaning of their global learning experiences, the skills they gained from these experiences, and the connections they made among them. The ePortfolio provides the student and the university with tangible multimedia evidence of the Global Learning Medallion's power as an integrative global learning habitat.

Peace Corps Prep

This certificate program prepares undergraduates for volunteer service in the Peace Corps or work in other international development contexts. To earn a certificate from the Peace Corps, undergraduates must successfully complete three global learning courses and a minimum of two semesters of college- or university-level courses in the same foreign language; participate in informational, networking, and mentorship opportunities; and complete a capstone research project on a global issue in one of six areas stipulated by the Peace Corps: education, health, environment, agriculture, youth in development, or community economic development (FIU Global Learning, 2017c; Peace Corps, 2016).

As with the Global Learning Medallion, a student was the impetus for innovating the Peace Corps Prep program and making it a success. In the program's original iteration, Peace Corps Prep students didn't know who else was pursuing the certificate, and this led to a weak sense of community and a low completion rate. Participants peppered Feldman with questions, and although he enjoyed working with students, Peace Corps Prep was only one of several global learning habitats he facilitated. Nannette Boza was a junior and chair of the Peace Corps Prep board when she expressed a need for the program to become more student centered. Boza wanted participants to feel more like a family or a team. Feldman suggested a cohort model. Cohorts help students create community and learn from their peers. At the same time, Feldman advised, a cohort model would require more coordination and cooperation on the part of participants and program facilitators. Despite the potential challenges, Boza thought that the cohort idea was the best approach and suggested that each board member could serve as a peer mentor. Feldman agreed that peer mentorship would provide participants with individualized attention and help board members acquire essential leadership skills. He also thought a cohort model would help students feel greater affiliation with the program, resulting in a higher proportion of students completing requirements and graduating with a Peace Corps Prep certificate.

Together, Feldman and Boza made a list of ideas to bring to the board for discussion and deliberation. They also conferred with Connie Penczak, an OGLI graduate assistant whose responsibilities included advising the Peace Corps Prep program and three other global learning clubs. She suggested students submit a résumé as part of the application process to enhance their initial and long-term commitment. A few weeks later, the board joined Feldman and Penczak in a conference room. The board included the global engagement chair, whose role is to find people from nonprofits and other local resources to connect with Peace Corps Prep students and speak at program events; the development chair, who focuses on what students need to do to enter the Peace Corps and gain access to other international development professions; the student engagement chair, who works on students' personal development and finds less involved Peace Corps Prep students to offer extra support; and the resource chair, who connects students to resources in FIU. The board had a wide-ranging discussion about leadership qualities, processes, and types of activities that help build affiliation in any organization, in short, best practices for creating a stable, vibrant organizational culture. After agreeing to institute a cohort model and a selection process for Peace Corps Prep applicants (a written application and an interview with the board), the board members homed in on two ideas to help build community in the program: a two-hour orientation session for each cohort and a peer mentorship program. An orientation would give all Peace Corps Prep students the same information simultaneously and allow them to engage in team building and leadership activities from the start. Mentors would be able to guide peers individually throughout the program and help them fulfill all the program requirements. Each board member would mentor seven to eight students.

The Peace Corps describes itself as "a service opportunity for motivated changemakers to immerse themselves in a community abroad, working side

by side with local leaders to tackle the most pressing challenges of our generation" (Peace Corps, n.d.-a). As the previous example demonstrates, allowing
students to decide for themselves how an integrative global learning habitat
should be conducted enables them to become agents of their own learning
and take ownership of their community's progress. In addition to tackling
problems in their own globally focused research activities, Peace Corps Prep
members were up to the challenge of designing and implementing strategies
to further their own growth and that of their peers. The motto of the Peace
Corps is "Make the Most of Your World" (Peace Corps, n.d.-b); certainly the
students participating in the innovation of the Peace Corps Prep program at
FIU did just that.

Global Living Learning Community

Established in the 2012–2013 academic year, the Global Living Learning
Community aims to develop globally competent leaders who actively seek
to increase their global awareness, perspective, and engagement; accept their
responsibilities as global citizens; and practice leadership methods that focus
on collaboration, inclusion, and intercultural competency (FIU Student
Affairs, 2017). About 30 students live in this community for one year.
During this time they take part in a menu of activities purposefully designed
to work in concert to create meaningful integrative global learning, including

- participating in global learning experiences during a weekend retreat
  at the beginning of the fall semester;
- attending monthly meetings that feature faculty, staff, and
  administrators who engage students in collaborative problem-solving
  activities;
- hosting cultural dinners in which the students prepare food from
  various parts of the world; and
- completing a semester-long globally focused project in which students
  collaboratively work with a local or global organization to analyze and
  address an issue that transcends borders.

The community meets as a group every other Tuesday, at times with a
guest speaker, to discuss global challenges that surface in Miami. The guest
speaker often has a connection to an organization working on the issue at
hand. When students identify with the challenge itself or the speaker's passion, they are sometimes prompted to work with the organization as part
of their semester-long project. At one of these meetings Ashaunte Stroman,
known on campus as the high-scoring center of the FIU women's rugby team
and as a two-time member of the U.S. Women's Collegiate All-American

rugby team, jumped at the chance to get involved in a project that led to what she described in an interview as the biggest transformation of her life. Eric Feldman, the speaker at this particular meeting, was there to talk about local organizations that students might become involved with, and one of these organizations was the Miami chapter of the Church World Service.

Founded in 1946, the mission of this international faith-based non-profit organization is to address hunger, poverty, displacement, and disaster throughout the world (Church World Service, n.d.). The organization assists refugee families with many of their resettlement needs, including finding low-rent apartments, jobs, furniture, and clothes. Church World Service also takes an active role in helping refugees with their transportation needs. In late 2015, Feldman volunteered to lead a bike drive effort at FIU, teaming up with the on-campus bicycle shop to solicit donations of new and used bikes, with the goal of getting 20 bicycles for the newly arrived refugees. At the Global Living Learning Community meeting, he talked about the bike drive as an opportunity for the students to make a concrete, positive difference in the daily lives of others.

Stroman was moved to become involved with the drive because she could personally relate to the problem: "It just really touched me because I don't have a car either. I have a bike, and I'm a student who doesn't have to go many places, so I can just imagine how it feels for them" (A. Stroman, personal communication, May 27, 2016). Stroman's role was to promote the bike drive across campus. She visited fraternities and sororities, contacted different departments, and spoke in classes. She held a fund-raiser at a fast-food restaurant and opened a Go Fund Me account to make it easy for students and staff to give donations online.

Stroman learned that solving even a small problem is challenging. The goal of the bike drive was 20 bikes—a goal she thought would have been easily met—but between donations and fund-raising, she was only able to obtain five bikes. Although she was disappointed at not meeting the goal, leading the marketing effort enabled her to learn how to implement charitable events and, more important, how to inspire her peers to open their eyes to others' plight. "I've never cared about helping others so much and it's just really rewarding," said Stroman. "It shows you what life is really about" (A. Stroman, personal communication, May 27, 2016). What Stroman learned from this experience encapsulates the goal of the Global Living Learning Community: to prepare global leaders by helping them personally connect to global issues and integrate incremental steps toward global problem-solving into their daily lives.

Other Global Learning Cocurricular Opportunities

Outside integrative global learning habitats, FIU students participate in global learning clubs and recurring discussion, lecture, seminar, film, and other arts and culture series. On their own, these activities can extend and enrich global learning and lead to deeper involvement in the future.

GlobeMed

In 2007 a group of Northwestern University undergraduates who had participated in medical mission trips to developing countries gathered with students from other universities to answer the following question: How can undergraduates best help to improve the health of people living in poverty around the globe? (GlobeMed, n.d.-a). The students knew of grassroots leaders all over the world who had started initiatives to improve health conditions in their own communities, but without access to essential resources such as technology, supplies, and funding, the initiatives had very limited success. The national organization GlobeMed was born from these students' collective will and creativity. The organization's mission is to "strengthen the movement for global health equity by empowering students and communities to work together to improve the health of people living in poverty around the world" (GlobeMed, n.d.-b, para. 5). GlobeMed carries out its mission by pairing universities with grassroots community organizations in developing countries to design and implement health improvement projects. Every summer, students from GlobeMed chapters travel to their partner communities. The U.S. Agency for International Development (2015) financially supports the interns' trips through its Global Health Fellows II program.

For Camila Uzcategui, the club's mission and vision, "a world in which health—the ability to not only survive but thrive—is possible for all people" (GlobeMed, n.d.-c, para. 4), were a perfect fit for her personal and professional goals. Like many of her classmates, Uzcategui, whose parents come from Uruguay, is a first-generation American. She told us the following:

> I always knew that I wanted to work in health care in some way. In March 2014, I received an e-mail from Eric [Feldman] about GlobeMed—and it sounded like an amazing organization in which you could work on a health issue somewhere in Latin America in partnership with a grassroots organization. I asked Eric about it, and he said that if you like this organization, you'll have to found a club for it at FIU. (C. Uzcategui, personal communication, May 25, 2016)

That's exactly what Uzcategui did. After completing what she called a "mind-bending" application consisting of open-ended questions involving leadership and cultural awareness as well as case studies on complex global health issues, Uzcategui had a telephone interview with a leader from the GlobeMed national office. At this point, having spent a lot of time and energy on the application process, she was determined to found the organization. Within two weeks, Uzcategui's application was accepted, and she was on a plane headed to GlobeMed's annual Global Health Summit in Evanston, Illinois. She called the summit eye opening for the following reasons:

> GlobeMed used to be only at Ivy League and other elite schools. At this time the organization was deliberately trying to engage Hispanic-serving institutions and HBCUs [historically Black colleges and universities]. The attendees were really aware of their privilege and talked about it. These conversations made me more aware of the spectrum between the really privileged and not-so privileged. We had open conversations about these important issues of power and privilege and shared lots of models on how to lead these types of conversations. (C. Uzcategui, personal communication, May 25, 2016).

Uzcategui returned to campus feeling part of a global community of self-aware and empathetic problem solvers. During that summer, she recruited members for FIU's GlobeMed chapter and assembled a team of peers for its executive board. In the fall, she and the chapter's copresident participated in the annual GlobeMed Leadership Institute. During that three-day weekend, they learned organizational and strategic planning skills that they and other FIU students would apply the following summer as grassroots on-site work interns with their partner organization, Escuela de la Calle, in Quetzaltenango, Guatemala.

Describing the relationship between GlobeMed's national office and the individual chapters, Uzcategui said, "It's the national organization that chooses the sites, but the chapters have input into the type of partnership and location they want. Once you're partnered with the organization, you have bi-weekly phone calls or Skype meetings" (C. Uzcategui, personal communication, May 25, 2016). In these meetings, GlobeMed members discuss their partners' local needs. "The first project that we worked on was fundraising for a health post," Uzcategui said, "because they had a little bit of infrastructure, but none of the supplies necessary, not just medical supplies, but the actual machinery—scales and OB/GYN types of equipment due to the high birthrate among young women in Guatemala" (C. Uzcategui, personal communication, May 25, 2016). The GlobeMed students created a budget for their project, developed a timeline, and held fund-raising events to raise money for their health post project, for a health clinic to support Guatemalan women with basic health needs, and to offset expenses for their trip. They also held regular talks on global health and social justice issues with their partners. As the time to leave for Guatemala drew near, the biweekly partner meetings became focused on their specific on-site project. "We decided to do a general health awareness workshop for the children and families in the community," Uzcategui said. But when she and the three other FIU GlobeMed students who made the trip arrived at their site, they saw that the aspects of health education they really needed to tackle were water and sanitation. "Once you get on the ground you see a lot of things that talking on Skype doesn't allow you to see," Uzcategui said (C. Uzcategui, personal communication, May 25, 2016).

She and her fellow FIU interns quickly learned that Quetzaltenango, at 7,640 feet above sea level and surrounded by mountains, has poor water access. Because of the relative lack of water in the city and the distance residents must travel to get it, many people in the community use contaminated water and suffer from waterborne diseases such as dysentery, giardia, and Guinea worm. With no advance planning, Uzcategui and her team collaborated with the local health clinic to conduct a series of workshops for community residents on effective strategies for proper hygiene. But the importance of hygiene education isn't all that Uzcategui learned while in Quetzaltenango; she said she also gained perspective consciousness (Hanvey, 1975):

> I thought that I was very Hispanic but when I got to Guatemala I realized that my culture is very different from Guatemalan culture, not only because they have a larger population of Native Americans, but because that population also has a different language, and they have a different way of viewing the world, and they have also been kind of merged with the Guatemalan culture. . . . I was very humbled by the experience. (C. Uzcategui, personal communication, May 25, 2016)

During the 2014–2015 academic year, FIU's GlobeMed chapter raised funds for water filters for everyone in their partner school in Guatemala. That summer the interns conducted workshops on using and maintaining the filtration systems. In the 2015–2016 academic year, they tackled aspects of sex and reproductive education. As the needs of their partners in Quetzaltenango evolve, so too will the projects that FIU's GlobeMed students work on, but the continuous dialogue and collaborative problem-solving in which GlobeMed students engage with their international partners will remain the same.

Tuesday Times Roundtable and Other Recurring Global Learning Activities

We've found that the keys to successful global learning cocurricular programming outside integrative habitats are regularity, high-quality content, and a variety of pedagogical strategies to engage students in active dialogue. We've learned this primarily from leading the OGLI's signature global learning cocurricular program, the Tuesday Times Roundtable, a weekly discussion of articles in the *New York Times* on global issues, events, and trends. Cosponsored by the *New York Times*, FIU Division of Libraries, the Office of the Provost, the OGLI, and the Student Government Association, it's the first cocurricular global learning activity the OGLI developed to integrate with global learning courses. When we implemented the series in 2010, it was a companion to the foundations course How We Know What We Know. The entire FIU community is now invited to participate in these multiperspective discussions moderated by faculty; staff; students; community members, and leaders of local, national, and international organizations.

The Tuesday Times Roundtable is part of FIU's *New York Times* Readership Program, which provides all students with digital copies of the daily paper, a light lunch for roundtable participants, faculty development, and an annual visit from a *New York Times* journalist. Petra Kohlmann Sanchez, former regional education manager for the *New York Times* whose accounts included FIU, inspired the idea for the roundtable when she told the OGLI about similar discussions held at Georgia College as part of their partnership with the AAC&U's American Democracy Project (P. Kohlmann Sanchez, personal communication, May 11, 2016). The American Democracy Project aims to promote civic engagement among college students and prepare them to be informed citizens (American Association of State Colleges and Universities, n.d.). As Kohlmann Sanchez explained, she was prompted to introduce the idea to Landorf and Doscher after "seeing that the discussion-based format for analyzing [*New York Times*] articles was very engaging for students and allowed them a safe space to talk about current issues of global and local concern" (P. Kohlmann Sanchez, personal communication, May 11, 2016).

Kohlmann Sanchez was right. According to surveys the OGLI has conducted with regular roundtable attendees, the top reasons they come are to (a) discuss current issues with an expert and their peers in a nonthreatening and nongraded environment, (b) receive credit in their global learning foundations course, and (c) receive activity points in their quest for a Global Learning Medallion. The regularity of the Tuesday Times Roundtable series schedule—it takes place in the same room and at the same time every Tuesday on the main Modesto Maidique Campus and every other Tuesday on FIU's Biscayne Bay Campus—allows attendees to easily add the event to their routines. This regularity has helped weekly roundtable attendance grow from an average of 20 per week in 2010 to 45 per week from 2014 to the present.

Having a dedicated person consistently oversee the Tuesday Times Roundtable also contributes to its success. When Eric Feldman began working at the OGLI in 2011 as a graduate assistant, his main responsibility was to assist Stephanie Doscher with the series' management. Soon, however, as Doscher's curricular responsibilities increased, Feldman took over the tasks of recruiting moderators, marketing the series, and running the sessions at the main campus. He expanded his role by creating a dedicated roundtable page on the OGLI's website (goglobal.fiu.edu/ttr) and developing and executing a plan to have every roundtable session videotaped and posted on an FIU global learning YouTube channel (www.youtube.com/user/GoGlobalFIU/videos). With the advent of fully online students at FIU, viewing Tuesday Times Roundtable sessions online has become a vital part of these students' global learning experience.

Another ingredient of the roundtable's success is the variety of pedagogical strategies moderators use to engage students in active discussion and draw out different perspectives on issues of local and global concern. In 2013 Feldman created a moderator guide with tips on how to choose a topic, title, and article and implement strategies for creating a safe space for meaningful, multiperspective discussions. In addition to making traditional PowerPoint introductions and posing open-ended questions, moderators present case studies for discussion; involve students in simulations; have groups of students debate the causes and effects of issues; and use art, music, and literature to make key points. Whichever pedagogical strategy moderators choose, they know the goal of the roundtable is to engage students in participatory dialogue and deliberative discussion.

The last ingredient for success is consistent high-quality content. By this we mean topics should be relevant, compelling, and thought provoking. Topics change from year to year and semester to semester depending on moderators and world events, but they must always lend themselves to rich discussions. What's more, regular attendees find themselves making connections among topics that are seemingly unrelated. Themes explored in a single semester have included voter turnout, global public health, the school-to-prison pipeline, social media and its influence on democratic knowledge, the five-year recovery after the Japanese tsunami of 2011, sexual assault, body image and self-esteem, and climate change. We believe that the quality of content in the roundtables is a reflection of the quality of the OGLI's relationships with departments, offices, and organizations throughout the FIU community. As you may recall from chapter 1, the OGLI is the node in a network of collaborative relationships with individuals and groups inside and outside the university. When Feldman sends out the call for moderators each semester, he receives positive responses almost immediately from people who believe in global learning and sincerely want to work with students. Feldman works with each volunteer to fashion an event that will appeal to students and give them opportunities to follow up by taking appropriate action. Moderators prompt students to enroll in a particular global learning course or in the Global Learning Medallion program, to volunteer, engage in advocacy, or pursue study abroad or internships. Steady increases in weekly attendance and the variety of topics covered, combined with attendees' willingness to express their opinions, listen to other perspectives, and pursue further global learning opportunities, provide the best evidence of the success of this weekly cocurricular activity.

In addition to the Tuesday Times Roundtables, students have other opportunities to attend lectures, seminars, and arts and culture events that fuel and inform their exploration of global dynamics and issues. The OGLI works with partners across the university to ensure that such activities take place. The Steven J. Green School of International and Public Affairs is a frequent collaborator, hosting many of these events and bringing in experts from across the United States and around the world to speak about international and global issues.

Pedro Botta, the school's senior director for strategic initiatives, told us that international programming is as important a contributor to student development as classroom learning. He said, "Students learn about issues a class may have briefly mentioned and are able to get a glimpse into possible careers by meeting experts in various professions" (P. Botta, personal communication, May 25, 2016). He said the guiding question in planning activities is, "How do we impact people so that they walk away thinking about something in a different way?"

These events often feature multiple experts in dialogue with a moderator. They use conversational presentation styles and sometimes incorporate art or music. The flagship Ruth K. and Shepard Broad Lecture series "provides students, faculty and the community with insights into the events and forces shaping contemporary global affairs" (Steven J. Green School of International and Public Affairs, n.d.). The series addresses issues such as the struggle for freedom in totalitarian regimes like the former Czechoslovakia, turmoil in the European Union resulting from Brexit, and the impact of the U.S. presidential election on Latin America. In addition to FIU faculty experts, presenters have included former presidents of Caribbean countries, locally based consuls general, political dissidents, and administrators of major organizations such as the International Monetary Fund. Other event series at the school focus on particular issues. For example, the Spanish and Mediterranean Studies program has a series funded by Total Bank to help students think about identity. Events explore topics such as what it means to be Hispanic in North America or the lives of Sephardic Jews in Latin America.

Conclusion

Colleges and universities must provide multiple, diverse, high-quality experiences in the curriculum and the cocurriculum, as well as habitats to connect these experiences, for integrative global learning to occur. This chapter provides a close look at how students regard and shape these opportunities and how they use them to enhance their personal and professional development. Philosopher Jiddu Krishnamurti asks, "What do you consider the end purpose of education? Is it not to bring about an integrated individual?" (Krishnamurti, 2017, p. 36). If the answer is yes, and we believe that it is, then integrative global learning can go a long way toward helping students achieve this purpose.

8

GLOBAL LEARNING IN THE
K–12 PIPELINE

The future of the world is in my classroom today. (Fitzwater as cited in Zbick, 2017, para. 9)

In previous chapters we discuss how to provide global learning to students once they've arrived on campus. But how can we in higher education help students participate in global learning before they enter college or even apply? At FIU, our solution has been to develop global learning partnerships that connect our faculty and students with teachers and students in K–12 schools. These partnerships also serve to cultivate college readiness pipelines and engender in students a sense of purpose and direction toward global learning once they matriculate.

FIU has been working in partnership with K–12 schools to promote global learning since 1979 because of the pioneering leadership of late education professor Jan L. Tucker. This chapter contains case studies of three different kinds of K–12 partnerships. The first case explores an initiative founded by Tucker, the Global Awareness Program (GAP), coordinated through the former Center for International Education in the School of Education, which prepared preservice and in-service teachers to imbue their public school students with a global perspective (Tucker, 1982). The second case describes a project that emerged from a single course in which FIU undergraduates collaborated with secondary school teachers and students in Miami, Florida, and Kingston, Jamaica, to integrate global engagement through digital participatory research (DPR) (Gubrium, Harper, & Otañez, 2016). The third case involves a cultural mentorship program for Haitian-American middle school students that was wholly initiated, designed, and implemented by a student organization (Tejedor, 2015).

We organize our discussion of these cases according to the four principles Tucker (1991b) considered essential to forming and sustaining successful global learning partnerships between K–12 schools and institutions of higher education. He asserted that successful partnerships should feature a shared commitment to

1. high-level and grassroots leadership and collaboration,
2. universal global learning,
3. mutually beneficial activities, and
4. a common conceptual framework.

You no doubt note the strong similarities between Tucker's principles and the precepts of this book and of collective impact (see chapter 3); we're pretty confident that if the collective impact methodology had been established back in 1991, Tucker would have written about partnerships in those terms. As you read through and glean ideas from these cases, we encourage you to think about how you might use the conditions of collective impact to implement new global learning partnerships with K–12 schools or to infuse global learning into pipeline programs already in place at your institution.

FIU's Global Awareness Program

Tucker's passion for global learning was the driving force behind the GAP, which he directed until his death in 1997. The GAP aimed to provide universal global learning to Miami-Dade County Public School (MDCPS) students by infusing global content, perspectives, and engagement into the training of preservice and in-service teachers. The GAP's curriculum model involved the following interrelated aspects:

- Information about differing beliefs, perspectives, and attitudes about the world
- Exploration of basic concepts concerning conflict, change, communication, and interdependence
- A teacher-chosen content organizing framework, such as area studies, global problems, U.S. history, Florida studies, or geography
- Basic skills development in reading, critical thinking, research, and teamwork
- Community engagement projects

To promote the model's implementation in schools, the multifaceted GAP involved revised core courses in the undergraduate teacher education curriculum; revised social studies courses in the undergraduate and graduate teacher education curricula; content workshops for in-service teachers; conferences for local, state, and national school and university participants; visiting scholar programs; international travel and study opportunities for teachers; library development; and professional development for teacher education faculty. The GAP also trained "master teachers who in turn provided school-based leadership" through a train-the-trainer model (Tye, 2009, p. 11). Lauded as "one of the oldest and most successful collaborations between schools and higher education in the nation" (Merryfield, 1992, p. 31), the GAP reached thousands of teachers and hundreds of thousands of students in MDCPS and other Florida districts (Cruz & Bermúdez, 2009).

How did Tucker accomplish all this? He didn't do it alone. Although he acknowledged that differing institutional cultures and reward systems usually doomed K–12 and higher education collaborations to failure, Tucker (1991b) thought that global learning provided a unique context to overcome traditional organizational challenges. Highlighting common goals and global learning's interdisciplinary nature, Tucker helped stakeholders at all levels see themselves in the initiative and determine ways they could get involved and contribute. The following describes how Tucker brought university and K–12 stakeholders together to implement this innovative global learning partnership.

High-Level and Grassroots Leadership and Collaboration

The GAP's initial impetus was provided by a Florida State Board of Education resolution calling for global education to be infused into elementary and secondary social studies curricula (Tucker, 1979). The resolution stipulated that global education should enable students as future citizens to develop "cooperative solutions, deeper understanding, greater patience, and an increase in global awareness in decision making" (p. 7) when addressing complex problems associated with "environmental protection, energy conservation, population, food, and satellite communication" (p. 7). It also specified that global education should be "concerned with the commonalities among humankind as well as the diversities of their cultures with their different value systems, frames of reference, and views of the world" (p. 7).

Armed with an explicit endorsement from the highest level of education leadership in the state, Tucker built a broad-based local coalition and marshaled a diversified set of resources to promote global learning in MDCPS. The GAP's leadership included prominent MDCPS administrators and FIU leaders from multiple units, including the International Affairs Center, the Latin American and Caribbean Center, the College of Arts and Sciences, the School of Education, the Departments of Political Science and International Relations, the Student Government Association, and the Division of Libraries. The initiative also featured an advisory board consisting of representatives from FIU, MDCPS, and community-based nongovernmental organizations (Tucker, 1982). Funding for various GAP activities was garnered from MDCPS, FIU, the Florida Department of Education, the U.S. Department of Education, and multiple private foundations.

Because the GAP's goal "was to improve student achievement through global education" (Kirkwood-Tucker, 2009, p. 121), grassroots leaders in MDCPS were able to buy into a common vision for global learning. This enabled them to accept generous, long-term, and much-needed support from university partners. Toni Fuss Kirkwood-Tucker (2009), the principal global learning trainer for district teachers, media specialists, and administrators, observed that,

> above all, the success of global education reform was due to the strong and unflinching support of administrators at the district, area, and building levels. Far-sighted administrators recognized the necessity to globalize curriculum and instruction in the age of globalization in order to prepare students to become well-informed, open-minded, flexible, skilled, and critical thinkers in an increasingly interdependent complex world. . . . Though taxed with uncountable daily responsibilities these committed administrative leaders believed in the importance of a global education program, thoughtfully and democratically designed, planned, and implemented by all participants that would increase student academic achievement and a sense of bonding often lacking in the setting of schools. (p. 133)

In turn, administrative backing motivated teachers to exert global learning leadership in their schools and classrooms. With support from FIU trainers and their own supervisors, "despite serious time constraints and diverse curricular interests the globally trained teachers recognized the value and importance of teaching and learning about the larger world . . . and were willing to give it their time and energy" (Kirkwood-Tucker, 2009, p. 134). Students reacted positively to their teachers' enthusiastic and creative efforts to stimulate their growth as citizens, and this encouraged school and university partners to maintain and expand their activities. Finally, community organizations were invited to become collaborators in the GAP. After informing parents, governmental, and nongovernmental organizations of the curriculum reform under way, school and university leaders invited these partners to bring their knowledge of the world and unique expertise to the planning and implementation table. The GAP's collaborative approach and combined high-level and grassroots leadership achieved a culture change that transformed the way individuals in MDCPS viewed global learning and their roles in facilitating it. Diego Garcia, principal of Miami High School, Miami's oldest secondary school, expressed his own awakening in the following: "Global education is not a course. It is more of a feeling that I am part of the world and the world is part of me, and we are all in this together" (Kirkwood-Tucker, 2009, p. 134).

School-Based Leadership

The Global Education Leadership Training Program "was the practical, school-based arm of GAP" (Cruz, 2018). The training program was composed of six components: conceptualization, inventory, design, implementation, assessment, and networking (Cruz & Bermúdez, 2009). During conceptualization, K–12 teachers and staff explored the meaning of global learning and global pedagogy. In the inventory phase, schools identified the physical, financial, human, and technological resources already in place and determined the additional resources needed to implement global learning such as maps, globes, almanacs, and money for field trips. Next, schools formed teams of volunteer or principal-appointed teachers and staff to design a universal global learning plan that would meet the needs of their particular school and context. These plans were integrated vertically throughout feeder patterns, the sequence of schools that students attend as they progress through grade levels, with common global themes or year-end projects or activities. During implementation, the leadership teams briefed their colleagues on the plan, arranged coaching and training from FIU, and invited speakers and experts from community organizations and cultural associations to provide additional preparation and guidance. Leadership teams also spent considerable time during this phase addressing teacher and staff concerns and exchanging success stories with other schools. The leadership training program also featured an established assessment plan, which involved

> (1) evaluation of university content workshops; (2) evaluation of school-site in-service training; (3) program and materials evaluation at school site; (4) pre-post tests of teacher attitudes and global knowledge gain; (5) pre-post tests of student attitudes and global knowledge gain; and (6) analysis of school plans and revealed effective results in realizing program goals. (Cruz & Bermúdez, 2009, p. 102)

Networking among the school global leadership teams, the GAP's director, and training facilitators enabled continuous communication of assessment data and ongoing improvement of professional development, teaching and training materials, and the GAP's support system for the training program.

Over a 10-year period, the Global Education Leadership Training Program was deployed in three phases. According to Kirkwood-Tucker (2009), the first phase involved three years of piloted activities in select district feeder patterns with the most ethnically diverse student bodies. The second phase expanded activities to the remaining schools in the north-central area, and the third phase added additional feeder patterns with unique needs or particularly strong enthusiasm and support for global learning. By the end of the 10-year period, two-thirds of MDCPS public schools had succeeded in infusing global learning into their curricula and instruction to varying degrees (Kirkwood-Tucker, 1998).

The GAP's Conceptual Framework

Tucker (1991a) believed that the acquisition of a global perspective, not content, was the purpose of global learning:

> Global education begins with the premise that information and knowledge about the rest of the world must make a feedback loop into our own consciousness so we can better understand ourselves and our relationships to each other and to other peoples, cultures, nations, and global issues. This feedback loop is the essential meaning of education for a global perspective. Without this feedback loop into our lives, simply studying about the rest of the world is not an adequate global education. (p. 46)

Robert Hanvey's (1975) five-dimensional model served as the conceptual framework underlying teacher training and the inventory phase of the leadership training program. The GAP trainers implemented strategies teachers could use in their classrooms to promote each of Hanvey's five dimensions: perspective consciousness, state of the planet awareness, cross-cultural awareness, knowledge of global dynamics, and awareness of human choices (Cruz & Bermúdez, 2009).

Benefits for MDCPS and FIU

The GAP's mission might appear unidirectional because its purpose was to use FIU resources to promote global learning in elementary and secondary schools. But the GAP provided many benefits for FIU as well. It prompted a significant update to teacher education core course work, including the addition of new content related to non-Western history, culture studies, and geography. Tucker developed a new course, Global Perspectives in Education, which explores teaching strategies that promote intercultural perspective taking and can be offered at all Florida state universities (Cruz & Bermúdez, 2009). Global Perspectives in Education is offered each semester at FIU as a designated global learning course that counts toward graduation requirements for students in all majors. The current syllabus maintains the same mission that Tucker envisioned:

> While establishing themselves as a new learning community, students and the professor will explore together the meaning of globalization, the interconnection between globalization and global education, and some of the

whys and hows of infusing a global perspective in ALL social studies curricula or in the student's particular discipline" (S. Mathews, personal communication, September 17, 2017).

The GAP also drew internal university partners together in new ways to collectively promote K–12 global learning. These partnerships ultimately laid the groundwork for collaborations that constitute the Global Learning for Global Citizenship initiative. Even the Student Government Association got involved; using their own budget, students organized a national conference titled Global Education: An International Necessity, featuring participants and presenters from local, state, and national entities (Tucker, 1982). The GAP provided FIU libraries with $25,000 to purchase books, films, teaching kits, documents, and other materials for undergraduates, teacher educators, and in-service teachers. Support for the professional development of teacher educators came in the form of funding for conference presentations and attendance, consultancies, research, and course development.

MDCPS provided FIU's School of Education with a living "laboratory for the development of a prototype in global education for materials compilation, program development, and teacher training program in a multiethnic and multicultural setting" (Tucker, 1982, p. 216). Tucker (1982) emphasized that teachers' value and ownership beliefs about the GAP's model were fundamental to its success and dissemination. "People, not textbooks, appear to be the primary carriers of the global education culture" (p. 213). At the same time, he contended in the following that colleges and universities play a special role in supporting grassroots global learning and problem-solving in the community and in K–12 schools:

> The long-term validity of higher education in the United States as a shaper of global futures hinges on whether these institutions can become more globally-minded. Colleges and universities in the United States should be at the vanguard of the change process in global education. The university can be a catalyst for change. It has many advantages—freedom of expression, expertise, status, resources, and continuing contact with cosmopolitan values. Other institutions such as the media, churches, and non-profit educational organizations can make contributions. But it is the formal education system, with universities leading the way, where the critical difference will be realized. Moreover, college of education and teacher education programs stand at the intersection of the need for change in both schools and in the universities. (p. 214)

As the GAP became established in MDCPS, it enabled FIU to provide preservice teacher field placements with experienced global educators, enhancing the preparation of individual teachers, the overall quality of the teacher education program, and the spread of global learning throughout MDCPS.

GAP's Legacy at FIU

Unfortunately, in recent years, state and national government support for global education in K–12 schools has diminished. The Global Education Leadership Training Program was a 10-year initiative with a planned conclusion, but the GAP ended in a more gradual fashion. Tucker's unexpected death in 1997 and a steep rise in emphasis on testing and accountability measures were blows to the program's sustainability (Cruz & Bermúdez, 2009). Despite the program's success in integrating global learning into MDCPS, the GAP ended in 2005 after public and private support for K–12 global education shifted to other areas.

Although the GAP no longer exists, the program achieved its primary goals of bringing global learning to MDCPS and to teacher education programs at FIU and across the state. A number of teachers who were involved in the GAP currently lead active global education programs in MDCPS, including the Global Studies Academy at G. Homes Braddock Senior High School; the Airbase K-8 Center for International Education; and international magnet programs at Sunset Elementary School and Coral Reef Senior High School. The GAP also influenced Hilary Landorf's decision to come to FIU in 2002 as an assistant professor of social studies education. She came at the urging of Donald Johnson, Jan Tucker's colleague and one of Landorf's professors in the PhD program in social studies and international education at New York University. Johnson knew of Landorf's commitment to global education and student success and felt that FIU would allow her to thrive and make a difference. Landorf was determined to carry on Tucker's legacy. Although she couldn't save the GAP in name, she was able to continue its multiple practices, including continuously improving undergraduate and graduate social studies education courses with updated global learning outcomes, content, and pedagogical strategies and leading global education workshops for teachers in MDCPS. Landorf's accomplishments in global education led to her appointment as director of the OGLI. The establishment of a permanent office for global learning at FIU is a testament to the continuing influence of Jan Tucker's work.

Fostering Global Learning Outcomes Through International DPR

A different kind of partnership begins with individual professors who involve undergraduate and K–12 students in global learning as part of a course or research project. One example is Sarah Mathews's (2016) project involving DPR at FIU. Mathews is an assistant professor of social studies education and has been the program's leader since her arrival at FIU in 2011. Following in the footsteps of Jan Tucker, Mathews brought her passion for global learning with her to FIU. In her former position as assistant professor of social studies education at Clemson University, Mathews was coinvestigator for the International Leaders in Education Program. Funded by the U.S. Department of State, the program brings secondary school teachers from throughout the world in multiple disciplines to universities in the United States for a five-month period, during which teachers hone their subject matter expertise, enhance their pedagogical skills, and increase their knowledge about the United States. In addition to overseeing the International Leaders in Education Program at Clemson, Mathews served as the international teachers' pedagogical instructor to facilitate the program participants' development of teacher training modules they would implement in their home countries.

Mathews' decision to come to FIU was similar to that of Hilary Landorf's in that she was attracted by Jan Tucker's legacy and the primacy of global learning at FIU. "I knew enough about the Global Learning for Global Citizenship initiative at FIU to understand that the university was not just talking about global learning, but was walking the walk, and I wanted to be part of that environment" (S. Mathews, personal communication, September 17, 2017). In 2014 she developed a multidimensional global learning study that involved FIU undergraduate preservice teachers majoring in social studies education and teachers in an MDCPS middle school and a high school in Kingston, Jamaica. Secondary students in both schools were also involved, as was Medjy Pierre-Louis, an undergraduate researcher who helped Mathews coordinate the project. The goals of the study were to help K–20 students develop a sense of civic efficacy and to increase their global awareness, perspective, and engagement through the use of DPR. Mathews's project addressed the following research questions:

1. What issues do youth document and address through DPR?
2. How does engaging in DPR affect students' perceptions of their civic efficacy?
3. In what ways, if any, do youth demonstrate global awareness, global perspective, and global engagement through DPR?
4. In what ways does coordinating a DPR project in cross-cultural settings prepare preservice teachers to help their students develop global citizenship?

Collaboration and Leadership

To appreciate Mathews' project goals and potential impacts, it's important to understand DPR. Also referred to as video participatory research or Photovoice (Wang & Burris, 1997), DPR combines the use of digital technology with participatory research, asks students to investigate assets and problems in their community, and facilitates civic participation by using problem-based and practice-oriented pedagogies (Mathews, 2016). In her use of the DPR method, Mathews adhered to the following five research principles of community-based research (Hacker, 2013) and youth participatory action research (Orleans, Mirra, Garcia, & Morrell, 2016):

1. Research is not a solo venture, but is conducted with others.
2. Research is participatory, meaning that it is a coconstruction between the researchers and participants, those affected by the issues being studied (Jagosh, MacAulay, & Pluye, 2012).
3. Researchers use a critical lens, examining loci of power.
4. Researchers examine issues from multiple perspectives.
5. Researchers and participants collaboratively construct knowledge.

To briefly describe the project, students from the Miami middle school and the high school in Kingston used iPads to document on video issues of concern in their local communities. Preservice teachers in one of Mathews's social studies education classes and the Miami students' social studies teacher Anthony Reid worked with local students to help them create and produce their videos. Mathews and Pierre-Louis worked in Kingston alongside the social studies and drama teachers to facilitate the Jamaican students' work.

Mathews's research project had many moving parts, and achievement of the research goals required collaboration at all levels and across groups. The following is a snapshot of the student collaboration sequence and process. First, small groups of students brainstormed challenges affecting their communities. Each group provided its list of challenges to the whole class to create a master list; then new groups formed based on their issues of interest. Second, the newly formed groups examined their chosen issues from different perspectives using an activity called Circle of Viewpoints (Mathews, 2016) in which students take on the perspectives of different people influencing or influenced by the issue. Students answered a series of questions from these different perspectives, exchanged answers with their group members, and determined the information they needed to know about their issue. Third, the students in both locations created storyboards outlining the scenes in their videos. They collaboratively edited their videos using technology such as WhatsApp, Flipagram, and Microsoft Moviemaker software. During the 10-day period of the project, students in each location communicated their thoughts and their progress with their international peers via Skype and WhatsApp (Mathews, 2016).

Another area of collaboration involved the FIU preservice teachers, Reid, and his students. At the beginning of the research process, the preservice teachers identified different methods of data collection for the students and explained essential research considerations, such as seeking permission from individuals to use information, photos, or video of them in their projects. At the end of the project they assisted in the production of the students' videos. Throughout the project, they helped the Miami students hone their ideas and supported them in implementing the DPR method.

Although Mathews and Pierre-Louis were in Kingston, they played much the same role as the preservice teachers in Miami. Unlike in Miami, however, where Mathews had an established collaborative relationship with Reid and his school's administration, she was not able to establish such a network in Kingston. Several factors worked against Mathews's efforts, including her professed limited knowledge of the politics and culture of the Jamaican K–12 school system; the physical distance between Miami and Kingston, which prevented her from visiting the research site more than once before she began her research; and very limited financial resources to develop and implement her research (S. Mathews, personal communication, September 17, 2017). Lacking a collaborative network in Kingston, Mathews found that expectations were harder to manage, and communication among the various parties was more difficult to coordinate. For example, on her preresearch visit, Mathews was told that laptops were available at the school, but when she and Pierre-Louis arrived to conduct their research, they found that the laptops were being used for another purpose. Mathews said, "The clearest lesson I learned was the importance of building strong collaborative connections before attempting to do participatory research in global learning" (S. Mathews, personal communication, September 17, 2017).

Despite these challenges, Mathews was able to make the project work. This wasn't happenstance; it depended on effective leadership. You might recall from chapter 4 that one of the traits of effective global learning leaders is that they embody the same global learning outcomes they want their students to achieve. As a leader, Mathews was challenged to increase her own global competence to help others understand how local and global issues interconnect in people's everyday lives (Mathews, 2016). She helped the teachers, preservice teachers, and students in Miami and Kingston find ways to analyze problems from multiple perspectives. Exhibiting global engagement, she successfully brought a diverse group of people together to identify, share, and reflect on ways to solve common problems such as environmental degradation that manifested in unique ways in different communities.

At the grassroots level, Mathews was able to rely on Anthony Reid's leadership abilities to carry the project forward in Miami. Reid is also an adjunct professor in FIU's social studies education program and has cofacilitated global learning workshops with Hilary Landorf in Miami K–12 schools. He has deep knowledge of and experience with the process of global learning and, like Mathews, exemplifies global learning outcomes in his own teaching. In Kingston, identifying grassroots leadership was more complex. Mathews's initial contact was the school's principal, with whom she communicated before she arrived at the site. The principal gave Mathews permission to conduct research in the school building and provided contact information for several of the teachers in the building. When Mathews and Pierre-Louis arrived at the school, however, they found themselves basically on their own (M. Pierre-Louis, personal communication, September 22, 2017). Luckily, a social studies teacher and a drama teacher volunteered their students and their classroom space for the research, which took place during the school day and after school hours. The two teachers generously gave their time, knowledge, and dedication to the students' personal and academic success throughout the research process (S. Mathews, personal communication, September 17, 2017).

Conceptual Framework

Mathews approached her research on the principle that civic engagement, along with global learning, are necessary outcomes of schooling. In fact, civic engagement is part of the National Council for the Social Studies College, Career, and Civic Life Framework (2013), which calls on social studies teachers to involve students in conducting research, evaluating sources, and addressing real-world problems.

Mathews assessed global competency in terms of FIU's global learning SLOs and evaluated civic competency using Westheimer and Kahne's (2004) conception of a good citizen. Westheimer and Kahne describe three types of citizens based on the ways they solve problems in their communities. A personally responsible citizen works within the law and supports the community in times of crisis, a participatory citizen takes a leadership role to accomplish tasks and motivate collective community power, and a justice-oriented citizen searches for injustice and views society with a critical eye. Mathews used these concepts in her analysis of the types of global learning and citizenship the students demonstrated while engaged in the DPR process.

Mutual Benefits of Research Collaboration

Mathews's research project produced multiple benefits for all involved. The preservice teachers in Miami acquired valuable experience teaching DPR skills, facilitating cross-cultural communication, and helping students increase their global competencies and civic participation. They also had the opportunity to develop their own global and civic competencies. The secondary school teachers in Miami and Kingston benefitted by developing collaborative international distance learning and research skills. The students in Miami and Kingston learned how to conduct research, use video technology, identify and examine issues with local and global implications, propose solutions, and communicate with international peers. Although the students did not learn all the background facts and history about the issues documented locally or by their international peers, they demonstrated an awareness of broad societal issues, an ability to understand others' perspectives, and a disposition toward local and global civic engagement (Mathews, 2016). In individual interviews, students in both locations reported to Mathews the ways citizens could participate in their community to promote positive change, such as circulating petitions and giving presentations on pollution or security issues at community meetings.

The Haitian Cultural Mentorship Initiative

Another type of partnership, the Haitian Cultural Mentorship Initiative (HCMI), is a student-led effort to encourage Haitian youths to learn more about their heritage and history. The HCMI was spearheaded by Taisha Gauthier, a gregarious Haitian-American student who transferred to FIU from nearby Barry University. Gauthier grew up in the United States but felt she had become assimilated to the point of losing sight of her roots (T. Gauthier, personal communication, August 3, 2016). She realized that her dual identity made her feel like an outsider in both of her cultures. As a Haitian-American, she said, "I live on the hyphen" (T. Gauthier, personal communication, April 18, 2016), referring to the punctuation mark used to link or bridge terms describing people's dual identities. She observed that Haitians in her home country think of Haitian-Americans as privileged and that when she went home to Haiti she was often referred to as a foreigner. She also didn't feel completely accepted as an American because of her Haitian background. She observed that it was not uncommon for her to encounter stereotypical beliefs that all Haitians practice voodoo or eat cats. These stereotypes are so internalized that "even the Haitian-American children believe they are true" (T. Gauthier, personal communication, April 18, 2016).

Gauthier was inspired to found the HCMI by a course she took at Barry University with Pamela Hall, a psychology professor whose research interests include Haitian adolescents' academic, social, and emotional development. Hall, along with Charlene Désir of Nova Southeastern University, ran the Haitian Empowerment and Literacy Project, a summer program for middle and high school students of Haitian descent designed to improve literacy and social skills through Haitian art, culture, and history instruction. After inviting Gauthier to become a project volunteer, Hall became Gauthier's mentor. Gauthier's involvement with the project led her to the realization that to succeed as a student and participate effectively as a global learner, she needed to better understand and integrate both parts of her identity and that younger people needed to do this, too. Gauthier's epiphany prompted her to launch the HCMI after her transfer to FIU.

The OGLI and the Kimberly Green Latin American and Caribbean Center provide financial and advising support to the HCMI. To recruit participants, Gauthier visits a local middle school with a high percentage of Haitian and Haitian-American students and works in partnership with FIU's precollegiate pipeline programs, such as the EV3 Robotics Program, a mathematics- and technology-focused program for low-income and minority middle school students, and the Educational Talent Search in FIU's Office of Pre-Collegiate, Grants and McNair Program. Typically about 40 students participate in the HCMI annually.

Mentoring a Marginalized Student Community

"We focus on their identity because for a lot of Haitian children growing up here, we tend to be marginalized" (T. Gauthier, personal communication, April 18, 2016). The HCMI's codirector, Mwai Osahar, an undergraduate enrolled in an accelerated bachelor's and master's program in public administration, added, "Once you know who you are, it has a domino effect on your life. You can stand strong and be proud of who you are" (Tejedor, 2015). Following in Désir's and Hall's footsteps, Gauthier established the HCMI as a summer program for Haitian and Haitian-American middle schoolers. One difference between the HCMI and the Haitian Empowerment and Literacy Project is that the HCMI is completely planned and implemented by volunteer members of the Haitian Student Organization. Gauthier explained that in Haitian culture there is a big difference between how children interact with adults and how they interact with their peers. Being mentored by college students allows younger children to be more open than they could be with adults or older family members.

In its first year, the HCMI was two weeks long. It was generally agreed that this wasn't enough time to fully explore Haitian culture, so the program was expanded to four weeks (T. Gauthier, personal communication, July 6, 2017). Gauthier and her Haitian Student Organization colleagues developed curricula and activities related to Haitian history, fine and performing arts, and oral and written language instruction. According to Gauthier, the program targets cultural identity, self-esteem, college readiness, and personal safety and violence prevention (T. Gauthier, personal communication, April 18, 2016). Many of the participants have never learned the positive characteristics of Haiti, so challenging their negative perceptions is an important part of the program. Gauthier described a drum circle workshop in which "the kids were not feeling it" (T. Gauthier, personal communication, April 18, 2016). She said the students associated drumming with voodoo, and because most of them were Christian, they felt uncomfortable participating. However, after a group of mentors taught them about the Haitian Revolution and the role that drumming played in communication, the students realized the significance and ingenuity of drumming and became willing to participate. It took time to break down the barriers created by negative stereotypes, but eventually the kids rejoiced and began to express their personalities through the dancing and drumming. As Gauthier reflected, "To know your worth you need to know yourself" (T. Gauthier, personal communication, April 18, 2016).

The depth and breadth of the student-developed HCMI curriculum is impressive. Table 8.1 summarizes the learning goal for each week and associated learning activities.

Benefits for Mentors

The HCMI program not only cultivates an appreciation of Haitian culture in its middle school participants but also opens the minds of Haitian Student Organization college volunteers. The organization welcomes all students as members, and many of the HCMI volunteers are not Haitian. Gauthier said the volunteers get exposure to Haitian culture during their preparation and training. They have a chance to live in another's shoes. Many of the mentors came to the program with some negative stereotypes and stigmas about Haiti, but once they learn about the richness of the culture, they realize that what they'd heard was often inaccurate. Gauthier said the mentors' involvement prompted them to ask, "If Haiti is like that and I thought it was terrible, what about Africa or other places?" (T. Gauthier, personal communication, April 18, 2016). The mentors and HCMI participants realized that it's important to acquaint themselves firsthand with other cultures rather than depending on hearsay or stereotypes for information.

TABLE 8.1

**Haitian Cultural Mentorship Initiative Weekly Learning
Goals, Content, and Activities**

HCMI Weekly Learning Goal	Learning Content and Activities
Week 1: By the end of the week, participants will be able to analyze and inventory their own thoughts and emotions to develop a greater sense of self-worth based on the value of their lived experience.	• Haitian history, trivia, and flag • Who Is Edwidge Danticat? activity • Inner Beauty art project • Guest speakers: Black Female Development Circle and FIU football team • Journey to Self Discovery activity • Paying It Forward activity • Journaling and literacy skills activities
Week 2: By the end of the week, participants will know the steps to take to successfully complete a college application and will be motivated to pursue higher education.	• What's Your College? research project • Guest speakers: FIU Haitian Student Organization and Phi Beta Sigma fraternity • Haitian Heritage and Culture • College: Getting In activity • College: Making It Through activity • Ropes course • Journaling and literacy skills activities
Week 3: By the end of the week, participants will be willing to lead their peers toward a safer community by preventing violent acts through the promotion of dialogue and civility in their schools and communities.	• Guest speakers: Miami-Dade Police Department • A Child's Life Here and Haiti activity • Dealing With Emotions poetry project • Haitian Revolutions: Crash Course in World History • Retrospect and Root Causes violence prevention activities • Journaling and literacy activities
Week 4: By the end of the week, participants will have a better understanding of their Haitian heritage and be motivated to have an impact on their communities after a connection has been strengthened.	• Guest speakers: Digital Library of the Caribbean staff • UNICEF Children of Haiti Summit activity • Create Your Own Flag art project • Haitian Pride Skits activity • Haitian cooking • Drumming circle • Field trip: FIU swimming pool • Journaling and literacy activities

Note. FIU = Florida International University; HCMI = Haitian Cultural Mentorship Initiative;
UNICEF = United Nations Children's Fund.

Conclusion

In this chapter we showcase three global learning partnerships between K–12 schools and FIU that originated from various parts of the university. We contend that such partnerships can be customized and innovated for higher education institutions and districts of any size or demographic. The impact of all three partnerships points to the fact that Jan Tucker (1991b) really was on to something with his four recommended principles for success: collaboration and high-level and grassroots leadership, universal global learning, mutually beneficial activities, and a common conceptual framework. To these, however, we would like to add a fifth ingredient: passion. We agree with Tucker that when it comes to forging global learning partnerships, his four principles can make it easier to manage differences in organizational structure and culture between K–12 and higher education institutions. But it's impossible to ignore the fact that the energy behind these principles and partnerships—the fuel that starts them and keeps them running—is the passionate dedication of leaders like Jan Tucker, Sarah Mathews, and Taisha Gauthier. If you look, you will probably find passionate leaders like these in your own institution, people who have been working on K–12 partnerships long before you planned a universal global learning initiative. Once you formalize a plan and things get under way, more people will become motivated to start their own visionary partnerships with K–12 schools. We encourage you to support these leaders and their efforts by assisting them in structuring their projects for success and including them in your conception of what universal global learning really means.

PART THREE

SUSTAINING AND EXPANDING
GLOBAL LEARNING

STUDENT LEARNING
ASSESSMENT AND
PROGRAM EVALUATION

We need assessment—systematic, usable information about student learning—that
helps us fulfill our responsibilities to the students who come to us for an education
and to the publics whose trust supports our work. (Astin et al., 1993, p. 2)

We all want our students to succeed and for our institution's universal global learning initiative to support high levels of student
achievement. Yet, this desire begs two essential questions: What
constitutes success? and How do we know the extent to which our students
and our initiative are successful? These questions and their answers undergird
student learning assessment and program evaluation and are the foci of this
chapter.

In regard to the first question, you know from previous chapters that
student learning is at the center of all we do. We measure success primarily
in terms of the global learning SLOs, the knowledge, skills, and attitudes
students demonstrate as a result of having participated in global learning
experiences. We also measure our universal global learning initiative's success
in terms of our program goals. Program goals "establish criteria and standards
against which you can determine program performance" (Centers for Disease
Control, n.d.). Program goals for universal global learning describe what the
institution intends to achieve or provide in support of all students' global
learning. Program goals and SLOs are completely interrelated. We cannot
stress enough that program goals should support all students' global learning
and their achievement of global learning SLOs.

Now to our second question: How do we gauge the extent to which
SLOs and program goals are being met? People often confuse three terms
when answering this question: *measurement, assessment,* and *evaluation.* Let's
clarify how we use these terms throughout this chapter. When we use the
term *measurement* (n.d.), we mean any process people use to determine the

extent or amount of something. Measurement can be conducted in the contexts of assessment and of evaluation. When we use the term *assessment*, we mean the process of collecting, understanding, and using measurement data to improve student learning (Suskie, 2004). Student learning assessment is a continuous, reflective process that has four steps: defining *SLOs*, giving students ample opportunities to achieve and demonstrate those SLOs, collecting and critically reflecting on direct and indirect evidence showing how well students are meeting the SLOs, and communicating and using evidence to continually improve student learning. These four steps are often referred to as an "assessment cycle" (Suskie, 2004, p. 4).

Although the purpose of assessment is to understand and improve student learning, evaluation is conducted to improve the environment that supports student learning. *Evaluation* is a "systematic method for collecting, analyzing, and using information to answer basic questions about a program and to ensure that those answers are supported by evidence" (Administration for Children and Families, 2010, p. 6). Similar to student learning assessment, program evaluation follows a cycle that involves formulating program goals, determining measures and strategies for evaluating goals, analyzing evaluation data, and communicating and using results to improve administrative and leadership decision-making (Trochim, 2006).

To reiterate, student learning assessment and program evaluation are fundamentally interconnected. Together we treat them as our initiative's shared measurement system, which, as you'll recall from chapter 3, is one of the five conditions of a successful collective impact initiative (Kania & Kramer, 2011). A shared measurement system is composed of a short list of common measurements and a common system of reporting performance. Shared measurement enables participants to hold each other accountable and to learn from others' successes and failures. As noted by Hanleybrown and colleagues (2012),

> Having a small but comprehensive set of indicators establishes a common language that supports the action framework, measures progress along the common agenda, enables greater alignment among the goals of different organizations, encourages more collaborative problem-solving, and becomes the platform for an ongoing learning community that gradually increases the effectiveness of all participants. (para. 40)

In this chapter, we explore the shared measurement system we use for student learning assessment and program evaluation. We describe the methods we use to measure progress on our SLOs and program goals, which constitute our common agenda. We also share highlights from the results we derive from these methods. Throughout the discussion, we address the following key questions that will arise as you develop your shared measurement system for your universal global learning initiative's common agenda:

- At what points during students' careers should student learning assessment data be collected and analyzed?
- At what points during the program should evaluation data be collected and analyzed?
- What kinds of measures and data collection and analysis methods are needed to conduct student learning assessment?
- What kinds of measures and data collection and analysis methods are needed to conduct program evaluation?

You will note that these questions do not address two critical aspects of the student learning assessment and program evaluation cycles: communicating and using results for the initiative's continuous improvement. Because communication and improvement are such rich topics, we're devoting an additional chapter to them, chapter 10. For now, remember that just as student learning assessment and program evaluation are inextricably bound, continuous communication and improvement are as well. It's useless to collect and analyze data if you don't share them with others and use them to enhance goals and outcomes. By the same token, communication and improvement cannot be conducted in the absence of timely, valid, and reliable student learning and program evaluation data. With these important points in mind, let's proceed with the discussion of our global learning assessment and evaluation measures, methods, and results.

Student Learning Assessment

Faculty begin assessing learning as soon as students enter the classroom. Whether observing how often students check their smartphones, noting the questions they ask, or identifying the points at which they take notes, faculty are always gauging the extent to which students are taking information in, processing it, and using it to make meaning. Yet the quickest way to drive colleagues out of a room is to start talking about the *A* word: assessment. Why does student learning assessment have such a bad rap? Many faculty, administrators, and staff associate it with accreditation, something imposed from the outside, an institutional requirement resulting in pointless additional paperwork (Wehlburg, 2011). We think of assessment differently, as a natural part of the ongoing process of teaching and learning.

When developing your initiative's assessment plan, one of the first things you'll have to consider is when student learning should be measured. At what points during students' academic careers should the institution gather data to ensure that everyone is making adequate progress toward the SLOs? Miller and Leskes (2005) enumerate five points or levels when assessment can take place, ranging from assessing an individual student's learning in a single course to assessing what all students have learned as a result of their entire college education (see Figure 9.1).

To determine the levels at which global learning assessment should take place at FIU, Landorf and Doscher consulted with the initiative's steering committee and with staff in the Office of Academic Planning and Accountability (APA), which supports all university quality improvement efforts, including student learning assessment. Together we worked to avoid overburdening faculty by streamlining the plan and building on processes and at levels already in place. We decided that the OGLI, the initiative's backbone organization, would collect data at Levels 3 and 5, the course and institution levels. When we submitted this plan to our regional accreditation body, the Southern Association of Colleges and Schools, its staff advised us to focus on Level 5 only, as course-level assessment would be too time consuming. But because we consider classroom learning to be the basic building block of institution-wide learning, we chose to collect data at both levels. We knew we wouldn't be able to make sense of institution-level data if we lacked insight into the quality of learning taking place in global learning courses.

Global learning assessment at FIU also occurs at other levels, but the OGLI doesn't collect or store those data. Levels 1 and 2 assessments, grading individual students in and across global learning courses, are left to faculty and departments. As for program-level assessment, the steering committee and the APA recommended against it for the following reasons: (a) Not every major had a capstone course or activity to facilitate this kind of assessment, (b) it would be too labor-intensive for the OGLI to coordinate, and (c) it would overburden department chairs who were still garnering acceptance for the new graduation requirement.

As the accrediting agency predicted, the OGLI has a lot of work with course- and institution-level assessment, but we don't regret this choice. Course-level assessment yields meaningful results that have led to numerous improvements for the initiative. We conduct assessment at the course level using our Global Learning Course Assessment Matrix (Appendix 9.A), the structure and results of which are described next. As student achievement of the graduation-level SLOs is addressed by one of our program goals, we'll discuss institution-level assessment in the next section on program evaluation.

Figure 9.1. Levels or points at which student learning assessment can be conducted.

Level 1. Assessing individual student learning in courses: investigations of what individual students are learning and how well they are meeting the goals of a course

Level 2. Assessing individual student learning across courses: investigations of what and how well individual students are learning during the progression of a particular program (e.g., general education, major) or over their years at college

Level 3. Assessing courses: investigation of the achievements of an entire class or the effectiveness of individual or multiple-section courses

Level 4. Assessing programs: investigation of the achievements of students within a particular program (e.g., general education, major)

Level 5. Assessing the institution: investigation of the achievements of all students in an institution, often undertaken for internal improvement or to meet external accountability demands

Global Learning Course Assessment Matrix

When FIU faculty wish to obtain a global learning designation for their course, they submit two documents to the Faculty Senate oversight committee, the GLCOC: a global learning syllabus and the Global Learning Course Assessment Matrix. Before we explain how the matrix works, let's take a quick look at the GLCOC's expectations for the syllabus to help you see how these documents differ and why they are both needed.

In addition to items normally included in a course syllabus, such as a grading scale, office hours, and policies and procedures, the GLCOC looks for items specific to global learning, such as

- a course description that includes a discussion of the faculty member's global learning approach to the course topic;
- three proposed global learning course outcomes aligned with the three graduation-level SLOs;
- a blend of traditional and authentic assessments;
- active, collaborative learning strategies; and
- content and readings featuring diverse perspectives.

As you read in chapter 7, global learning foundations course syllabi must also include an integrative cocurricular component.

Although the syllabus specifies what faculty will provide for students, such as readings, lectures, assignments, and so on, the matrix homes in on the first two questions of backward curriculum design: What do students need to know and be able to do, and how will faculty know students have achieved these outcomes? The matrix helps faculty maintain a student-focused approach to course design and leads them through the four steps of the assessment cycle (Suskie, 2004). It also helps faculty maintain a close alignment among course outcomes and assessment tasks, which is critical to the validity of assessment results. Validity refers to the "extent to which conclusions drawn from research provide an accurate description of what happened or a correct explanation of what happens and why" (Jupp, 2006, p. 311). For assessment results to be valid depictions of what students know and can do, the assessment activity must give students appropriate opportunities to demonstrate the learning outcome. The form's structure helps the GLCOC evaluate the relationship between outcomes and assessments and make well-informed, collegial suggestions for revision, if necessary.

The matrix is composed of three pages, one for each of the three graduation-level SLOs: global awareness, perspective, and engagement. Appendix 9.A shows the matrix and the directions for filling out each cell. Faculty use this document at two points in time—when they prepare a model matrix as part of their course proposal and when they complete a matrix and submit it to the OGLI after the course is taught.

Preparing the Matrix for the Course Proposal

Faculty learn how to prepare a model matrix for the proposal during the Global Learning Course Design and Instruction Workshops described in chapter 5. For the proposal, faculty fill out only the matrix's header and the sections labeled Course Learning Outcome and Assessment Method.

Course Learning Outcome. In this cell, faculty propose a global learning course outcome that aligns with the course's subject matter and with the graduation-level SLO stated in the cell above. The GLCOC evaluates each proposed course learning outcome based on its alignment with the graduation-level SLO and whether it meets the following criteria:

- Student centered, specifying what the student will be able to demonstrate on completion of the course, not what the faculty will do for the student or the activities in which students will participate
- Essential and significant, describing knowledge, a skill, or an attitude that is foundational to students' personal, professional, or academic success
- Clear and focused, meaning it can be understood by the layperson, and each outcome addresses only one type of knowledge, skill, or attitude

- Observable or quantifiable, describing something that can be assessed through measurement or observation

The GLCOC also evaluates whether the outcomes are written in a way that allows all faculty teaching future course sections to develop the global learning assessments, activities, and content they deem appropriate. At FIU all faculty teaching sections of global learning courses must teach with the course's three GLCOC-approved outcomes in mind, but they may do so in any way they choose as long as they adhere to the university's definition of *global learning* and the previously stated components of a global learning syllabus.

Assessment Method. In this column, faculty describe one or more methods they use to assess the course outcome. The methods specified in the proposal matrix will serve as models for future faculty. We have mentioned several times that global learning courses need a balance of traditional and authentic assessments, and the reason is simple. Because the graduation-level and course-level global learning outcomes are complex and require critical thinking skills such as analysis, synthesis, creation, and evaluation, valid assessments of these outcomes must give students ample opportunity to demonstrate these cognitive attributes. For the most part, such assessments are authentic, meaning they are

> engaging and worthy problems or questions of importance, in which students must use knowledge to fashion performances effectively and creatively. The tasks are either replicas of or analogous to the kinds of problems faced by adult citizens and consumers or professionals in the field. (Wiggins, 1993, p. 229)

In contrast, traditional assessments are the conventional testing methods most commonly seen in education: multiple choice, true or false, fill in the blank, and short-answer questions as well as essays and papers. In general, traditional assessments are good for measuring the background knowledge students need to achieve global learning outcomes. Authentic assessments are more appropriate for measuring the outcomes themselves. Table 9.1 compares the attributes of traditional and authentic assessments in the context of global learning. Figure 9.2 offers some examples of authentic assessments faculty can use in global learning courses. The GLCOC looks for evidence of traditional assessments of background knowledge and authentic assessments of global learning course outcomes in proposed syllabi and matrices.

Once the GLCOC is satisfied that a course adheres to all required global learning elements, it recommends it for global learning designation to the Faculty Senate. When the Faculty Senate awards a course the global learning designation, the approved syllabus and matrix are posted on FIU's global learning website as models for future faculty. This is also where faculty find and download their course's matrix to complete and submit it to the OGLI after the course is taught.

Completing a Matrix After the Course Is Taught

The OGLI asks faculty to submit a completed matrix after the first semester they teach a newly designated course, after they've completed a Global Learning Course Design and Instruction Workshop (the workshop's $250 stipend is dependent on submission of a matrix), and in preparation for the GLCOC's Triennial Review Process (discussed in chapter 10). To complete a matrix, faculty fill in the header with their name and the semester and year of the report, edit the Assessment Method column to reflect what they implemented in their course section, and fill out the Results column and Use of Results for Improving Student Learning cell at the bottom of the form.

Use of Results is the most important section of the matrix. This is where faculty reflect on their successes and challenges, providing the OGLI with the information it needs to improve its work in support of the initiative. Stephanie Doscher reads every completed matrix, takes notes on results and their use, and replies by e-mail to every faculty member who submits a form. This process is also discussed in more detail in chapter 10.

Results of Student Learning Assessment at the Course Level

Completed matrices provide an indispensable view into courses, helping us understand which global learning strategies work, which don't work, and under what conditions. Some results aren't unique to global learning. Global learning faculty face the same struggles as other faculty. They find it hard to get students to read and participate in discussions. They're challenged by large enrollments and the need to adapt to shortened summer schedules and hybrid and online modalities. And as is the case on many campuses, it's difficult to involve commuter and working students in cocurricular activities. Global learning faculty also use many of the same methods others use to improve teaching and learning. They scaffold content and chunk projects, clarify assignment directions and expectations, and seek help from colleagues to bolster students' research, writing, and public speaking skills.

At the same time, the OGLI finds it challenging to collect completed matrices from all of the faculty we ask. Sometimes faculty only fill out the form's first page or neglect to complete the Use of Results section. Some forms are carbon copies of those submitted in prior semesters or only provide superficial information. But these are outliers. Most faculty exert great

TABLE 9.1

**Comparison of Characteristics of Traditional Versus
Authentic Assessments of Students' Global Learning**

Traditional Assessments	Authentic Assessments
Students select a response	Students perform a task
Involves recall, recognition	Involves construction, application
Responses are instructor structured	Responses are student structured
Indirect evidence of student learning	Direct evidence of student learning

Figure 9.2. Examples of authentic assessments that can be used in global learning courses.

- Story or poem
- Original research paper
- Literary analysis
- Book or article review
- Case study
- Speech
- Journal response
- Art exhibit
- Portfolio
- Conference proposal
- Letters to editor or opinion pieces
- Musical composition
- Lab report
- Strategic plan
- Mediation
- Editorial
- Peer editing
- Poster presentation
- Video
- Podcast
- Mock trial
- Digital storytelling
- Debate
- Role-playing
- Wikipedia entry or editing
- Blog
- Advertising campaign
- Building a prototype
- Modeling
- Experiment
- Service-learning
- Interviews

effort reflecting on students' global learning because they know someone in the OGLI is going to read what they write and respond with comments and suggestions. Next, we present some major themes that have emerged over seven years of collecting hundreds of matrices, organized according to our three graduation-level SLOs.

Global Awareness

When it comes to this outcome, faculty report that globalization and the interrelated causes and effects of global problems are difficult for students to conceptualize in the abstract. Faculty across disciplines are experimenting with content, teaching, and assessment strategies to help students understand complexity and make connections among seemingly disparate actors, ideas, and dynamics.

Regarding content, many instructors initially think that global awareness emerges naturally from the mastery of knowledge in their field but quickly realize that this outcome requires more than that. To develop global awareness, students do need a grasp of foundational concepts, theories, and information, but they must also be able to detect relationships among this knowledge and far-flung, even conflicting ideas, events, and disciplines (see chapter 1). For this reason, textbooks aren't quite cutting it. Faculty seek to expand course content to include materials that explore current events and emergent theories and dynamics through multiple perspectives. They're increasingly turning to documentaries, podcasts, blogs, international news sources, scholarly articles, and magazine articles for these perspectives. To boost interdisciplinarity, faculty look to the OGLI to connect them with guest lecturers in other departments. Faculty are also reducing the amount of content students are required to consume to provide them with more time and space to digest and make sense of it.

Faculty are constantly seeking teaching strategies that incorporate the real-world knowledge and experience our diverse students bring to class. Many achieve this through strategies that flip the classroom or get students to consume content before class so that in-class time can be spent applying and expanding on it collaboratively with diverse others (Berrett, 2012). They are also challenging students to distill information and connect concepts by composing class discussion questions, leading peers in case study analysis, and making PechaKucha presentations, a style in which 20 slides are shown for 20 seconds each for a total presentation length of 6 minutes and 40 seconds (PechaKucha, n.d.).

Test questions and essay prompts are being revised to require students to make explicit connections across time, geography, discipline, and so forth. Sometimes, instead of asking students to deconstruct cases or articles about global topics, faculty task students with filling in gaps in other thinkers' analyses or placing local or domestic challenges in an international or global context or vice versa. Faculty mind-sets about global awareness have shifted so much that many are assessing this outcome by having students contribute to the world's knowledge and learning network. Students are editing or creating new Wikipedia entries through WikiEdu, writing blogs, submitting editorials and letters to editors, and preparing policy briefs and conference presentations.

Global Perspective

Faculty often say that students have more difficulty developing a global perspective than they do global awareness. Some observe that these outcomes are developmentally related, finding that students who grasp the interconnectedness of global problems are more likely to perceive a need to understand and address them through multiple viewpoints. Many report that they successfully guide students toward a global perspective when they begin with perspective consciousness (Hanvey, 1975). They facilitate this by asking students to compose and share personal, scholarly, or professional self-reflections. When students realize that others' thoughts or values differ from their own or differ from what they'd assumed or had been taught they'd be, they experience cognitive dissonance, psychological stress associated with conflicting beliefs, behaviors, or attitudes (Festinger, 1957). Faculty have learned to plan such activities early in the semester so they have time to help students resolve dissonance by analyzing the sources of their assumptions and embracing new perspectives.

Faculty tell us that they sometimes must tweak assignments multiple times over multiple sections and semesters before they hit on effective teaching strategies for global perspective. Role-playing is a strategy, however, that seems to work right off the bat and across disciplines. Students experience transpection (Hanvey, 1975) when acting out scenarios or writing in the first person from another person's point of view. Guest speakers can also be very powerful, whether they appear in person or via video conferencing technology. We've lost track of the number of times we've read that a speaker has transformed students' perspectives, motivating them to volunteer for an organization or apply for an internship, or even prompting them to change their major.

Global Engagement

In the early years of our initiative, faculty frequently complained that they couldn't figure out how to weave global engagement into their syllabi. Now they commonly reflect that this is where global learning truly comes together. Global awareness and perspective are developed and strengthened by engaging students in collaborative problem-solving activities related to the course's topic. Faculty observe that role-playing, field trips and field research, mock trials and town hall meetings, and volunteering and service-learning increase students' willingness to engage in global problem-solving with others through the act of doing it. A college education shouldn't only be about preparing students to address problems after they graduate, it should also help them to do so while still in college.

As successful as these strategies may be, they are also time and resource intensive. Faculty need additional support from their academic departments, student affairs, and national and community organizations. One of the central functions of the OGLI is to connect faculty to this support. As a result of this work, we've witnessed a significant uptick in the use of cutting-edge pedago-gies for global engagement such as City as Text (Machonis, 2008), Reacting to the Past (Carnes, 2014), and digital storytelling (digitalstorytelling.coe .uh.edu/index.cfm).

Faculty say the key here is to make sure the problems students address are those that affect their lives in some way. Some focus on campus-based engagement, such as the environmental studies professor who has students analyze construction materials used in campus buildings and make recom-mendations to administration for sustainable alternatives. Instructors encour-age students to bring friends along on campus and to off-campus excursions, bolstering interest and commitment. Films and documentaries are reportedly powerful influencers of empathy toward others, but faculty observe that for maximum impact these must be accompanied by readings that help students understand the reality of problems portrayed on screen and how they can act to address them. Faculty note that over time students appear more com-fortable with global engagement activities, although they aren't sure if this change is because of improvements in their teaching skills or students' prior experience with global learning courses. This is something the OGLI is just beginning to explore through institution-level research.

Program Evaluation

In this era of dwindling resources for education, it's particularly important for institutions to support the value proposition of universal global learning initiatives. Program evaluation is essential to determining how your initia-tive improves people's lives, produces benefits, and is differentiated from other projects of its kind. At FIU we determined the following measurable goals that describe what we intend our universal global learning initiative to accomplish. We resolved that if successful our initiative would (a) provide a sufficient number of courses to allow students to fulfill their two-course global learning graduation requirement, (b) increase cocurricular oppor-tunities available for integrative global learning, (c) provide high-quality global learning professional development for faculty and staff, and (d) increase levels of student achievement of the graduation-level global learn-ing SLOs. Note that institution-level student learning is the subject of one of our program goals. This is because the purpose of program evaluation is to measure the efficiency and the effectiveness of the activities you engage in to support student learning. In this section, we describe the measures and methods we use to evaluate our program goals, and we discuss significant results we've found. We take up the discussion of how we share these find-ings with stakeholders and use them to improve our work in chapter 10.

Program Goal 1: Provide a Sufficient Number of Global Learning Courses

In Florida a state statute stipulates that students must pay a surcharge for each credit hour taken in excess of the number required to complete their degree program (Fla. Stat. § 1009.286, 2016). The OGLI was charged with leading the development of an ample number of global learning courses and ensuring they were embedded in programs of study to minimize time to graduation and the prospect of excess credits. In 2009, a year before FIU began phasing in the requirement, the OGLI worked with the Offices of Analysis and Information Management and the APA to develop a five-year strategic plan to meet this goal. We thought this would be a straightforward process. Using the total number of undergraduate students projected to enroll in the university, the plan outlined the total number of global learning foundations and discipline-specific courses we would need to make available. The plan also included an analysis of courses in the catalog that appeared to address at least two of the graduation-level SLOs and seemed suitable for possible global learning designation. Moreover, the plan projected the percentage of seats freshmen and transfer students would have to fill in these courses each year to signal adequate flow.

When FIU submitted this plan to the accrediting agency, however, the chair of our onsite visit committee made 28 requests for additional information, including

- a master schedule projecting the academic year in which every global learning foundations course and every discipline-specific course in every major degree program would be developed and approved for implementation over the proceeding five years, and
- a detailed projection of the annual number of global learning course sections that would need to be offered by each major degree program and the number of seats that would need to be filled in each of these sections for the proceeding five years (E. Rugg, personal communication, February 23, 2010).

Fulfilling this request stretched our collective knowledge, resources, communication skills, access to data, and patience, but in the long run we developed a superior strategic plan for course offerings. This plan drove our efforts to meet this program goal, and it also became the yardstick for measuring the extent to which we were achieving the goal. The following is how we developed the plan. To start, because many departments had not determined five-year student enrollment projections for their programs, the OGLI made projections in collaboration with chairs based on a forensic analysis of student enrollments during the previous three-year period. Next, to facilitate section projections, the OGLI asked heads of each department to choose from the following course development models:

- Model 1: Identify a minimum of two existing courses that are required of all students that will be submitted for global learning designation
- Model 2: Identify a minimum of one required course and one elective course available to all students that will be submitted for global learning designation
- Model 3: Ensure that all students may take a minimum of two elective global learning courses available in other academic departments

Once department administrators had chosen a model and identified courses, the OGLI projected the number of unique sections and seats to be filled in each program for the next five years. Ultimately, the OGLI was able to fulfill the accrediting agency's information request and, what's more, include brief narratives describing how each college or school would help its students meet the graduation requirement. Figure 9.3 shows an excerpt of the plan for FIU's School of Hospitality and Tourism Management, which in 2010 had one undergraduate degree, the bachelor of science in hospitality management.

To determine whether students are meeting the graduation requirement in a timely manner, the OGLI annually compares the number of seats filled by freshmen and transfer students in all global learning courses to the total number of freshmen and transfer students entering the university during that same period. Benchmark figures of 50% freshman enrollment and 75% transfer enrollment signal adequate progress to graduation.

As for Program Goal 1 results, our five-year plan stipulated that FIU would need to develop at least 95 courses designated global learning by the end of the 2011–2012 academic year. We overshot this goal, with the GLCOC approving 102 courses by the end of that year. Since then, faculty have continued to submit proposals, bringing the total number of global learning courses approved to 194 as of June 1, 2017. Of that number, 146 courses have multiple sections, and all global learning courses are offered at least once every two years per GLCOC policies and procedures. Faculty continue to seek the designation because they believe in the power of global learning. Additional benefits include using the designation to recruit students into courses and degree programs, provide opportunities for students to earn the Global Learning Medallion or Peace Corps Prep certificate, or enhance their own instructional résumé for tenure and promotion.

Figure 9.3. School of Hospitality and Tourism Management, Model 1.

OGLI projects that HFT 3503 and HFT 4323 will be approved as discipline-specific global learning courses and first offered during the 2011–2012 academic year. These courses are required for all students in the School of Hospitality and Tourism Management (SHTM). Historical data from the last three academic years show that the average capacity for HFT 3503 (768 students) exceeds the anticipated head count projections for entering students in the SHTM for the 2011–2012 academic year (504 students). Additionally, OGLI projects that eight (8) sections of HFT 4323 will be offered during the 2011–2012 academic year, resulting in a projected capacity (560 students) that exceeds anticipated head count projections (504 students). Consequently, entering students in the Hospitality Management BS Degree Program will meet the global learning requirement by taking HFT 3503 and HFT 4323.

Bachelor of Science Hospitality Management (Required)						
	Avg Enrl	Avg CAP	Avg # Sections (min–max)	Avg CAP per Section	Curriculum Approval	GL Course Initiation
HFT 3503	570	768	14 (11–18)	55	Fall 2010	Spring 2011
HFT 4323	422	488	7 (6–8)	70	Fall 2010	Spring 2011

Source. FIU and SACSCOC, internal communication, January 22, 2011

In terms of enrollment flow, FIU has well exceeded its freshman and transfer benchmarks every year since the initiative's implementation in 2010. The number of seats filled in global learning courses by freshmen has ranged from 61% in 2012 to 110% in 2013 (proportions exceeding 100% indicate that some students have taken more than one global learning course in that year); seats filled by entering transfer students have ranged from 79% in 2011 to 107% in 2015. On average, fewer than 15 students per year have requested a waiver for either their foundations or discipline-specific course requirement. Hilary Landorf discusses exceptions with advisers on a case-by-case basis. FIU has stood by its commitment; there has never been an instance when the OGLI prevented a student from graduating on time or required the student to take excess credits to meet the global learning requirement.

Program Goal 2: Increase Cocurricular Opportunities for Integrative Global Learning

The OGLI conducts online surveys of student affairs directors and faculty to estimate the number of global learning cocurricular activities available to students and to gauge how faculty are integrating them into global learning courses. Directors describe the offerings sponsored by their departments and report whether staff collaborated with faculty to develop or implement them. Similarly, faculty describe the cocurricular activities they integrate into their courses and report any student affairs or community partners they have worked with to develop or implement them. FIU defines *cocurricular activities* as any activity that engage students with their surrounding campus, local, national, or international communities. The OGLI also analyzes results from the cocurricular scale of the Global Perspective Inventory (GPI), a survey it delivers annually to a minimum 10% sample of incoming freshmen, transfers, and graduating seniors.

As for Program Goal 2 results, in the years since our first survey at the end of academic year 2010–2011, FIU has witnessed a 294% increase in the number of global learning cocurricular activities offered by student affairs departments. Of the faculty who responded to the cocurricular survey, on average 75% reported having integrated a cocurricular activity as part of either their foundations or discipline-specific global learning course.

Items on the GPI's cocurricular scale ask students to report the number of semesters they participate in the following while at FIU: cultural events or activities, community service, campus organized discussions on diversity issues or international or global affairs, leadership programs stressing collaboration and teamwork, and religious or spiritual activities. Since academic year 2012–2013, graduating seniors report having participated in these activities on average at least one semester while at FIU. Academic year 2014–2015 was the first in which we detected a statistically significant increase over the 2010–2011 senior rates of participation in one activity in particular: campus-organized discussions of international or global affairs. We've continued to see this significance ever since.

Program Goal 3: Provide High-Quality Global Learning Professional Development

As you recall from chapter 5, the OGLI provides Global Learning Course Design and Instruction Workshops to all faculty who are developing course proposals or teaching sections of previously designated global learning courses. Student affairs staff and graduate teaching assistants are welcome to attend these workshops as well. Although we provide a wide array of other professional development events, the design and instruction workshops anchor our initiative and are the focus of this program goal. We define *high-quality professional development* as enabling participants to develop courses and activities that address the global learning SLOs and adhere to FIU's definition of *global learning* and the GLCOC's requirements for global learning syllabi. The OGLI evaluates the extent to which we've achieved this goal through two methods: postworkshop paper-and-pencil Likert scale surveys and focus groups conducted at the end of every semester. All global learning faculty and staff are invited to attend one of three 90-minute focus group discussions offered each semester. This allows educators to provide detailed feedback concerning the workshops' long-term impact on their practice.

In regard to Program Goal 3 results, a total of 651 faculty and staff members have attended 87 Global Learning Course Design and Instruction Workshops between summer 2009 and June 1, 2017. Survey respondents overwhelmingly concur that the workshops provide high-quality professional development. Over the past eight years, faculty and staff have consistently and strongly agreed on Likert scale items that the workshops help them understand the meaning of global learning (96%), help them understand the graduation-level global learning SLOs (98%), prepare them to assess the global learning SLOs (94%), prepare them to develop problem-based themes for their courses (95%), and prepare them to design active, collaborative learning strategies (95%). In open-ended responses, participants consistently praise the workshops' hands-on nature. They value opportunities to experience active learning strategies with colleagues from other disciplines and across the academic–student affairs divide. The most common suggestions for improvement have been to lengthen the duration of workshops, provide more examples of global learning syllabi, and provide additional global learning strategies workshops.

Over the past seven years, 217 faculty and staff members have attended focus groups about the workshops. Thematic analysis of responses has led the OGLI to four major conclusions concerning our workshops. First, the workshops' use of the backward curriculum design approach (Wiggins & McTighe, 2005) enables faculty to thoroughly integrate global learning throughout their course rather than relegating it to a unit or so. Second, the workshops help them recognize what they may already be doing in terms of facilitating the process of global learning and bolster their confidence that incremental changes in teaching practice implemented over time can have a strong positive influence on student learning. Faculty report that the workshops inspire them to experiment with authentic assessment and give them ideas for meaningful tasks, and they attribute their motivation to conduct ongoing course improvement to the OGLI's feedback on matrices. Third, faculty are always eager for more ideas for active, collaborative learning strategies. New teaching strategies are often cited as the workshops' most useful elements. Participants consistently agree that methods for flipping the classroom such as TBL foster student engagement and shift class time from content delivery toward active learning. Fourth, faculty and staff want more strategies for facilitating substantive discussions that involve diverse people and perspectives in face-to-face and online modalities alike. They observe that students are reluctant to bring up controversial subjects on their own but are willing to actively participate when faculty members initiate such discussions. Faculty and staff are increasingly interested in doing this as research substantiates their own experience that meaningful encounters with difference have a significant impact on students' global learning (Braskamp & Engberg, 2011; Glass & Braskamp, 2012).

Program Goal 4: Increase Student Achievement of the Global Learning SLOs

Institution-level student learning assessment requires a high level of institutional commitment in terms of time, resources, and goodwill on the part of administrators, faculty, staff, and students. The OGLI couldn't have managed the large-scale assessment necessary for a university of our size were it not for the consistent support of our president, provost, Faculty Senate, and the Student Government Association, as well as the coordinated assistance of units such as the APA, undergraduate education, and the Division of Student Affairs.

FIU uses two instruments, the GPI and the Case Response Assessment (CRA), to conduct a pretest-posttest study of our universal global learning initiative's influence on all students' graduation-level SLOs. Beginning in 2010 with the initiation of the graduation requirement, we have administered the GPI and CRA annually as a pretest to a minimum 10% sample of freshmen entering FIU with no previous college credits, that is, first time in college freshmen (FTIC) and incoming transfer students. We also deliver these instruments as a posttest to a minimum 10% sample of graduating seniors. Freshmen complete the assessments during orientation, and seniors do so as part of their graduation packet. We deliver either the GPI or the CRA to cluster samples of transfer students in large enrollment classes. We knew from the outset that we'd have to wait to begin our gains analysis until the academic year 2013–2014 at the earliest, when the first group of students subject to the requirement would begin graduating. We also knew from our four- and six-year graduation rates that these samples would be relatively small for the next few years after that. Nevertheless, we analyzed response trends and waited patiently as greater numbers of FTICs and transfer students graduated. Our persistent investigations have yielded some very useful results.

GPI

When developing FIU's institution-level assessment plan, Landorf and Doscher sought existing instruments that would provide indirect evidence of student learning, that is, surveys of students' perceptions of their knowledge, skills, attitudes, and experiences, and direct evidence, or tangible, visible, standards-based measures of learning (Deardorff, 2015). We conducted an extensive review of instruments and selected the GPI survey (Braskamp, Braskamp, & Engberg, 2014) for indirect assessment because its items most closely aligned with our SLOs (Landorf & Doscher, 2013a). We negotiated an annual site license contract with the developers so that we could collect our own data and analyze and store the data in our own systems.

The GPI asks respondents to rank 48 statements on a 5-point Likert scale, which takes about 15 minutes to complete. It assesses students' development in three domains: cognitive, interpersonal, and intrapersonal. Each domain is divided into two scales, one reflective of cultural development theory and the other of intercultural communication theory (Braskamp et al., 2014). Our own studies and those conducted by the instrument's developers found sufficient evidence of test-retest reliability, internal consistency of the scales, and face validity to convince us that scores in the different domains could be considered valid reflections of our three graduation-level SLOs (Braskamp et al., 2014; Landorf & Doscher, 2013a). The cognitive domain, which we consider to be aligned with our global awareness outcome, addresses the question, How do I know? It centers on respondents' perceptions of their knowledge and how they use knowledge to create meaning. The intrapersonal domain addresses the question, Who am I? and focuses on how individuals become self-aware and integrate their belief system, values, and sense of self into their life. We consider this domain aligned with one's global perspective. Global engagement is aligned with the interpersonal domain, which addresses the question, How do I relate to others? Questions in this domain prompt reflection about how respondents interact with those whose values, beliefs, and perspectives are different from their own (Braskamp et al., 2014). In addition to measuring students' holistic development in these three domains, the GPI also surveys students' perceptions of their college community and their involvement in various curricular and cocurricular opportunities.

The CRA

We developed our own assessment task and instruments in house to directly assess students' global awareness and perspective because we couldn't find an existing alternative that fit our needs. The CRA tasks students with reading a complex case study—one as part of the pretest form and another for the posttest—and responding to two essay prompts. One of the question prompts corresponds to global awareness and the other to global perspective.

Although fictional, the case study narratives explore real-world problems that can be analyzed and addressed from multiple disciplinary, theoretical, and cultural points of view. The CRA takes about 45 minutes to complete. A panel of trained faculty raters evaluates responses on a scale from 0 to 4 using two FIU-developed rubrics, one for each outcome (see Appendix 9.B). The rubrics are also used for course-level assessment because they can be customized and applied to performance tasks in multiple disciplines.

The CRA's development began as soon as faculty started designing global learning courses. Faculty wanted criteria to assess global awareness and perspective through tasks ranging from research papers and mock trials to debates, online discussions, and advertising campaigns. They also wanted a common language to discuss these outcomes with colleagues across the institution. Stephanie Doscher led the effort to develop the CRA and the rubrics, drawing from her experience developing a statewide performance assessment in Oregon and writing case studies in her field of educational leadership (Doscher, 2008, 2012). She composed parallel cases for the CRA pretest and posttest forms and worked with faculty to determine criteria for two holistic rubrics to assess essays. The rubrics' criteria and scores are aligned with Bloom's (1956) taxonomy of cognitive development. A quasi-experimental study comparing average learning gains of students enrolled in global learning courses with those enrolled in non-global-learning courses demonstrated that the rubrics yield valid and highly reliable measures of students' global awareness and perspective (Doscher, 2012).

Program Goal 4 Results
Before we present results, we want to underscore two points. First, as we alluded to previously, institution-level assessment of universal global learning is a long-term proposition. It is unlikely that you will see significant effects in only one or two years. Be prepared to analyze student performance trends over time and across varied contexts to build evidence of the added value of your initiative. Second, aspects of your institution's organizational and administrative environment—factors that may be outside your control—may influence the quality and validity of the data you derive from institution-level assessment. These factors include (a) data management policies and procedures, (b) the culture surrounding assessment, and (c) administrative support for implementing assessments (Peterson & Einerson, 1997). These points will become clearer as you read the next sections.

Global Perspective Inventory Results
Academic year 2013–2014 was the first in which FIU was able to analyze an FTIC student cohort that entered in 2010–2011 and graduated under our

two-course global learning requirement. Using an independent sample *t*-test, we found a statistically significant increase ($p < .01$) in students' scores on all GPI scales between the time they entered the university and when they graduated in 2013–2014. This trend continued for students who entered in 2010–2011 and graduated in 2014–2015 or in 2015–2016. Table 9.2 shows the results comparing the GPI scores of FTICs entering in 2010–2011 with those of students graduating in 2015–2016, the most recent year for which we have statistics as of the publication of this book.

The OGLI has also conducted a paired sample *t*-test on a subgroup of students who took the GPI as FTICs and again as seniors. In academic year 2015–2016, the OGLI was able to analyze a pooled sample of students ($n = 267$) who took the GPI as a pretest as FTICs entering between academic year 2010–2011 and 2013–2014, and again as a posttest as seniors graduating in either 2014–2015 or 2015–2016. This test also revealed statistically significant increases ($p < .05$) in students' average GPI scores for all scales (see Table 9.2). This is strong statistical evidence that our universal global learning initiative is having a significant positive effect on students' global awareness, perspective, and engagement.

Over the years, we have also conducted regression analyses exploring the relationship between students' demographic identity and their scores on the various GPI scales. Academic year 2014–2015 was the first year we detected any significant relationships. In that year and the year following, we found that students who self-identified as African American, African, or Black scored significantly higher than Whites on two GPI scales: intrapersonal identity, which reflects one's level of awareness of their unique identity and sense of purpose, and *interpersonal social responsibility*, defined as one's level of interdependence and social concern for others. In 2015–2016, African American, African, or Black students also reported significantly higher rates of participation in cocurricular activities than Whites and Hispanic or Latinos. In 2014–2015 and 2015–2016, we found that international students scored significantly higher in cognitive knowledge—one's degree of understanding and awareness of various cultures—than non-international students.

We also analyzed the relationship between students' reported participation in the curricular and cocurricular activities and their scale scores. The most consistent trend we've found is that increased engagement with two global learning strategies—intensive classroom dialogue among students with different backgrounds and beliefs and attendance of events or activities reflecting a cultural heritage different from one's own—are significantly positively correlated ($p < .05$) with increases in students' perceived proficiency in all three graduation-level SLOs. These findings are consistent with recent

TABLE 9.2
Pretest-Posttest GPI Average Score Results, 2010–2016

GPI Scales	Independent Sample		Paired Sample	
	2010–2011 FTIC, N = 1,719	2015– 2016 Seniors, N = 1,190	2010–2011 to 2014– 2015 FTIC, N = 267	2014–2015 to 2015– 2016 Seniors, N = 267
Cognitive knowing	3.08	3.54**	3.38	3.58**
Cognitive knowledge	3.77	4.03**	3.78	3.98**
Intrapersonal identity	4.22	4.36**	4.23	4.30*
Intrapersonal affect	3.76	4.02**	3.79	3.99**
Interpersonal social responsibility	3.76	3.91**	3.79	3.87*
Interpersonal social interaction	3.68	3.86**	3.67	3.82**

Note. FTIC = first time in college freshmen.
$^*p < .05.$ $^{**}p < .01.$

research concluding that meaningful encounters with difference are powerful contributors to students' development as global citizens (Braskamp & Engberg, 2011; Glass & Braskamp, 2012).

CRA Results
Doscher's (2012) study of the validity and reliability of students' CRA scores yielded very useful results. The study compared the average global awareness and perspective gains of students enrolled in two global learning foundations courses with the gains experienced by students enrolled in two non-global- learning courses concerning the same subject matter. When Doscher simply compared average pretest-posttest gains, she didn't find significant differences between the groups. However, when she compared gains of students within groups, she found the most convincing evidence possible that global learning strategies positively influence global awareness and perspective and that students' rubric scores are valid and reliable reflections of that influence. She found that on average students in a global learning course who scored above 1.728 on the global awareness pretest earned significantly and disproportionately higher posttest scores than predicted for students who earned the same pretest score in a non-global-learning course.

Students in a global learning course who scored below 1.728 on the pretest did not experience those gains. Similarly, on average, students in a global learning course who scored above .533 on the global perspective pretest experienced significantly and disproportionately higher posttest scores than predicted for students with the same score in a non-global-learning course. This was not the case for global learning students who earned a lower pretest score. Rubric scores of 1.728 and .533 correlate with the knowledge level of Bloom's (1956) taxonomy of cognitive development. The conclusion is that the more global learning courses a student takes the better. For some students, one course isn't enough. Some need at least one course just to gain the background knowledge necessary to succeed in subsequent courses. Students who enter a global learning course able to at least define the meanings of *global awareness* and *perspective* are significantly more likely to advance in their understanding and application of these concepts than either those who enter with no background knowledge or those who take a non-global-learning course on the same subject. This finding is also consistent with the literature on the importance of background knowledge; it is the "glue that makes learning stick" (Lent, 2012, p. 30).

Unfortunately, our institution-level study using the CRA did not yield such useful results. We found that students who entered the university as FTICs in 2010 earned decreased posttest scores on global awareness and perspective when they graduated as seniors in 2013–2014 and thereafter. We found the same result in independent sample and paired sample analyses.

These results were disappointing, but they weren't entirely surprising. Course-level assessment results and the results of the GPI gave us good reason to believe that CRA scores weren't valid reflections of our students' global learning. There are two reasons the implementation of the CRA and the nature of the task itself produced invalid results, and we present them as a caution for those contemplating a similar institution-level assessment activity. First, we get a higher response rate to the GPI because it is brief and easy to complete; students decline to take the CRA because it is lengthy, demanding, and essentially a no-stakes assessment. Research substantiates the contention that students aren't motivated to perform well on low-stakes tests (Hoyt, 2001; Schiel, 1996) and that low levels of motivation negatively affect assessment scores (Duckworth et al., 2011; Kane, 2006; Wise & Demars, 2005). A large number of seniors' CRA responses had to be thrown out because they were too brief to score, didn't address the topic, or addressed only one of the questions asked. Second, although the CRA cases are written to make it easy for students to approach them from different disciplines, the problems at the center of the cases often have little to do with the student's major program of study or academic interest. We suspect that students who view these problems as outside their expertise are even less motivated to excel on the CRA posttest. The bottom line is that although we continue to promote the case method of instruction as a global learning pedagogy and the rubrics as course-level assessment instruments, we no longer deliver the CRA as an institution-level student learning assessment.

Conclusion

Global learning enables students to construct meaning by making connections between their knowledge and experiences. It's important to note, however, that meaning does not lie in knowledge and experience themselves—it emerges from reflection on them. The same is true of student learning assessment and program evaluation. You won't find answers to your questions about the value and implications of your work in the data you collect, but you will discover consequential elements through the act of reflecting on that data. Even if your conclusion is that your methods yield adverse, invalid, or unhelpful results, which was our experience after reflecting on five years of CRA data, you will learn from your mistakes. The process of reflection will lead you to make revisions that will likely become improvements to your initiative, and continuous improvement is really the purpose of assessment and evaluation, regardless of the nature of your results. Just remember: Success is not final and failure is not fatal. It's the courage to continuously improve that counts.

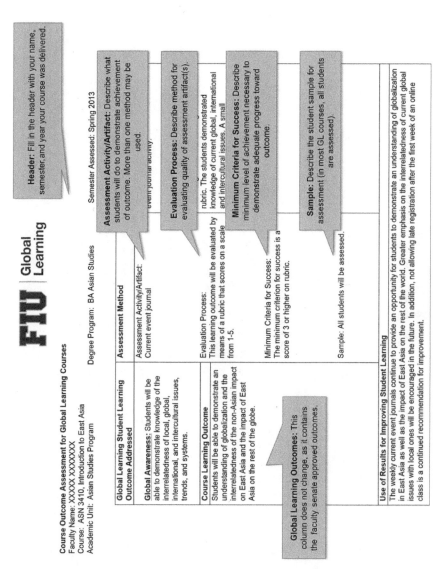

FIU | Global Learning

Course Outcome Assessment for Global Learning Courses
Faculty Name: XXXXX XXXXXXX
Course: ASN 3410, Introduction to East Asia
Academic Unit: Asian Studies Program

Degree Program: BA Asian Studies

Semester Assessed: Spring 2013

Header: Fill in the header with your name, semester, and year your course was delivered.

Global Learning Student Learning Outcome Addressed	Assessment Method
Global Awareness: Students will be able to demonstrate knowledge of the interrelatedness of local, global, international, and intercultural issues, trends, and systems.	Assessment Activity/Artifact: Current event journal
Course Learning Outcome Students will be able to demonstrate an understanding of globalization and the interrelatedness of the non-Asian impact on East Asia and the impact of East Asia on the rest of the globe.	Evaluation Process: This learning outcome will be evaluated by means of a rubric that scores on a scale from 1-5.
	Minimum Criteria for Success: The minimum criterion for success is a score of 3 or higher on rubric.
	Sample: All students will be assessed.

Assessment Activity/Artifact: Describe what students will do to demonstrate achievement of outcome. More than one method may be used.

Evaluation Process: Describe method for evaluating quality of assessment artifact(s).

rubric. The students demonstrated knowledge of current global, international and intercultural issues. A small

Minimum Criteria for Success: Describe minimum level of achievement necessary to demonstrate adequate progress toward outcome.

Sample: Describe the student sample for assessment (in most GL courses, all students are assessed).

Global Learning Outcomes: This column does not change, as it contains the faculty senate approved outcomes.

Use of Results for Improving Student Learning
The weekly current event journals continue to provide an opportunity for students to demonstrate an understanding of globalization in East Asia as well as the impact of East Asia on the rest of the world. Greater emphasis on the interrelatedness of current global issues with local ones will be encouraged in the future. In addition, not allowing late registration after the first week of an online class is a continued recommendation for improvement.

FIU | Global Learning

Course Outcome Assessment for Global Learning Courses
Faculty Name: XXXXX XXXXXXX
Course: ASN 3410, Introduction to East Asia
Academic Unit: Asian Studies Program

Degree Program: BA Asian Studies

Semester Assessed: Spring 2013

Global Learning Student Learning Outcome Addressed	Assessment Method	Assessment Results
Global Perspective: Students will be able to conduct a multi-perspective analysis of local, global, international, and intercultural problems.	**Assessment Activity/Artifact:** One of six 1-page reflection papers	The majority of the students participated in these in-class papers (some students were absent).
Course Learning Outcome Students will be able to conduct a multi-perspective social issues	**Evaluation Process:** This learning outcome will be evaluated by means of a rubric that scores on a scale from 1–5.	All students who participated were able to meet the minimum criteria for success by scoring a 3 or above on the rubric. Those students who were evaluated exhibited critical analysis of the contemporary social issues affecting East Asia.
	Assessment Results: Summarize assessment results in quantitative and/or qualitative form, as appropriate. Describe in a way that is meaningful for you and others who may teach the course. ...s is an ...ubric.	
	Sample: All students will be assessed.	

Use of Results for Improving Student Learning
Students were able to analyze contemporary social issues in East Asia such as: Orientalism, Social Problems of Communist China, Reverse Orientalism, Asian Globalization, and Japan and the Environment. By expressing their ideas through reflection papers, students were able to conduct a multi-perspective analysis of current global and intercultural problems in Asia. Greater emphasis on analyzing East Asian social issues in the United States will improve students' understanding of contemporary social issues in Asia as a whole. Some improvement is needed in regard to relating global East Asian social issues to these same issues in the United States. Additional time will be spent on comparing and contrasting social issues in East Asia and the United States.

Use of Results for Improving Student Learning: Reflect on the implications of the results and make recommendations for future semesters. Recommendations may include changes to content, teaching strategies, or assessments.

FIU | Global Learning

Course Outcome Assessment for Global Learning Courses
Faculty Name: XXXXX XXXXXXX
Course: ASN 3410, Introduction to East Asia
Academic Unit: Asian Studies Program

Degree Program: BA Asian Studies

Semester Assessed: Spring 2013

Global Learning Student Learning Outcome Addressed	Assessment Method	Assessment Results
Global Engagement: Students will be able to demonstrate willingness to engage in local, global, international, and intercultural problem solving.	**Assessment Activity/Artifact:** Site Visit: Students will be required to make one site visit (as individuals or in a group) during the semester and write one at-home Reflection Paper in response to the visit.	22 students out of 28 demonstrated a willingness to engage in contemporary local and global issues by completing the site visit and the required reflection paper for the visit.
Course Learning Outcome Students will demonstrate a willingness to engage in contemporary local and global issues by making a site visit.	**Evaluation Process:** This learning outcome will be evaluated by means of a rubric that scores on a scale from 1–5.	Each completed assignment met the minimum criteria needed for success by maintaining scores of 3 or higher on the rubric, though a few students suffered from deduction of points because of late submission. Overall, they did best in this assignment, as most participants proved themselves to be keen observers and fairly decent writers.
	Minimum Criteria for Success: The minimum criterion for success is an average score of 3 or higher on rubric.	
	Sample: All students will be assessed.	

Use of Results for Improving Student Learning

In spite of awkwardness in dealing with conceptual and theoretical issues, the students proved themselves to be keen observers and thoughtful writers when it comes to communicating and expressing their own experience. Although their expectation for this assignment was initially low, many of the students seem to have found their visits unexpectedly enjoyable and stimulating, and their engaging attitude make it an unexpectedly enjoyable experience for me to read their reports. That makes me think in incorporating more visual and practical elements, in addition to readings, in my lecture to stimulate students' interest.

FIU | Global Learning

Global Awareness: Knowledge of the interrelatedness of local, global, international, and intercultural issues, trends, and systems.

0	(Knowledge/Comprehension) 1	(Application) 2	(Analysis) 3	(Synthesis/Evaluation) 4
• Does not demonstrate knowledge of issues influencing the problem Student accomplishes the following: ✓ fails to cite issues influencing the problem ✓ fails to depict interrelatedness of issues influencing the problem	• Demonstrates incorrect or incomplete knowledge of issues influencing the problem Student accomplishes the following: ✓ presents incorrect or incomplete depiction of issues influencing the problem ✓ presents incorrect or incomplete depiction of the interrelatedness of issues influencing the problem	• Demonstrates, with generalizations, knowledge of issues influencing the problem Student accomplishes the following: ✓ generally describes limited number of issues influencing the problem ✓ implies or generally describes the interrelatedness of issues influencing the problem	• Assembles an analysis of the problem based on the interrelatedness of influencing issues Student accomplishes the following: ✓ accurately explains issues influencing the problem ✓ provides specific evidence of or references to interrelated issues influencing the problem	• Synthesizes and/or evaluates differing interpretations of the problem based on the interrelatedness of influencing issues Student accomplishes previous and one or more of the following: ✓ presents more than one interpretation of the problem ✓ bases evaluation of the problem(s) on the interrelatedness of influencing issues

Global Perspective: Ability to develop a multi-perspective analysis of local, global, international, and intercultural problems.

0	(Knowledge/Comprehension) 1	(Application) 2	(Analysis) 3	(Synthesis/Evaluation) 4
• Does not recognize or does not acknowledge the legitimacy of differences in perspectives pertaining to the problem Student accomplishes the following: ✓ identifies one perspective and does not recognize other perspectives pertaining to the problem	• Identifies a limited number of perspectives pertaining to the problem Student accomplishes the following: ✓ identifies a limited number of perspectives pertaining to the problem ✓ identifies only those perspectives explicitly stated in article	• Identifies multiple perspectives pertaining to the problem however, does not analyze the influences on differing perspectives Student accomplishes the following: ✓ identifies multiple perspectives pertaining to the problem ✓ may identify perspectives not discussed explicitly in case	• Assembles an analysis of multiple perspectives pertaining to the problem Student accomplishes previous and one or more of the following: ✓ explains the influences on differing perspectives ✓ compares and/or contrasts differing perspectives	• Integrates multiple perspectives into a multifaceted interpretation of the problem and/or solution(s) Student accomplishes previous and one or more of the following: ✓ presents a synthesized discussion of multiple perspectives ✓ offers possible solution(s) for the problem ✓ evaluates the problem and/or solution(s)

FIU | Global Learning

Explanation of Case Response Rubric Scoring Scale

The rubric's scoring scale (0-4) is based on Bloom's Taxonomy of Cognitive Development (1956). Bloom's Taxonomy attempts to divide cognitive objectives into subdivisions ranging from the simplest behaviors (knowledge) to the most complex (evaluation). The rubric's scoring criteria and descriptors are also based on the taxonomy.

Score	Cognitive Level	Definition	Behaviors
0	N/A	N/A	Student fails to address prompt or provide evidence of knowledge or skill.
1	Knowledge/Comprehension	Student can recall and may grasp the meaning of previously learned material.	Student can explain, list, or summarize common terms, facts, basic concepts, and/or principles stated in case.
2	Application	Student can use learned material in new and concrete situations.	Student can use previously learned concepts, principles, or skills to explain or summarize new cases.
3	Analysis	Student can break down material into its component parts so that its organizational structure may be understood.	Student can identify parts, the relationship between parts, and may distinguish organizational principles involved in a case. Student may recognize unstated assumptions, logical fallacies in reasoning, and/or distinguish between facts and inferences.
4	Synthesis/Evaluation	Student can put parts together to form a new whole and may judge the value of material.	Student can produce a scheme for organizing or classifying a set of abstract relations gathered from a case. Student may form judgments based on definite criteria, which may be internal (observed in the case) or external (relevant to the purpose).

10

CONTINUOUS COMMUNICATION AND IMPROVEMENT

To improve is to change, so to be perfect is to have changed often.
(Winston Churchill as cited in Humes, 1994, p. 15)

It's seldom possible to produce anything that's perfect. It's almost always possible, however, to perfect the things we produce. If you're committed to achieving the ambitious goal of universal global learning, you should also be committed to improving your initiative over the long term. Large initial investments, and ongoing reinvestments, of time, energy, and creativity are crucial if you want to involve all your stakeholders in achieving inclusive excellence through universal global learning. In truth, the pursuit of universal global learning is ceaseless, but, unlike Sisyphus's endeavor, it's not a futile enterprise. Through the ongoing process of perfecting your work, often referred to as *continuous improvement*, the impact of your universal global learning initiative will be much greater than the sum of its imperfect parts. According to the Kaizen Institute (2017), "Big results come from many small changes accumulated over time" (para. 2). This chapter aims to help you identify and develop strategies for incorporating those many small changes into the design and implementation of your initiative.

Let's start by clarifying what we mean by continuous improvement. When applied to education, it "refers to any school- or instructional-improvement process that unfolds progressively, that does not have a fixed or predetermined end point, and that is sustained over extended periods of time" ("Continuous Improvement," 2013, para. 1). Continuous improvement involves a constant effort to enhance the extent to which individuals and groups are achieving their intended objectives. Improvement isn't all about ends, though; the means are just as important. Even if you have a common agenda in place with well-articulated program goals and SLOs, your initiative will likely fizzle out or fail if you haven't built in processes for evaluating and assessing those objectives

211

as well as analyzing and using results for improvement. Continuous improvement processes should enable faculty, staff, and administrators to integrate quality enhancement efforts into their regular work activities. They should also help them take on a continuous improvement mind-set that motivates them to overcome obstacles by addressing their sources rather than dismissing them as isolated events. You'll recognize this mind-set when you observe people taking frequent small steps to increase the efficiency, effectiveness, equity, and safety of their own work and that of the universal global learning initiative as a whole (Park, Hironaka, Carver, & Nordstrum, 2013).

Continuous improvement is built on a foundation of continuous communication. Stakeholders need timely access to information that helps them determine how their work contributes to the common agenda. They also need regular opportunities to exchange and reflect on that information with others while working on the agenda. Communication helps people discover relationships among their various activities and improve their agenda by increasing coordination, collaboration, and mutual reinforcement. Communication also engenders trust. Stakeholders working across reporting lines toward a common agenda need to "see that their own interests will be treated fairly, and that decisions will be made on the basis of objective evidence and the best possible solution to the problem, not to favor the priorities of one organization over another" (Kania & Kramer, 2011, p. 40).

Once again, it takes significant time, energy, and creativity on the part of dedicated backbone personnel to facilitate continuous communication and improvement. It also helps to know at the outset that these personnel will face obstacles that are inherent to educational institutions. Communication and improvement are sometimes difficult to accomplish in higher education because

- work tends to be conducted in silos;
- high-level administrators and policy makers want immediate results;
- time needed to achieve complex program goals and SLOs is in short supply;
- data are not accessible or provided quickly enough to allow stakeholders to make incremental changes to their practices; and
- performance-based accountability structures promote a search for cure-alls and low-cost solutions rather than long-term approaches (Park et al., 2013).

Temponi (2005) adds one more obstacle to this list—faculty and administrators often disagree about the degree to which students should influence strategic planning and continuous improvement. Some bristle at the idea of treating students like customers, worrying they will cede authority over curricular and other decisions under the guise of quality enhancement. Others view students as central to the institution's mission and demand their voices be heard at the planning table.

Continuous improvement is also hard for some faculty to buy into because they view students holistically as complex people, not products. These faculty don't believe it's possible to ascertain the quality of teaching and learning by a few objective measures. How does one calculate the relevance of course content, the power of an inspirational lecture, or the impact of a serendipitous aha moment? They worry that too much assessment, evaluation, and analysis will undermine the initiative by destroying student motivation and faculty innovation. Education is indeed a complex, dynamic, long-term endeavor that doesn't necessarily involve standardization (Roffe, 1998). Education is also a social phenomenon, making it impossible to control all the variables influencing the extent to which students achieve SLOs. And when accountability looms large over program evaluation and student learning assessment, people avoid dialogue about improvement out of fear of punitive measures. They want to stay under the radar, and they resist making changes that could upset the status quo, however mediocre that status may be.

Still, we are educators. We are in the business of teaching, and we "have not taught if our students have not learned" (Brown & Marshall, 2008, p. 205). Dialogue about students' learning, how they learn and how we can best facilitate learning, is an essential part of our job. We view universal global learning as adding value to this dialogue; therefore, we take an asset-based rather than an accountability-oriented approach to communication and continuous improvement. As we proceed with our discussion of methods we use for this approach, we discuss communication and improvement simultaneously because we view them as fundamentally interconnected. We discuss these twin foci in the contexts of student learning assessment and program evaluation, and we highlight some positive changes to our initiative that have resulted from these methods. We also tackle the following critical questions:

- How can leaders help stakeholders exchange information in timely, engaging ways for improvement?
- What methods can leaders use to enable individuals and groups to reflect on assessment and evaluation results?
- How can leaders help stakeholders generate innovative ideas and sustain a culture of continuous improvement?

Improvement implies change, and change demands that we break away from previous forms of thought and behavior and adopt new ones. As Keynes

(1935) observed, the difficulty of change lies not so much in embracing "new ideas, but in escaping from the old ones" (p. 5). We would be lying if we said it's possible to embrace universal global learning without also letting go of many ideas and practices that are currently the norm for your institution. Universal global learning is a bold, daring concept; even if stakeholders endorse the idea, they have to make ongoing adjustments to beliefs and behaviors to make this vision a reality. What follows are some of the communication strategies we've found helpful in enabling people to make adjustments and to continuously improve the realization of universal global learning.

Student Learning Assessment

Our analysis of student learning assessment results has taught us not to assume that students are achieving high levels of global awareness, perspective, and engagement just because they've taken a global learning course or two. At the same time, we've learned that if we want faculty to maintain or improve the power of their global learning experiences, we must recognize their work. People need validation to feel that their efforts are valuable and worthwhile. For this reason, we treat all global learning educators at FIU as a community of practice (Wenger, McDermott, & Snyder, 2002). The OGLI facilitates this community's exchange of information about student learning and the assessment instruments, pedagogical strategies, and content used in global learning courses and cocurricular activities. We do this to help faculty and staff ascertain the connection between what they and others are doing to promote students' achievement of the SLOs and to honor this connection. We engage in continuous communication with our community of practice to help global learning educators

- build relationships and increase interaction with a wide network of peers;
- learn from their peers, develop replicable tools and strategies, and in some cases become involved in each other's work;
- coordinate activities and take action as a community; and
- create new knowledge in our fields by exchanging information across disciplinary boundaries and exploring new collaborations, technologies, practices, and ideas (Cambridge, Kaplan, & Suter, 2005).

As you know from chapter 9, the OGLI coordinates student learning assessment at the course and institutional levels. Although we use slightly different strategies to exchange information at each level, our purpose for doing so is the same: to produce ideas for improvement that faculty and staff can apply to their work. To begin, we describe course-level methods, which are the Global Learning Course Assessment Matrix and the GLCOC's triennial review process. We discuss communication and improvement associated with institution-level student learning assessment in the next section on program evaluation.

Global Learning Course Assessment Matrix

The OGLI begins the process of communication and improvement at the course level each semester by reading every completed matrix, taking notes on major insights, and sending an e-mail response to every faculty member who submitted one. If multiple faculty submit a matrix for sections of the same course, we send one e-mail to the entire group to encourage dialogue and learning among colleagues, which is especially important for adjunct faculty who seldom communicate with other faculty in their department. Every semester we receive notes of thanks for our support. The power of this e-mail strategy is so great that we want to tell you exactly how we do it.

We introduce the matrix reply e-mail with a greeting, some words of thanks for submission, and a reminder that we use the data they provide in order to continuously improve the course and the initiative. We then summarize and validate the major points faculty have expressed in their matrix and recommend how they might improve, expand, or share their work. These recommendations include ideas for revising an assignment; links to additional teaching, assessment, or content resources; e-mail introductions to other faculty, the global learning librarian, student affairs professionals, or a community organization; and suggestions for possible conference presentations or publications. Because we take an asset-based approach to our responses, when we note something less than satisfactory in the matrix, perhaps a failure to fill out all pages or reporting that only traditional assessments were used, we seldom ask the faculty to resubmit unless the course is slated for the GLCOC triennial review. Instead, we diplomatically remind them of what the GLCOC expects from a course and proceed with giving them ideas for future semesters. We close the e-mail with announcements of new and existing resources, workshops, and events for faculty and students.

This kind of communication with faculty leads to course improvements. Every semester, faculty members tell us in e-mails, matrices, and focus groups how they've applied our suggestions and used the information we've provided. They invite us to observe their courses and activities so we can witness the fruits of their work. Although it is time and labor intensive, we highly recommend you build strategies into your initiative to regularly communicate with faculty members about what is happening in their courses. This helps individuals feel they aren't alone in their experiences and that a community of peers supports them. It also builds trust, and when there's trust, faculty are more open to the data pointing them in the direction they need to move their instructional practices. A global learning initiative's backbone organization, in our case the OGLI, should then provide the support faculty need to make these improvements as well as recognize and validate their efforts (Edmondson & Zimpher, 2014).

Data in the matrices have also led to improvements in how the OGLI supports the initiative overall. Faculty members' reflections are the best source of information we have about the kinds of consultation and professional development they want. We noticed that many faculty reported that they and their students were having problems locating appropriate content for global learning courses; we gave that information to the FIU libraries division, whose staff voted to hire a dedicated global learning librarian. In another example, faculty have reported that the transition of face-to-face courses to hybrid and fully online modalities has been difficult. This led the OGLI to search for a pedagogy that would make the move a benefit rather than a burden. We found what we were looking for in the collaborative online international learning model (Connell, 2014), which uses technology and the Internet to connect students and faculty with their peers across national borders. Courses in this model enable intercultural teams to work on meaningful projects that increase their knowledge of the world and help them better understand and empathize with other people's perspectives. We never would have known about the need for or potential interest in this new pedagogy if we had not continuously communicated with faculty through the course assessment matrices.

The GLCOC Triennial Review

FIU's GLCOC, a standing Faculty Senate committee, has two main responsibilities: evaluate proposals for global learning designation and ensure that courses are offered regularly and conducted with fidelity. The GLCOC fulfills this second responsibility through its triennial review process. Every three years after a course is approved, the committee evaluates the course's latest syllabi and completed matrices using the same checklists it used to confer global learning status in the first place. Although teaching strategies, assessments, and content may have evolved over the years, as long as the documents adhere to the items on the checklist, the committee will vote to maintain the course's designation. The committee also reviews course offering and enrollment data. To maintain the global learning designation, courses must be taught at least once every two years, resulting in a vibrant collection of courses readily available to students so they can make timely progress toward graduation.

What happens if the GLCOC finds that a course doesn't adhere to the checklist or isn't being taught in regular rotation? The committee communicates with faculty and department chairs to rectify the situation. Most of the time the department staff want to retain the designation and work diligently and collegially with the committee to maintain fidelity. Once or twice each year department personnel request for the designation to be removed (as of June 2017, the designation has been removed from 12 courses). Most commonly this is requested because of departmental changes, such as adjustments to degree requirements or changes in the composition and expertise of faculty. If removing the course's designation has any potential impact on students' ability to fulfill the graduation requirement, the GLCOC refers the department to the OGLI to help identify another course to take its place.

The OGLI provides administrative support to the GLCOC and acts as a liaison between the committee and departments. The office staff compiles the syllabi, matrices, and course offering and enrollment data for the committee's review. The OGLI determines the triennial review calendar and tracks the committee's decisions. When department administrators need to make significant revisions to a course, the GLCOC refers them to the OGLI for help developing a plan of action to respond to GLCOC recommendations. This sometimes involves providing additional professional development workshops to faculty.

Although the matrices go a long way toward facilitating continuous communication and improvement of courses, the GLCOC has a different and important kind of influence. Even though the committee remains collegial—all five members, who serve two-year renewable terms, are global learning faculty—it also has the power to remove a designation that department heads and students greatly value. In the committee's early years, GLCOC members didn't have much personal experience with global learning. Some had only taught their own courses a couple of times, and they hadn't seen many syllabi from other faculty, so they had a steep learning curve in terms of how to conduct an effective course review. Now the committee's members have vast experience, and they know global learning when they see it in a syllabus or matrix. The GLCOC and its triennial review process are critical to maintaining the fidelity and vitality of our expanding collection of global learning courses.

Program Evaluation

People don't usually take part in program evaluations unless they're compelled to do so for accountability purposes. But we contend that even if prompted by outside forces, you can make program evaluation meaningful and useful by balancing the need to address external requirements with a focus on internal interests and goals.

Institutions should conduct program evaluation to "improve, not just prove" (Edmondson & Zimpher, 2014, p. 159). To achieve this, your plan must go beyond data collecting and reporting procedures to include ways you will use data to achieve your common agenda. Just as student learning assessment has a cycle, program evaluation is cyclical as well. There are many models of program evaluation cycles, but it is important to use one that requires you to "regularly evaluate key systems, processes, and outcomes by adhering to an established framework and methodology in order to create a basis for the strategic and continual improvement of the organization's performance" (Temponi, 2005, p. 19). To facilitate continuous improvement at the institution level, you will need methods for communicating with high-level leadership and with the broader stakeholder community. These methods need to help people see themselves in the initiative and motivate them to get involved, take ownership, and advocate for its importance. These methods should promote a continuous improvement mind-set that tears down silos and brings partners together throughout the institution to implement universal global learning (Park et al., 2013).

Annual Impact Reports

It's been said that reports are where ideas go to die. Although this may be a truism, there is a kernel of truth in every cliché. We agree that enshrining a great idea on a piece of paper can effectively wall it off from further action. Writing a program plan or evaluation report can take all your time and energy and be a stressful and harrowing experience. This was pretty much the case when we submitted our original plan for universal global learning to FIU's accreditation body, the Southern Association of Colleges and Schools. After a major report is finished, its contributors want a break. They want to rest and take care of other responsibilities they set aside. This makes it hard to restart people's motors and bring ideas on paper to life.

Still, reports are the main way we communicate our plans and our program evaluations to internal and external parties. We decided to make our initial plan for the accrediting agency, our subsequent annual impact reports, and the agency's required fifth-year impact report integral aspects of our continuous communication and improvement cycle. We wanted the reports to drive the cycle and for the cycle itself to be reflected in the reports' structure. We also decided to make these reports working documents the OGLI and internal and external stakeholders would refer to frequently. So let's take a glimpse at the structure of our annual impact reports, how we use them to drive the continuous improvement cycle, and the improvements that have come about as a result of their use.

Structure

The Southern Association of Colleges and Schools required us to follow specific organizational structures for the initial plan for universal global learning and the fifth-year impact report. We were happy these structures were simple, easy to follow, and included the steps of a continuous improvement cycle. We decided early that if we followed the structure of the fifth-year report for our internal annual reports as well, writing all the documents would be much easier. Our instinct proved correct: Using the same format year after year made report writing feel familiar and allowed year-over-year comparisons. Our office has developed an efficient annual time line for collecting and analyzing data and starting and completing drafts, and we've been able to divvy up research and writing responsibilities equitably. All our reports are available on our website, goglobal.fiu.edu.

Our reports are organized as follows:

- Executive summary: Retained from our original plan submitted to our accrediting agency, this is a one-page description of our universal global learning initiative, its purpose, our program goals and SLOs, major actions to be implemented, and institutional resources and support.
- Program goals and intended SLOs: These tables display the goals, SLOs, and methods we use to evaluate and assess them.
- Significant developments: We include brief descriptions of the changes to the initiative we implemented to address points raised in previous years' program evaluations and institution-level assessment results, the university's strategic plan, and any changes in institutional or global context.
- Impact on learning and the environment supporting student learning: We share the results of program evaluation and institution-level student learning assessments.
- Use of results to facilitate continuous improvement: We propose actions for the following year to improve achievement of our goals and SLOs.

Based on our experience, we recommend keeping your reports simple and straightforward so you spend less time preparing them and more time discussing your findings with internal and external stakeholders and following through with proposed actions. We keep the report in draft form up until submission so we can seek input on the use of results for improvement from various stakeholder groups, including the GLCOC and the Office of the Provost. OGLI staff members also incorporate the proposed actions into their human resource performance excellence goals for the following year. We also recommend that you write your reports in concise layperson's language so people will actually read it. Avoid educational jargon. The report doesn't have to be flashy, but if you have the budget to work with a designer, you can get very creative. We know that information in our reports could be communicated better through data visualization, but currently we don't have funding for a designer. Another reason we didn't go down the design route is that we knew the Southern Association of Colleges and Schools didn't want too many graphics in the fifth-year impact report. However, in the spirit of continuous improvement, because our fifth-year report has been approved and we're no longer beholden to the accrediting agency for a report, we may get more artistic in the future.

Improvements

This section discusses some selected improvements we've made to the initiative that weren't part of our initial plan for universal global learning. These changes were prompted by our adherence to the continuous improvement cycle, facilitated by our annual impact reporting process.

Program Goal 1: Provide a sufficient number of global learning courses. The initial plan for universal global learning called for the OGLI to lead the development of global learning courses, but it didn't include strategies for enabling students to easily identify and locate these courses. The OGLI now works with admissions to promote global learning before students enroll and with orientations and parent programs to acquaint them with the graduation requirement during their first interactions with the university. The OGLI is also responsible for tagging courses with the global learning designation in the online catalog and promoting semester lists of offerings on our website, social networking sites, and the student electronic mailing list. The OGLI worked with academic affairs to ensure that required and elective global learning courses were emphasized in all students' programs of study, which at FIU are known as Major Maps, a centerpiece of FIU's Graduation Success Initiative, which helps undergraduates find their right major and stay on track to graduate on time (O'Neill, 2014). OGLI staff and student volunteers also promote courses through periodic meetings with academic advisers; at informational tables during events such as Week of Welcome,

International Education Week, and Diversity Week; and classroom visits to first-year experience courses.

Program Goal 2: Increase cocurricular opportunities for integrative global learning. Although in our original plan we envisioned integrative global learning, it took several years and many attempts at different strategies to figure out how best to achieve this goal. Our initial approach was to simply increase the number of global learning activities available to students, particularly those cocreated by faculty and student affairs professionals. To this end, we included faculty and student affairs staff in our Global Learning Course Design and Instruction Workshops, thinking this would initiate connections and collaborations. We formed a committee of representatives from the OGLI, the Center for the Advancement of Teaching, and the Division of Student Affairs to update workshop content. The executive director of the Center for Leadership and Service, Beverly Dalrymple, was brought on as a workshop cofacilitator, and the vice president of the Division of Student Affairs encouraged staff attendance. This resulted in a few interesting projects, but we soon faced challenges. Student affairs staff had more difficulty taking time to attend workshops than faculty did, and they were far outnumbered by faculty, which created an imbalance of power. Because only a limited number of student affairs departments provided programming to undergraduates, we soon ran low on the number of people to include in the workshops.

Still, integrative learning was our goal. Based on feedback from workshop surveys and work by Denise (1999) and Thalheim (2008), Dalrymple and Doscher reconceptualized faculty and staff collaboration as the following four-stage developmental continuum of individually significant activities rather than as an end in itself:

1. Informing, exchanging information for mutual understanding
2. Consulting, advising to stimulate joint thinking
3. Coordinating, networking and independently altering activities to achieve a common purpose
4. Collaborating, working cooperatively to mutually enhance capabilities and achieve a common purpose

This continuum now informs how the OGLI supports faculty and staff in their efforts to facilitate integrative global learning. The OGLI acts as a conduit for information exchange by showing staff how to access the global learning course list, view specific course syllabi, send invitations to faculty and students to activities, and coordinate programming schedules with class meetings. When consultation is needed, the OGLI introduces faculty to student affairs staff with the appropriate expertise. Such introductions have led to several projects that faculty and staff members collaborate on, such as service-learning components of global learning courses. To energize all aspects of the continuum, in 2011 the OGLI brought faculty and staff together to implement a university-wide project commemorating the 10th anniversary of September 11, 2001. Titled Unity/Diversity: Reflecting on the Meaning of 9/11, this month-long series of events included art exhibits, musical performances, lectures, discussions, an essay contest, a teach-in, and multidenominational prayer services and ceremonies honoring victims and first responders. Faculty and student affairs staff served on the coordinating committee and worked together to produce all the events in the series.

The OGLI continues to support the stages of the collaborative continuum between faculty and staff, but we've learned that the key to facilitating integrative learning is creating the habitats we discussed in chapter 7. These have breathed new life and purpose into how the OGLI supports collaboration, and from the standpoint of continuous improvement, our focus is now on bringing faculty and staff together to maximize the depth, breadth, and variety of the habitats available to all students.

Program Goal 3: Provide high-quality global learning professional development for faculty and staff. Beginning in the second year of our initiative, we discovered that many faculty assigned to teach sections of global learning courses hadn't attended a Global Learning Course Design and Instruction Workshop. When we investigated, we found that department heads had not told these instructors about the course's designation or that they were entitled to attend a workshop to prepare them to teach the course. Department administrators had spent so much energy with lead faculty getting courses approved in the first year, they didn't take time to develop mechanisms to communicate information to the new faculty assigned to the courses in subsequent years. The OGLI worked with chairs to develop intradepartmental communication processes and assumed partial responsibility for communicating with all new faculty. Each semester the OGLI obtains a list of all faculty assigned to global learning courses as soon as schedules are released. The OGLI then determines which faculty haven't yet taken a workshop. The office sends a workshop invitation to these faculty, summarizing the agenda and reminding them of the stipend they're eligible to earn. With this strategy we are down to just a handful of faculty each semester who still need a workshop.

Chapter 5 discusses the differentiated professional development offerings the OGLI provides to meet our faculty's evolving needs, which we learned about primarily through faculty reflections in the matrices. Our end-of-semester focus group dialogues taught us that professional development is most powerful when faculty themselves communicate their teaching challenges and innovations to colleagues. This led us to develop a call for proposals for 75-minute brown-bag lunch workshops led by any adjunct or full-time global learning instructor. The call offers a $500 stipend for workshops that explore a specific global learning strategy that develops global awareness, perspective, or engagement; addresses diverse perspectives, collaborative learning, or global problem-solving; and can be implemented in courses across the undergraduate curriculum. Among the 12 well-attended workshops conducted thus far, faculty have taught their colleagues how to facilitate the Photovoice method for qualitative research and social change (see Photovoice.org), how to teach research and media literacy skills by having students edit and contribute to Wikipedia articles, and how to use Web-based tools for online collaboration.

The focus groups also led to the development of our Global Learning Fellowship program. Faculty frequently reported they were bringing their primary research into their global learning classes to great effect, and support for undergraduate research mentorship is one of our institution's strategic priorities. In response, we established the fellowships, which provide awards of up to $4,000 for research collaborations between faculty and undergraduate students exploring global problems. Funded projects generate new knowledge in the researchers' field and involve teaching strategies that bring results into the classroom to facilitate students' global learning. Abstracts of fellowship projects are available on our website at goglobal.fiu.edu.

Program Goal 4: Increase student achievement of the graduation-level global learning SLOs. This goal is really the heart of FIU's universal global learning initiative, so it is vitally important that data analyses enable us to identify the processes and practices that yield positive results. As Edmondson and Zimpher (2014) note, "Datasets are just the raw material; it is the *analysis* by people on the ground that gets us moving in the right direction" (p. 49). Every year Landorf and Doscher meet with stakeholders to present institution-level assessment results and discuss ways to improve and expand universal global learning. We scrutinize GPI results in various ways, discussing response trends on individual items and, their relationship to demographic variables. We use Braskamp and colleagues' (2014) interpretative framework to identify actions to be taken in the curriculum, cocurriculum, and campus community.

Here are some examples. In response to our finding that increased attendance of events or activities reflecting a cultural heritage different from one's own has a significant positive impact on all three SLOs, the OGLI's Eric Feldman increased methods for guiding Global Learning Medallion and Peace Corps Prep students to service activities and cultural events that would have maximum impact on their global awareness, perspective, and engagement. When GPI results indicated that courses featuring materials and readings on race and ethnicity issues are significantly positively correlated to global awareness, the OGLI devoted more time in professional development workshops to this subject and provided more resources to help faculty locate diverse materials and incorporate them into their syllabi. The finding that community service activities have a significant positive influence on global engagement led the OGLI to hire a graduate assistant for the express purpose of guiding and expanding our work sponsoring globally focused service clubs.

The most important lessons we've learned from institution-level assessment, however, are these: More global learning is better, and more is better for all students. Our GPI results underscore that all students, regardless of demographic category, benefit from global learning. To ensure these benefits, global learning must be built into all students' undergraduate programs. Our assessment results demonstrate that simply providing all students with a single common global learning course or activity isn't enough. For those who undertake a global learning course or activity with a minimum level of understanding of the SLOs, one course or activity alone may lead to significant SLO development (Doscher, 2012). But for the majority, one global learning experience won't be enough to develop robust, transferable SLOs. Students most often need several foundational global learning experiences just to develop sufficient familiarity with the SLOs to take their learning and collaborative problem-solving skills to the next level. This is why we haven't put the brakes on the development of global learning courses and activities. On the contrary, the OGLI actively encourages expansion of the global learning curriculum and cocurriculum. The OGLI's task is to keep pace with this expansion by providing the human, physical, technological, and financial resources that students, faculty, and staff need to facilitate and participate in these opportunities.

GoGlobal Scorecards

Although we have become quite used to working with a lot of data, we fully agree with Edmondson and Zimpher (2014) that data can be intimidating, especially to people in education "where numbers are most often used as a hammer instead of a flashlight" (p. 73). For the most part, we've been able to avoid this data trap and help build a culture of continuous improvement by subscribing to what Edmondson and Zimpher (2014) dub the Three I's:

1. identifying data to be collected from all partners, rather than information from individual organizations,
2. interpreting data and communicating it in an easy to understand format, and
3. improving by helping others adjust their activities to address new understandings.

We think the story of the GoGlobal scorecard is a good illustration of the Three I's in action. In fall 2014, after the OGLI had conducted its first true pretest-posttest study of a student cohort that entered and graduated under the two-course global learning requirement, the office turned its attention to how it could help academic departments continuously improve their contributions to universal global learning. Based on consultations with chairs, the OGLI identified key data points that would help departments choose actions that would mutually reinforce their own goals as well as those of the initiative, including (a) the number of global learning courses the department offered, (b) the frequency with which courses are taught, (c) the number of course sections offered, (d) the number of faculty teaching courses who have participated in a Global Learning Course Design and Instruction Workshop, and (e) the average enrollment in each global learning course. The OGLI uses these data to calculate a GoGlobal score for each department, composed of a weighted average of each of these data points. With the help of the external relations department, the OGLI designed an easy-to-read customized graphic handout (also available online at goglobal.fiu.edu) for each department that features the data that constitute the department's score and suggestions for how the department can work with the OGLI to improve its score. Hilary Landorf makes house calls to discuss the scorecard and plan activities. Because of this collaborative approach to continuous improvement, chairs always leave the meetings with actionable items, such as using GoGlobal scorecard results in marketing and recruitment efforts, committing to revise additional courses for the global learning designation, and advertising the Global Learning Medallion and Peace Corp Prep programs to all students in their degree and certificate programs.

Storytelling

According to Keller and Aiken (2015), "When we choose for ourselves, we are far more committed to the outcome (almost by a factor of five to one)" (p. 34). People with a continuous improvement mind-set feel motivated to increase the impact of their own work and the initiative as a whole. We use storytelling to encourage that mind-set. Leithwood and Mascall (2008) said that stories are a powerful influence on motivation because they influence two sets of personal beliefs:

1. capacity beliefs, which are people's opinions about their own self-efficacy that determine their ability to achieve goals, and
2. context beliefs, or people's ideas about the extent to which their work situation supports their ability to fulfill their responsibilities

The OGLI works hard to tell the story of universal global learning at FIU to internal and external audiences. We want to bolster the positive capacity and context beliefs of our students, faculty, staff, alumni, and interconnected local and global communities to expand the extent to which we provide global learning to all. We tell stories that fall into four main categories:

1. Purpose, stories that show why people's efforts are worthwhile, highlighting the link between individual efforts and the achievement of program goals, SLOs, and universal global learning
2. Role models, inspirational stories about global learning students and faculty throughout the university, or people who walk the talk
3. Evolving reinforcement, announcements of new projects, new goals, achievements, and financial and nonfinancial awards and supports
4. Skill building, stories that tell how big goals have been achieved through incremental advancements and how people have innovated and experimented with new strategies (Lawson & Price, 2003)

FIU's Division of External Relations, which is responsible for the university's internal and external communications, helps the OGLI develop and implement ways to tell global learning stories. An external relations account representative was embedded in the OGLI for 10 hours per week for several years to provide technical expertise and consulting. Still, effective communication is sometimes a hit-or-miss endeavor. We encourage you to try a variety of strategies, even simultaneously, until you find the ones that work for different audiences and purposes. And once you've found them, don't get complacent, because people's communication habits shift in response to changes in technology and circumstances.

Internal storytelling. In a university the size of ours with two campuses, programs abroad, hundreds of adjunct faculty, and tens of thousands of online and transfer students, getting stories across to people is a challenge. But no matter the size of your institution, it's always difficult to decipher and locate people outside your immediate orbit or reporting line who need or want to know what's going on inside your unit. Some of our internal communication methods are targeted toward specific audiences, but others are scattershot approaches. We are happy to connect with people even if it's serendipitous.

In the OGLI's early days, our goal was to create broad awareness of our initiative and the new graduation requirement. We wanted our logo, slogan, and website everywhere so that people would want to read the articles and e-mails they received about global learning and accept Landorf and Doscher's requests for meetings and presentations. We installed a large mural on a wall at the entrance to our main library. We put banners on light posts, table tents in cafeterias and meeting areas, and a decal on every office window. Alumni relations installed a beautiful copper sculpture of our logo at the entrance to our student center, and other globally themed artworks in the university's collection were repositioned in prominent areas. We asked staff in units with video messaging monitors to add our digital media to their feeds. Of course, we also established a social media presence through Facebook, Instagram, Twitter, and Flickr. We've never had much of a budget for promotional swag, but the money we have has been spent on things that are useful and highly visible, such as T-shirts, mouse pads, umbrellas, sunglasses, string bags, coffee and espresso cups, key chains, lunchboxes, and even eyeglass cleaning cloths in the shape of a globe.

We estimate the impact of these methods in part by monitoring user statistics on our website. At first the site was just a landing page explaining the purpose and nature of the initiative, and it housed our original plan for universal global learning. Over the years, the site has evolved into a communications tool to inspire students through purpose-driven stories and empower them with essential information. Nearly everyone involved in global learning at FIU must visit the website for some reason or another. Faculty use it to enroll in professional development workshops and access course proposal information, additional course design resources, model syllabi, and their Global Learning Course Assessment Matrices. Students use it to find out about the graduation requirement, semester course offerings, and cocurricular activities. The website is the online headquarters for the Global Learning Medallion and Peace Corps Prep programs, and it provides links to the video recordings of Tuesday Times Roundtable discussions and Global Learning Conference presentations in addition to announcements for the brown-bag lunch workshops and the Global Learning Fellowship programs. The OGLI's reports, research, and publications can be found there, too. Comparing the period of May 31, 2012 to May 31, 2013, the earliest year of our data, to the same period in 2016–2017, we found a 27% increase in the number of unique users of the site and a 35% increase in the total number of page views.

The stories of our Global Learning Medallion and Peace Corps Prep students' achievements are among the most powerful the OGLI has to tell. In chapter 7 you read about the impact of ePortfolios on the students who create them. To inspire others, the OGLI publishes Global Learning Medallion ePortfolios on its website and organizes them according to students' capstone projects. The Peace Corps Prep student leadership committee now uses VoiceThread (2017) to engage its membership, and there are plans to use the software to serve online Global Learning Medallion students. VoiceThread is a secure social networking platform that allows people to converse about images, documents, and videos using any mix of text, audio, video, or even a phone call. So far the committee has developed two VoiceThread modules for Peace Corps Prep participants that provide students with information and allow committee members to provide peer mentorship and guidance by exchanging stories about course requirements and global engagement projects.

External storytelling. Communication with external audiences should not be unidirectional. The OGLI wants to promote FIU's universal global learning story to raise the university's profile and to increase opportunities for research, recruitment, and advancement. But we also want to speak with external colleagues and partners to improve our work. One of the ways we've done this is through conference presentations and workshops. The OGLI's Landorf, Doscher, and Feldman, along with colleagues in and outside FIU, regularly interact with peers at meetings of professional organizations such as the AAC&U, Association of International Education Administrators, NAFSA: Association of International Educators, Comparative and International Education Society, American Council on Education, Florida Consortium of International Education, and NASPA: Student Affairs Administrators in Higher Education. At these events, the OGLI exchanges trifold color brochures about our initiative for the contact information or business cards of session attendees. With their permission, we add them to our external audience electronic mailing list, which we use to make major announcements or issue calls for project collaborators.

Our website is a platform for telling our story to external audiences, but we need strategies for driving people to visit it. In addition to conference presentations, we publish book chapters and research and opinion articles, and we serve as reviewers and evaluators for other institutions engaged in global learning or other curriculum internationalization initiatives.

Conclusion

We offer you a final thought about communication and its relationship to the launch and continuous improvement of your universal global learning initiative. Remember the collaborative continuum that we presented earlier in the chapter? We think it's critical over the long term for you to make your communications about more than simply informing. Your messaging should be consultative in nature; you want your stakeholders to feel that your backbone organization is dedicated to their needs and successes. The information you provide should be backed by a willingness to support your stakeholders as they act on that information. This is key to communication that leads to action and continuous improvement. How do we know this to be true? Because our students and faculty have told us so. Our students, in particular, have dispelled the truism that e-mail is dead. They tell us that because the OGLI's e-mails go beyond promotion and feel like personalized consultation, they motivate them to get involved and go the extra mile. The following reflection excerpts from our summer 2017 Global Learning Medallion students should help you understand what we mean:

> I would like to say thank you to Eric Feldman, for always keeping us apprised of any opportunities in the community. His dedication to work with the students is extremely amazing. Almost every day I wake up, I know I'm going to receive some e-mails from Eric. I don't know how he does that, but I know he never stops to look for internships and creates liaison [*sic*] with others to bring it to us.

> The Global Learning Journey has been such a blessing in disguise. What started off as an extra credit sit-in for one of my professors became the highlight of my collegiate experience. The first three years of my collegiate career, I was the student that went to school and came home immediately afterwards. After the first roundtable meeting and learning what the global medallion distinction was and the benefits, I wanted to do more. Eventually, I met different people and [am] beginning to become more involved in other activities. . . . Eric Feldman did a great job keeping the group informed of upcoming dates and events around campus or around the city. He was always polite, courteous, knowledgeable, always returned phone calls and replied to e-mail.

> I liked that Eric gives us a lot of updates on internships and opportunities both at FIU and outside. . . . It is really one of the most helpful things of being in this program.

I enjoyed going to all of the lectures at FIU, which were sent to me via Global Learning Medallion e-mail.

Please do not lower the number of e-mails you . . . send out. . . . Students who are genuinely interested in global learning will appreciate and look forward to them.

From these reflections, it's clear that e-mail can be just as effective a tool as any other for motivating and inspiring. We leave you with one final observation from journalist Sydney J. Harris about the difference between simply using communication to inform your stakeholders and using it for continuous improvement: "The two words 'information' and 'communication' are often used interchangeably, but they signify quite different things. Information is giving out; communication is getting through" (as cited in Green, 2017, p. 140).

CONCLUSION

It is said that this is a "hinge moment"—on one hand a terrifying time of building walls, of exiting any common search for a shared wholeness. But it is also the moment to champion our unique role in higher education to assert our essential responsibility of championing values and practices that reinforce searches for truth and justice. (Harward, 2017, para. 30)

When we started writing this book in 2015, terms like *diverse*, *interconnected*, and *global* were used frequently and relatively freely in the public realm to describe our world. In higher education, we used these words to describe the forces that compelled us to increase the relevance and responsiveness of our research, teaching, and service practices. What a difference a couple of years have made. Now these terms are politically charged dynamite. Some reject them out of hand as contrary to national safety, prosperity, and moral strength. Globalism, cosmopolitanism, and multiculturalism have been dubbed anarchic notions, associated with liberals, intellectuals, "bureaucrats and bankers, working together to flatten national boundaries and, indeed, to flatten the nation–state itself" (Pinkerton, 2016, para. 75).

How are educators to respond to this change? How should we, who consider ourselves part of the world's knowledge and learning network and duty bound to prepare students for responsible local and global decision-making, respond to the British prime minister's claim that "if you believe you're a citizen of the world, you're a citizen of nowhere. You don't understand what the very word 'citizenship' means" (May, 2016, para. 3). Or to the prime minister of Hungary's question about his country's children, "Will they understand that the only way we can avoid being the slaves of other peoples—and the only way we can remain an independent nation—is if, first and foremost, we declare ourselves to be Hungarian?" (Orbán, 2017, para. 15). Or to the U.S. president's proclamation:

> We hear a lot of talk about how we are becoming a "globalized world." But the relationships that people value in this country are local. . . . There is no global anthem. No global currency. No certificate of global citizenship. We pledge allegiance to one flag and that flag is the American flag. From now on it is going to be: America First. Okay? America first. We're going to put ourselves first. (Hains, 2016, paras. 5, 7, 8)

Has the moment for global learning passed? Is global citizenship an unrealistic goal? Are our efforts to facilitate universal global learning and global engagement a waste of our time, money, and political capital? Are these increasingly scarce resources better spent elsewhere? The short answer is that now, more than ever, we need global learning.

We need global learning to produce scholarship that substantiates the compatibility of national and global citizenship. These concepts are not mutually exclusive; people can possess local and global identities that motivate them to advance the interconnected common good of their own communities and of others worldwide. Global learning enables students to understand and make connections between local and global concerns, analyze pressing issues from multiple perspectives, and grapple collaboratively with the problems experienced in their neighborhood and around the globe.

We need global learning to comprehend the nature and impacts of diversity, interconnectedness, and globalization, and we also need it to understand the reasons for the backlash against them. Keith Revell, associate professor of public administration at FIU, whose course we profiled in chapter 6, said that global learning is the best way to prepare students with the "habits of mind" and "cooperative habits of work" students need to make a "positive impact on the global future." He added that

teaching global learning courses has made me somewhat cautious about that future. It is hard for me to imagine citizenship without some sort of institutional context. "Global" does not manage itself. At this moment, we do not have much of a global institutional context where terms of togetherness, of mutual obligation and standards of behavior, fairness, or even the basic rules of the game are debated, let alone codified. A voluntary effort like global learning is intended, in part, to fill that gap. However, it looks to me like global processes are far from benign. From the perspective of the management of cities, the global game looks more like a competition in which some people are able to organize themselves to take advantage of what a globalized world has to offer and other people are unable to do so, resulting in extreme and growing inequality, and that inequality makes it increasingly difficult for the losers in this process to play the game successfully. At this point, global institutions (or, rather, the lack of them) are set up to allow that process to play out to the advantage of the winners, no matter the cost. If we are not careful about how we present the promises and possibilities of "global" to our students, we run the risk of giving them the impression that the playing field is level and that we all enter upon it as autonomous individuals with approximately the same chances of success, assuming we have global awareness and a global perspective. I don't think that the field is level or that people participate as individuals, except in very, very rare cases: one's chances are very much determined by which team you are on. How to organize to confront global competition is therefore something that we need to address in more concrete terms. We need a debate about what kinds of institutions are necessary and possible to deal with a world that "global" has made vastly smaller and thus vastly more competitive. (K. Revell, personal communication, December 6, 2017)

Global learning can provide a framework for a debate in which the terms, obligations, rules, and institutions surrounding citizenship, competition, and success are deliberated from diverse points of view. Such a debate would certainly have to address the standards and structures governing technology's impact on people's lives. But the outcome of this debate might be frustrating; rather than helping us figure things out, global learning can increase our knowledge of what we cannot know. The news is rife with stories of the unintended, unforeseen sociopolitical consequences of new technologies, such as the negative impacts of Facebook on the 2016 U.S. presidential election, of self-driving cars on organ donor availability, and of smartphone geo-tag data on violence and theft (Curtis, 2017). When diverse perspectives come together to interpret complex issues and events, the process can reveal evidence of the butterfly effect, a phenomenon in which "small events can have large, widespread consequences" (Dizikes, 2008, para. 1). These consequences are seldom linear or easily traceable to their initial inciting incident. Complex human and natural systems are composed of innumerable interconnected variables, making it possible, in theory, for the mere flap of a butterfly's wings to cause a tornado. The introduction of even a small error or disturbance to a system, much less a large innovation such as self-driving cars, can lead to unpredictable outcomes. Those who perceive that they've been caught off guard and negatively affected by globalization, diversity, and interconnectedness—leaders struggling to resolve flaring international or interracial conflicts, factory workers who've suddenly lost their jobs, or people who can't find a job unless they are bilingual—are most vocal in their criticism of these dynamics. But before we blame globalization for all our troubles, global learning can teach flexibility within the context of ambiguity and instability. Together, people can discover how to address other variables, such as institutionalized bias, unequal distribution of information and economic resources, and funding for K–16 education and job training, to increase well-being within the context of increasing diversity, interconnectedness, and change.

Finally, we need global learning to achieve the greater purposes of education. The process of global learning is essential to fulfilling these goals, whether you believe they're limited to knowledge acquisition and career development or that they include increasing students' psychosocial well-being and sense of civic purpose. In the introduction we walked you through the map-based global learning strategy depicted on the book's cover to illustrate an important point: Every individual needs to solve the complex problem of developing a nuanced understanding of the world and his or her identity in it, but no one person can solve this problem alone. We each need to interact with demographically and cognitively diverse others to help us figure out who we are. To this end, all students' education should involve purposeful strategies to ensure that everyone's unique perspective is expressed, given credence, and used to achieve the greater purpose of self-understanding. This is what universal global learning is really all about.

During the AAC&U's 2017 Global Engagement and Social Responsibility Conference, President Lynn Pasquerella and Don Harward, founding director of Bringing Theory to Practice, an independent project that supports and encourages institutions to link students' learning, well-being, and civic development, posed an essential question for our geopolitical moment: Are higher education's efforts to advance global engagement and global citizenship un-American? Their response was the same as ours: an unequivocal no. Harward (2017) added this meant that every institution must develop organizational practices that make good on its commitment to advance students' global citizenship and engagement, and that

> the challenging work for each campus to be a global community is in it becoming a context and a learning culture where the emancipation of a student as a global citizen is anticipated—even expected—that "global citizenry" is realized as a dimension of each student's identity. (para. 32)

This has been our purpose in writing this book: to offer institutions a comprehensive approach to educating for global citizenship through universal global learning.

We began by tracing FIU's path toward mutually supporting global learning SLOs and program goals. We discussed the importance of adopting a theory of organizational change that involves all stakeholders in the achievement of these goals and outcomes and described how we use collective impact for this purpose. We delved into the potential human, physical, financial, and information technology resources needed to provide global learning for all, and we explored ways to provide global learning professional development to all faculty and staff. Finally, we described methods for conducting student learning assessment and program evaluation and strategies for implementing continuous communication and improvement, all necessary to sustaining and expanding universal global learning over the long term. This is our model for achieving universal global learning, a model that emerged from our research, our personal experience, and our knowledge of the challenges faced by leaders of global learning initiatives at colleges and universities in differing institutional contexts.

Despite the changing landscape of higher education and the swirling political cross-winds throughout the world, we're optimistic that global learning can become foundational to all students' higher education. We're optimistic because we know we aren't in this alone. Global learning is related to a variety of other types of teaching and learning approaches, practices, and research, and these relationships can and should be developed and made mutually reinforcing. We discuss a few of these potential associations next, and we conclude with our thoughts about the future of universal global learning.

Universal Global Learning Is Not a Zero-Sum Game

We often meet colleagues at conferences and other institutions who ask what they'll have to give up to pursue universal global learning. If they open an office to support global learning, will they need to close the office of civic engagement or social innovation? Our response is that the institution doesn't have to give up anything. In fact, the opposite is true. These offices should join forces and collaborate in whatever ways they perceive possible. Universal global learning is not a zero-sum game. Just as cognitively diverse teams are able to reach better solutions to complex problems, differentiated educational approaches to the same complex learning outcomes lead to superadditive effects. More students and faculty are reached, and richer, more effective teaching and learning occurs.

With whom should global learning leaders and educators seek to work? Concepts fundamental to global learning, such as perspective taking, diversity, collaboration, and problem-solving, are embedded in other efforts similarly aimed toward responsible global citizenship and the greater purposes of higher education. You'll likely find willing partners in those who are already applying techniques such as service-learning, publicly engaged scholarship, civic engagement, multicultural education, design thinking, education for sustainable development, human rights education, the human capability approach to education, inclusive education, and social innovation, to name just a few. Look for faculty and staff who are implementing practices such as deliberative dialogue, big data analysis, and culturally responsive instruction. You may even find creative partnerships with researchers working on topics such as the anatomical origin of empathy (Hynes, 2006). Positive emotions such as gratitude and appreciation, "close cousins of empathy" (Markham, 2016, para. 10), have been found to have salubrious effects on heart and brain functions. Researchers studying the relationship among technology use (Grieff, Fischer, Stadler, & Wüstenberg, 2015), cognitive diversity (Page, 2017), and complex problem-solving and collaboration will also likely influence the way educators think about facilitating global learning and the people and offices with whom we collaborate.

The OGLI has a particularly strong relationship with FIU's Center for Leadership and Service, which is located in the Division of Student Affairs. Tangible results of this collaboration include our Global Living Learning Community and the Global Civic Engagement Mini Grant program, funded by Wells Fargo "to expand global awareness and community engagement by supporting student-led service projects" (FIU Student Affairs, n.d., para. 1). The OGLI has also joined forces with FIU's Office of Engagement on K–12 global learning pipeline programs, internships, and service-learning with local community organizations. Global Learning for Global Citizenship plays an essential role in the curricular and cocurricular aspects of FIU's Carnegie Community Engagement Classification, administered through the Office of Engagement, and laid the groundwork for the university's designation as an Ashoka U Changemaker Campus in 2016.

Support for multiapproach collaborations can be found at the national level too. One example is the American Council on Education's (n.d.) At Home in the World: Educating for Global Connections and Local Commitments initiative, which funded three-year dialogues at eight institutions to enhance collaboration among campus stakeholders involved in multicultural education and global education. In 2015 Washington University in St. Louis, Missouri, and Duke University in Durham, North Carolina, convened the Think Tank on Social Innovation and Civic Engagement to explore connections between the fields to facilitate teaching and learning for social change (Gephardt Institute for Civic and Community Engagement, 2017).

We know that full *collaboration*, as we defined it in chapter 10, requires a lot of time, which is a valuable resource that might not be available to you. Like most of us in higher education, you probably work in a stressful environment marked by the hustle to meet deadlines and adhere to external mandates. Collaboration is also a long-term commitment. But if you can take small steps on the collaborative continuum—informing, consulting, coordinating—toward integrative global learning, these will pay off in long-term dividends for your students. Remember Lillie Garvin, the Global Learning Medallion recipient who had an internship with the Alliance for Global Justice? Her work resulted in a research publication and acceptance into the master of science degree program in public health at FIU, where she is now enrolled. Ashaunte Stroman, the Global Living Learning Community resident and mentor, has launched her own personal training business,

Grind2DaGreen. She credits her project securing used bicycles for newly arrived Syrian refugees with helping her build the confidence and skills she needed to become an entrepreneur (A. Stroman, personal communication, December 10, 2017). And Camila Uzcategui, the first-generation college student who helped start FIU's GlobeMed chapter, is now pursuing a PhD in material science and engineering at the University of Colorado Boulder, funded by a full scholarship from the National Science Foundation. Like many Global Learning Medallion alumni, she keeps in touch with the OGLI. She recently wrote to let us know that her involvement with GlobeMed fueled her ability to secure her fellowship and her particular interest in stereolithographic 3D printing for cartilage and bone tissue engineering (C. Uzcategui, personal communication, December 10, 2017).

Mapping the Future of Global Learning

In the global learning strategy depicted on the book's cover, you'll recall from the introduction that students were challenged to address the following critical question: What are the implications of different portrayals of maps for different people around the world? Now that you've spent some time exploring our definition of *global learning*, glimpsed what universal global learning can look like, and acquired tools to chart a course toward universal global learning at your own institution, we'd like to end our journey together by posing a critical question to you: How can educators and institutions form a community of practice to achieve universal global learning?

The community we envision would build relationships and increase interaction among a diverse network of peers, including Hispanic-serving institutions, historically Black colleges and universities, tribal colleges and universities, for-profit colleges, community colleges, technical schools, colleges and universities with religious affiliations, large urban and rural public research institutions, and small private liberal arts colleges. The community's mission would be to enable peers to exchange information about how they organize and lead their initiatives, develop replicable tools and strategies, and even collaborate to facilitate faculty and staff's professional development and students' global learning. This community would take action to communicate the value of global learning to governmental and nongovernmental organizations and to private citizens. A community of practice for universal global learning would be dedicated to producing new knowledge in our field and to mapping the terrain of global learning taking place around the world.

We know that we've set forth a bold vision for the future of global learning. But we are unafraid and unabashed in presenting it because we know who we are talking to. We are educators. We have devoted our lives to guiding our students' developmental journey toward understanding themselves and the world around them, to aiding their search for truth and justice. We're most successful in doing these things when we engage in inclusive excellence, helping our students in myriad ways to form deep, familiar connections with people and ideas that were once unknown to them. We can apply this same expertise, passion, and set of values to forming a community of practice around universal global learning. In so doing, we make ourselves true champions of the greater purposes of education and claim this hinge moment as one heralding greater well-being for all.

REFERENCES

Adams, J. M., & Carfagna, A. (2006). *Coming of age in a globalized world: The next generation.* Bloomfield, CT: Kumarian Press.

Administration for Children and Families. (2010). *The program manager's guide to evaluation.* Retrieved from http://www.acf.hhs.gov/sites/default/files/opre/program_managers_guide_to_eval2010.pdf

Age Discrimination Act, 42 U.S.C. § 6101 (1975).

Agnew, M. (2013). Strategic planning: An examination of the role of disciplines in sustaining internationalization of the university. *Journal of Studies in International Education, 17,* 183–202.

Albertine, S. (2014, October). *Global learning in college: Cross-cutting capacities for 21st century students.* Speech presented at the Association of American Colleges & Universities Global Learning in College Conference, Washington DC.

Allen, D. (2016). Toward a connected society. In E. Lewis & N. Cantor (Eds.), *Our compelling interests: The value of diversity for democracy and a prosperous society* (pp. 71–105). Princeton, NJ: Princeton University Press.

Allen, I. E., Seaman, J., Lederman, D., & Jaschik, S. (2012). *Conflicted: Faculty and online education, 2012.* Retrieved from http://www.onlinelearningsurvey.com/reports/conflicted.pdf

Alliance for Global Justice. (2013). *About.* Retrieved from http://afgj.org/about

Allport, G. W. (1954). *The nature of prejudice.* Cambridge, MA: Addison-Wesley.

Alonso, I. (2017). *ECS 3021: Women, culture and economic development.* Retrieved from https://goglobal.fiu.edu/resources/syllabi-assessments/

Alwin, D. F., Cohen, R. L., & Newcomb, T. L. (1991). *Political attitudes over the life span.* Madison: University of Wisconsin Press.

American Association of State Colleges and Universities. (n.d.) *American democracy project.* Retrieved from http://www.aascu.org/ADP

American Council on Education. (n.d.). *At home in the world: Educating for global connections and local commitments.* Retrieved from www.acenet.edu/about-ace/special-initiatives/Pages/At-Home-in-the-World.aspx

American Council on Education. (2012). *Mapping internationalization on U.S. campuses.* Washington DC: Author.

American Council on Education. (2017). *Internationalization toolkit.* Retrieved from http://www.acenet.edu/news-room/Pages/Internationalization-Toolkit.aspx

Americans with Disabilities Act, 42 U.S.C.A. § 12101 *et seq.* (1990).

Amodio, D. M. (2014). The neuroscience of prejudice and stereotyping. *Nature Reviews Neuroscience, 15,* 670–682.

Anand, S., & Sen, A. (1994). *Human development index: Methodology and measurement.* New York, NY: United Nations Development Programme.

Anderson, R. D. (1992). Perspectives on complexity: An essay on curriculum reform. *Journal of Research in Science Teaching, 29*, 861–876.

Andrew W. Mellon Foundation. (2015). *Report of the Andrew W. Mellon Foundation.* Retrieved from https://mellon.org/media/filer_public/63/cd/63cd225d-d20e-4594-892f-88af167f9172/awmf-ar-2015.pdf

Antonio, A. L., Chang, M. J., Hakuta, K., Kenny, D. A., Levin, S., & Milem, J. F. (2004). Effects of racial diversity on complex thinking in college students. *Psychological Science, 15*(8), 507–510.

Appiah, K. A. (2006a). *Cosmopolitanism: Ethics in a world of strangers.* New York, NY: Norton.

Appiah, K. A. (2006b). *The case for contamination.* Retrieved from http://www.nytimes.com/2006/01/01/magazine/the-case-for-contamination.html

Applebaum, B. (2016). *Critical Whiteness studies.* Retrieved from http://education.oxfordre.com/view/10.1093/acrefore/9780190264093.001.0001/acrefore-9780190264093-e-5

Ariz. Rev. Stat. § 11-1051 (2010).

Asmar, C. (2005). Internationalising students: Reassessing diasporic and local student difference. *Studies in Higher Education, 30*, 298–309.

Association of American Colleges & Universities. (n.d.). *Making excellence inclusive.* Retrieved from https://www.aacu.org/making-excellence-inclusive

Association of American Colleges & Universities. (2007). *College learning for the new global century.* Washington DC: Author.

Association of American Colleges & Universities. (2017a). *Integrative learning value rubric.* Retrieved from http://www.aacu.org/value/rubrics/integrative-learning

Association of American Colleges & Universities. (2017b). *Making excellence inclusive.* Retrieved from http://www.aacu.org/making-excellence-inclusive

Association of American Colleges & Universities. (2017c). *Shared futures: Global learning and social responsibility.* Retrieved from http://www.aacu.org/shared-futures

Association of American Colleges & Universities & Carnegie Foundation for the Advancement of Teaching. (2004). *A statement on integrative learning.* Retrieved from http://gallery.carnegiefoundation.org/ilp/uploads/ilp_statement.pdf

Astin, A. W. (1993). Diversity and multiculturalism on campus: How are students affected? *Change, 25*(2), 44–49.

Astin, A. W., Banta, T. W., Cross, P. K., El-Khawas, E., Ewell, P. T., Hutchings, P., . . . Wright, B. D. (1993). Principles of good practice for assessing student learning. *Leadership Abstracts, 6*(4), 1–3.

Baker, R. (2008). *Getting started with global citizenship: A guide for new teachers.* Oxford, England: Oxfam.

Banaji, M. R., & Greenwald, A. G. (2013). *Blindspot: Hidden biases of good people.* New York, NY: Delacorte.

Barkley, E. F., Cross, K. P., & Howell Major, C. (2014). *Collaborative learning techniques: A handbook for college faculty.* San Francisco, CA: Jossey-Bass.

Bauman, G. L., Bustillos, L. T., Bensimon, E. M., Brown, M. C., & Bartee, R. D. (2005). *Achieving equitable educational outcomes with all students: The institution's roles and responsibilities*. Retrieved from http://www.aacu.org/sites/default/files/files/mei/bauman_et_al.pdf

Becher, T., & Trowler, P. R. (2001). *Academic tribes and territories: Intellectual enquiry and the culture of disciplines*. Buckingham, England: Open University.

Bennett, A. (2012). *How to live on 24 hours a day*. Mineola, NY: Dover.

Bernstein, A. R. (2016). Addressing diversity and inclusion on college campuses: Assessing a partnership between AAC&U and the Ford Foundation. *Liberal Education, 102*(2), 26–33.

Berrett, D. (2012, February 19). How "flipping" the classroom can improve the traditional lecture. *Chronicle of Higher Education*. Retrieved from http://www.chronicle.com/article/How-Flipping-the-Classroom/130857

Bhabha, H. K. (1994). *The location of culture*. New York, NY: Routledge.

Blaine, B. E. (2013). *Understanding the psychology of diversity*. Thousand Oaks, CA: Sage.

Bloom, B. S. (Ed.). (1956). *Taxonomy of educational objectives: The classification of educational goals, by a committee of college and university examiners*. New York, NY: Longmans, Green

Botkin, J. W., Elmandjra, M., & Malitza, M. (1979). *No limits to learning: Bridging the human gap*. Oxford, England: Pergamon Press.

Bourn, D. (2014). *The theory and practice of global learning*. London, England: Development Education Research Centre, Institute of Education.

Bowman, N. A. (2013). How much diversity is enough? The curvilinear relationship between college diversity interactions and first-year student outcomes. *Research in Higher Education, 54*, 874–894.

Braskamp, L., Braskamp, D. C., & Engberg, M. E. (2014). *Global perspective inventory (GPI): Its purpose, construction, potential uses, and psychometric characteristics*. Chicago, IL: Global Perspective Institute.

Braskamp, L. A., & Engberg, M. E. (2011). How colleges can influence the development of a global perspective. *Liberal Education, 97*(3/4), 34–39.

Braslavsky, C. (2003). *The curriculum*. Retrieved from http://www.unhas.ac.id/hasbi/LKPP/Hasbi-KBK-SOFTSKILL-UNISTAFF-SCL/Hasbi-UNISTAFF-DOCUMEN/MODUL%20UNISTAFF%20SURABAYA%202006/QTL/curriculum%20development/cecilia%20e.pdf

Breslin, T. A. (1984). Florida International University. In E. L. Backman (Ed.), *Approaches to international education* (pp. 135–150). New York, NY: Macmillan.

Brooks, C. (2011). Space matters: The impact of formal learning environments on student learning. *British Journal of Educational Technology, 42*, 719–726.

Brooks, M. G., & Brooks, J. G. (1999). The courage to be constructivist. *Educational Leadership, 57*(3), 18–24.

Brown, J. F., & Marshall, B. L. (2008). Continuous quality improvement: An effective strategy for improvement of program outcomes in a higher education setting. *Nursing Education Perspectives, 29*, 205–211.

Brown, T. (2011, November 15). Why social innovators need design thinking [Web log post]. Retrieved from https://ssir.org/articles/entry/why_social_innovators_need_design_thinking

Bruffee, K. A. (1995). Sharing our toys: Collaborative versus cooperative learning. *Change, 27*(1), 12–18.

Bruffee, K. A. (1998). *Collaborative learning: Higher education, interdependence, and the authority of knowledge.* Baltimore, MD: Johns Hopkins University Press.

Burkholder, P. (2016, May 16). Backward design: Forward progress [Web log post]. Retrieved from https://www.facultyfocus.com/articles/instructional-design/backward-design-forward-progress/

Cambridge, D., Kaplan, S., & Suter, V. (2005). *Community of practice design guide.* Retrieved from https://www.educause.edu/ir/library/pdf/NLI0531.pdf

Campbell, K. P. (2010). Stereotypes, student identity, and academic success. *Diversity & Democracy, 13*(2), 21.

Carleton College. (2013). *Carleton College awarded Mellon grant in support of global initiative* [Press release]. Retrieved from http://apps.carleton.edu/media_relations/press_releases/?story_id=1062934

Carnes, M. C. (2014). *Minds on fire: How role immersion games transform college.* Cambridge, MA: Harvard University Press.

Cavagnaro, L. B., & Fasihuddin, H. (2016). A moonshot approach to change in higher education: Creativity, innovation, and the redesign of academia. *Liberal Education, 102*(2), 8–17.

Centers for Disease Control. (n.d.). *Developing program goals and measurable objectives.* Retrieved from https://www.cdc.gov/std/Program/pupestd/Developing%20Program%20Goals%20and%20Objectives.pdf

Chang, M. J. (2002). The impact of an undergraduate diversity course requirement on students' racial views and attitudes. *Journal of General Education, 51,* 21–42.

Chickering, A., & Braskamp, L. A. (2009). Developing a global perspective for personal and social responsibility. *Peer Review, 11*(4), 27–30.

Church World Service. (n.d.). *History.* Retrieved from https://cwsglobal.org/about/history

Clarke, C. G., & antonio, a. l. (2012). Rethinking research on the impact of racial diversity in higher education. *Review of Higher Education, 36,* 25–50.

Clayton-Pederson, A. (2009). Rethinking educational practices to make excellence inclusive. *Diversity & Democracy, 12*(2), 1–3.

Clifford, V. A. (2009). Engaging the disciplines in internationalising the curriculum. *International Journal for Academic Development, 14,* 133–143.

Community Center for Education Results. (2015). *The Road Map Project.* Retrieved from http://www.roadmapproject.org/wp-content/uploads/2013/08/Road-Map-Project-One-Page-Summary-Sheet.pdf

Compton, E., Bentley, M., Ennis, S., & Rastogi, S. (2013). *2010 census race and Hispanic origin alternative questionnaire experiment.* Retrieved from https://www.census.gov/2010census/pdf/2010_Census_Race_HO_AQE.pdf

Connell, C. (2014). New windows on the world. *International Educator, 23*(3), 26–38.

Continuous improvement. (2013). Retrieved from http://edglossary.org/continuous-improvement

Cosgrove, D. (2001). *Apollo's eye: A cartographic genealogy of the Earth in the Western imagination.* Baltimore, MD: Johns Hopkins University Press.

Council for Aid to Education. (n.d.). *Instructions for the voluntary support of education survey.* Retrieved from http://cae.org/images/uploads/pdf/Reporting_standards_VSE_2016.pdf

Cruz, B. (2018). Global visionary: The life and work of Jan L. Tucker. In Toni Fuss Kirkwood-Tucker (Ed.), *The Global Education Movement: Narratives of Distinguished Global Scholars* (pp. 37–58). Charlotte, NC: Information Age.

Cruz, B., & Bermúdez, P. (2009). Teacher education in the United States: A retrospective on the global awareness program at Florida International University. In T. F. Kirkwood-Tucker (Ed.), *Visions in global education: The globalization of curriculum and pedagogy in teacher education and schools* (pp. 90–115). New York, NY: Peter Lang.

Curtis, M. (2017, May 23). The butterfly effect of new technology: How innovation could lead to worrying consequences. *International Business Times.* Retrieved from http://www.ibtimes.co.uk/butterfly-effect-new-technology-how-innovation-could-lead-worrying-consequences-1623014

Deardorff, D. (2015). *Demystifying outcomes assessment for international educators.* Sterling, VA: Stylus.

Denise, L. (1999). *Collaboration vs. C-three (cooperation, coordination, and communication).* Retrieved from http://www.sccharterschools.org/assets/documents/collaborationvsthe3cs.pdf

Denson, N. (2009). Do curricular and co-curricular diversity activities influence racial bias? A meta-analysis. *Review of Educational Research, 79,* 805–838.

Dizikes, P. (2008, June 8). The meaning of the butterfly: Why pop culture loves the 'butterfly effect,' and gets it totally wrong. *Boston Globe.* Retrieved from http://archive.boston.com/bostonglobe/ideas/articles/2008/06/08/the_meaning_of_the_butterfly/?page=full

Dominguez, F. (2014, April 2). Doors open to a dream career [Web log post]. Retrieved from https://goglobal.fiu.edu/2014/04/02/doors-open-dream-career

Doscher, S. P. (2008). Knowledge versus national security: The case of Androscoggin High School. *Journal of Cases in Educational Leadership, 11,* 97–105.

Doscher, S. P. (2012). *The development of rubrics to measure undergraduate students' global awareness and global perspective: A validity study* (Doctoral dissertation). Available from ProQuest Dissertations and Theses database. (UMI No. 3517005)

Downey, G. L., Lucena, J. C., Moskal, B. M., Parkhurst, R., Bigley, T., Hays, C., . . . Nichols-Belo, A. (2006). The globally competent engineer: Working effectively with people who define problems differently. *Journal of Engineering Education, 95,* 107–122.

Duckworth, A. L., Quinn, P. D., Lynam, D. R., Loeber, R., & Stouthamer-Loeber, M. (2011). Role of test motivation in intelligence testing. *Proceedings of the National Academy of Sciences of the United States of America, 108,* 7716–7720.

Eagan, K., Stolzenberg, E. B., Lozano, J. B., Aragon, M. C., Suchard, M. R., & Hurtado, S. (2014). *Undergraduate teaching faculty: The 2013–2014 HERI faculty survey*. Retrieved from http://www.heri.ucla.edu/monographs/HERI-FAC2014-monograph.pdf

Eagly, A. H., & Chaiken, S. (1993). *The psychology of attitudes*. Fort Worth, TX: Harcourt Brace Jovanovich College.

Edmondson, J., & Zimpher, N. L. (2014). *Striving together: Early lessons in achieving collective impact in education*. Albany, NY: SUNY Press.

Edsall, R. M. (2007). Iconic maps in American political discourse. *Cartographica, 42*, 335–347.

Einstein Educational Enterprises. (n.d.). What is IF-AT? Retrieved from http://www.epsteineducation.com/home/about/Default.aspx

Engberg, M. E. (2004). Improving intergroup relations in higher education: A critical examination of the influence of educational interventions on racial bias. *Review of Educational Research, 74*, 473–524.

Espenshade, T. J., & Radford, A. W. (2009). *No longer separate, not yet equal: Race and class in elite college admission and campus life*. Princeton, NJ: Princeton University Press.

Espinosa, L. L., Gaertner, M. N., & Orfield, G. (2015). *Race, class, and college access: Achieving diversity in a shifting legal landscape*. Washington DC: American Council on Education.

Ewell, P. T. (2001). *Accreditation and student learning outcomes: A proposed point of departure*. Retrieved from http://www.chea.org/userfiles/Occasional%20Papers/EwellSLO_Sept2001.pdf

Falk, R. (1994). The making of global citizenship. In B. V. Steenbergen (Ed.), *The condition of citizenship* (pp. 127–140). London, England: Sage.

Fanning, D. (1994). Go back to Mexico! [Television series episode]. *Frontline*. Boston, MA: WGBH Educational Foundation.

Festinger, L. (1957). *A theory of cognitive dissonance*. Stanford, CA: Stanford University Press.

Fink, L. D. (2003). *Creating significant learning experiences*. San Francisco, CA: Jossey-Bass.

Fischer, K. (2012, June 27). Colleges' efforts to internationalize slip in some areas. *Chronicle of Higher Education*. Retrieved from http://hchronicle.com/article/Colleges-Efforts-to-Globalize/132661

Fla. Stat. § 1009.286 (2016).

Florida International University. (1970). *The birth of a university and plans for its development*. Miami, FL: Greenleaf/Telesca.

Florida International University. (1972). *Introductory catalogue (Florida International University [1972–1973]*. Retrieved from digitalcommons.fiu.edu/cgi/viewcontent.cgi?article=1059&context=catalogs

Florida International University. (2010). *Florida International University's quality enhancement plan: Global learning for global citizenship*. Retrieved from https://goglobal.fiu.edu/wp-content/uploads/sites/16/2014/03/QEP_Report-Final.pdf

Florida International University. (2015a). *INR 4013 Development of international relations thought.* Retrieved from http://catalog.fiu.edu/2015_2016/undergraduate/Steven_J_Green_School_of_International_and_Public_Affairs/Undergraduate_Politics_and_International_Relations.pdf

Florida International University. (2015b). *POT 3302 Political ideologies.* Retrieved from http://catalog.fiu.edu/2015_2016/undergraduate/Steven_J_Green_School_of_International_and_Public_Affairs/Undergraduate_Politics_and_International_Relations.pdf

Florida International University Global Learning. (2017a). *Earn a prestigious global distinction.* Retrieved from https://goglobal.fiu.edu/medallion/

Florida International University Global Learning. (2017b). *eportolio & reflection.* Retrieved from https://goglobal.fiu.edu/medallion/eportfolio/

Florida International University Global Learning. (2017c). *Peace Corps Prep @ FIU.* Retrieved from https://goglobal.fiu.edu/pcp/

Florida International University Interama Campus Planning Office. (1974, January). International. . . . It's our middle name [Press release]. Miami, FL: Author.

Florida International University Online. (n.d.-a). *Blackboard exemplary.* Retrieved from http://online.fiu.edu/faculty/quality-commitment/blackboard-exemplary.php

Florida International University Online. (n.d.-b). *Quality matters program.* Retrieved from http://online.fiu.edu/faculty/quality-commitment/quality-matters.php

Florida International University Student Affairs. (n.d.). *Global civic engagement mini grants.* Retrieved from https://studentaffairs.fiu.edu/get-involved/leadership-and-service/make-a-difference/global-civic-engagement-mini-grants/index.php

Florida International University Student Affairs. (2017). *Living learning communities.* Retrieved from http://studentaffairs.fiu.edu/get-involved/leadership-and-service/classes-and-communities/living-learning-communities/index.php

Florida, R. (2015, September 22). America's leading immigrant cities. *Atlantic CityLab.* Retrieved from http://www.citylab.com/politics/2015/09/americas-leading-immigrant-cities/406438

Frost, R. A., Strom, S. L., Downey, J., Schultz, D. D., & Holland, T. A. (2010). Enhancing student learning with academic and student affairs collaboration. *Community College Enterprise, 16*(1), 37–51.

FSG. (2014). *Setting a common agenda.* Retrieved from http://collectiveimpactforum.org/sites/default/files/Setting%20a%20Common%20Agenda.pdf

Gadsby, H., & Bullivant, A. (Eds.). (2010). *Global learning and sustainable development.* London, England: Routledge.

Garvin, S. (2016, November 4). My internship viral mapping Zika. *FIU News.* Retrieved from https://news.fiu.edu/2016/11/my-internship-viral-mapping-zika/106022

Georgia Tech University. (2012). *Global learning for first-generation college students at Georgia Tech is funded by $1.3 million grant from the Coca-Cola Foundation.* Retrieved from http://inta.gatech.edu/sites/default/files/attachments/coca_cola_scholarship_press_release.pdf

Gephardt Institute for Civic and Community Engagement. (2017). *A think tank on social innovation and civic engagement.* Retrieved from https://gephardtinstitute .wustl.edu/about-us/10-year-anniversary/a-think-tank-on-social-innovation-and-civic-engagement/

Gerlach, J. M. (1994). Is this collaboration? *New Directions for Teaching and Learning, 59,* 5–17.

Gibson, C., Smyth, K., Nayowith, G., & Zaff, J. (2013, September 19). To get to the good, you gotta dance with the wicked. *Stanford Social Innovation Review.* Retrieved from https://ssir.org/articles/entry/to_get_to_the_good_you_gotta_ dance_with_the_wicked

Gibson, K. L., Rimmington, G. M., & Landwehr-Brown, M. (2008). Developing global awareness and responsible world citizenship with global learning. *Roeper Review, 30*(1), 11–23.

Glaser, B., & Strauss, A. (1967). *The discovery of grounded theory: Strategies for qualitative research.* New York, NY: Aldine.

Glass, C. R., & Braskamp, L. (2012, October 26). Foreign students and tolerance. *Inside Higher Ed.* Retrieved from http://www.insidehighered.com/views/2012/10/26/ essay-how-colleges-should-respond-racism-against-international-students.

GlobeMed. (n.d.-a). *About: History and growth.* Retrieved from http://globemed .org/about/history

GlobeMed. (n.d.-b). *Mission statement.* Retrieved from http://globemed.org/about

GlobeMed. (n.d.-c). *Vision statement.* Retrieved from http://globemed.org/about

Golich, V. L., Boyer, M., Franko, P., & Lamy, S. (2000). *The ABCs of case teaching.* Washington DC: Institute for the Study of Diplomacy.

Gottfredson, N. C., Panter, A. T., Daye, C. E., Allen, W. A., Wightman, L. F., & Deo, M. E. (2008). Does diversity at undergraduate institutions influence student outcomes? *Journal of Diversity in Higher Education, 1*(2), 80–94.

Green, M. F. (2012, January). Global citizenship: What are we talking about and why does it matter? *Trends & Insights for Higher Education Leaders.* Retrieved from http://www.nafsa.org/_/File/_/ti_global_citizen.pdf

Green, S. (2017). *Culture hacker.* Hoboken, NJ: Wiley.

Green, W., & Whitsed, C. (2013). Reflections on an alternative approach to continuing professional learning for internationalization of the curriculum across disciplines. *Journal of Studies in International Education, 17,* 148–164.

Greenman, E., & Xie, Y. (2008). Is assimilation theory dead? The effect of assimilation on adolescent well-being. *Social Science Research, 37*(1), 109–137.

Grieff, S., Fischer, A., Stadler, M., & Wüstenberg, S. (2015). Assessing complex problem-solving skills with multiple complex systems. *Thinking and Reasoning, 21,* 356–382.

Grutter v. Bollinger, 539 U.S. 306 (2003).

Guarasci, R. (2001). Recentering learning: An interdisciplinary approach to academic and student affairs. *New Directions for Higher Education, 116,* 101–109.

Gubrium, A., Harper, K., & Otañez, M. (Eds.) (2016). *Participatory visual and digital research in action.* New York, NY: Routledge.

Gurin, P. (1999). *Theoretical foundations for the effect of diversity.* Retrieved from http://diversity.umich.edu/admissions/legal/expert/theor.html

Gurin, P., Dey, E. L., Gurin, G., & Hurtado, S. (2004). The educational value of diversity. In P. Gurin, J. S. Lehman, & E. Lewis (Eds.), *Defending diversity: Affirmative action at the University of Michigan* (pp. 97–188). Ann Arbor: University of Michigan Press.

Gurin, P., Dey, E. L., Hurtado, S., & Gurin, G. (2002). Diversity and higher education: Theory and impact on educational outcomes. *Harvard Educational Review, 72,* 330–366.

Gurin, P., Nagda, B. A., & Zúñiga, X. (2013). *Dialogue across difference: Practice, theory, and research on intergroup dialogue.* New York, NY: Russell Sage Foundation.

Hacker, K. (2013). *Community-based participatory research.* Los Angeles, CA: Sage.

Hains, T. (2016, December 1). *Trump: There is no global flag, no global currency, no global citizenship. We will be united as Americans.* Retrieved from https://www.realclearpolitics.com/video/2016/12/01/trump_there_is_no_global_flag_no_global_currency_no_global_citizenship_we_are_united_as_americans.html

Hanleybrown, F., Kania, J., & Kramer, M. (2012, January 26). Channeling change: Making collective impact work [Web log post]. Retrieved from https://ssir.org/articles/entry/channeling_change_making_collective_impact_work

Hanvey, R. G. (1975). *An attainable global perspective.* Retrieved from ERIC database. (ED116993)

Haring-Smith, T. (2012). Broadening our definition of diversity. *Liberal Education, 98*(2), 6–13.

Hartmeyer, H. (2008). *Experiencing the world: Global learning in Austria: Developing, reaching out, crossing borders.* Münster, Germany: Waxmann.

Hart Research Associates. (2013). *It takes more than a major: Employer priorities for college learning and student success.* Retrieved from http://www.aacu.org/sites/default/files/files/LEAP/2013_EmployerSurvey.pdf

Hart Research Associates. (2015). *Falling short? College learning and career success.* Retrieved from http://www.aacu.org/sites/default/files/files/LEAP/2015employerstudentsurvey.pdf

Harward, D. W. (2017). *Are higher education's efforts to advance global engagement, and global citizenship, un-American?* Retrieved from http://www.bttop.org/news-events/october-13-2017-are-higher-education's-efforts-advance-global-engagement-and-global

Hawawini, G. (2011). *The internationalization of higher education institutions: A critical review and a radical proposal.* Institut européen d'administration des affaires. Retrieved from https://sites.insead.edu/facultyresearch/research/doc.cfm?did=48726

Hazza, B. (n.d.). *Sorta like a dream? No, better.* Retrieved from http://hazzaborja.wixsite.com/mysite/reflection

Hemmati, M. (2007). *Participatory dialogue: Towards a stable, safe, and just society for all.* New York, NY: United Nations.

Herbert Wertheim College of Medicine. (2017). *Green Family Foundation Neighbor-hoodHELP.* Retrieved from https://medicine.fiu.edu/education/md/undergraduate-medical-education/curriculum/service-learning/neighborhoodhelp/index.html

Ho, A. K., Roberts, S. O., & Gelman, S. A. (2015). Essentialism and racial bias jointly contribute to the categorization of multiracial individuals. *Psychological Science, 26,* 1639–1645.

Hofmeyer, A. (2014, April 2). Banking for the future [Web log post]. Retrieved from https://goglobal.fiu.edu/2014/04/02/banking-future

Horton, A. (2013, September 25). Help us build the collective impact community (and 8 new case studies) [Web log post]. Retrieved from https://www.fsg.org/blog/help-us-build-collective-impact-community-and-8-new-case-studies?__hssc=&__hstc=&hsCtaTracking=8a1c1292-0011-4f6c-8aa2-f1094ef1e9dd|4c1d6185-0608-45e9-9a7f-8e3ca4e251cc

Hovland, K. (2006). *Shared futures: Global learning and liberal education.* Retrieved from http://www.aacu.org/publications-research/publications/shared-futures-global-learning-and-liberal-education

Howell, C. M., Harris, M. S., & Zakrajsek, T. (2015). *Teaching for learning: 101 intentionally designed educational activities to put students on the path to success.* New York, NY: Routledge.

Hoyt, J. E. (2001). Performance funding in higher education: The effects of student motivation on the use of outcomes tests to measure institutional effectiveness. *Research in Higher Education, 42,* 71–85.

Huber, M. T., Hutchings, P., & Gale, R. (2005). Integrative learning for liberal education. *Peer Review, 7*(4), 4–7.

Hudzik, J. K. (2011). *Comprehensive internationalization: From concept to action.* Washington DC: NAFSA: Association of International Educators.

Humes, J. C. (1994). *The wit and wisdom of Winston Churchill: A treasury of more than 1,000 Quotations.* New York, NY: HarperCollins.

Humphreys, D. (2003). Reality check: Learning civic engagement without diversity? *Peer Review, 5*(3), 29.

Hutchins, P. (2005, October). *Building habits—and habitats—of integrative learning.* Plenary address presented at the Association of American Colleges & Universities Network Conference on Integrative Learning, Denver, CO.

Hynes, C. (2006). Differential role of the orbital frontal lobe in emotional versus cognitive perspective-taking. *Neuropsychologia, 44,* 374–383.

Immigration Act of 1924, 153 U.S.C. § 68-139 (2012).

Inayatullah, S. (2000) Corporate networks or bliss for all: The politics of the futures of the university. In S. Inayatullah & J. Gidley (Eds.), *The university in transformation: Global perspectives on the futures of the university* (pp. 221–234). Westport, CT: Bergin & Garvey.

Information technology. (2017). Retrieved from http://www.businessdictionary.com/definition/information-technology-IT.html

Institute of International Education. (2017). *Fast facts: 2017.* Retrieved from http:// www.iie.org/Research-and-Insights/Open-Doors/Fact-Sheets-and-Infographics/ Fast-Facts

Jagosh, J., MacAulay, A. C., & Pluye, P. (2012). Uncovering the benefits of participatory research: Implications of a realist review for health research and practice. *Milbank Quarterly, 90,* 311–346.

Jaschik, S. (2013, November 11). To be a Black man at UCLA. *Inside Higher Ed.* Retrieved from http://www.insidehighered.com/news/2013/11/11/students-video-leads-discussion-race-ucla

Jaschik, S. (2015, April 13). UCLA faculty approves diversity requirement. *Inside Higher Ed.* Retrieved from http://www.insidehighered.com/news/2015/04/13/ ucla-faculty-approves-diversity-requirement

Johnson, D. W., & Johnson, R. T. (1988). Critical thinking through structured controversy. *Educational Leadership, 45*(8), 58–64.

Jones, E., & Killick, D. (2013). Graduate attributes and the internationalized curriculum: Embedding a global outlook in disciplinary learning outcomes. *Journal of Studies in International Education, 17,* 165–182.

Jones, W. A. (2011). *Examining the relationship between student body racial diversity and college/university retention and graduation rates* (Doctoral dissertation). Available from ProQuest Dissertations and Theses database. (UMI No. 3576893)

Jupp, V. (Ed.). (2006). *The Sage dictionary of social research methods.* London, England: Sage.

Kahlenberg, R. D. (2015, June 4). Race-based admissions: The right goal, but the wrong policy. *The Atlantic.* Retrieved from http://www.theatlantic.com/ education/archive/2015/06/race-based-admissions/394784

Kaizen Institute. (2017). *What is kaizen?* Retrieved from https://ci.kaizen.com/ about-us/definition-of-kaizen.html

Kalantzis, M., & Cope, B. (2002). Towards an international and inclusive higher education. In Michael Singh (Ed.), *Worlds of learning: Globalisation and multicultural education* (pp. 11–37). Champaign, IL: Common Ground.

Kane, M. (2006). Content-related validity evidence in test development. In T. M. Haladyna & S. M. Downing (Eds.), *Handbook of test development* (Vol. 1, pp. 131–153). Mahwah, NJ: Erlbaum.

Kania, J., & Kramer, M. (2011). Collective impact. *Stanford Social Innovation Review, 9*(1), 36–41.

Katznelson, I. (2016). Diversity and institutional life: Levels and objects. In E. Lewis & N. Cantor (Eds.), *Our compelling interests: The value of diversity for democracy and a prosperous society* (pp. 182–191). Princeton, NJ: Princeton University Press.

Kaye, D. (1981). *The traveling woman.* Des Plaines, IL: Bantam Books, Inc.

Keeling, R. P., Underhile, R., & Wall, A. F. (2007). Horizontal and vertical structures: The dynamics of organization in higher education. *Liberal Education, 93*(4), 22–31.

Keller, S., & Aiken, C. (2015). The inconvenient truth about change management. In J. E. Lane (Ed.), *Higher education reconsidered: Executing change to drive collective impact* (pp. 27–59). Albany, NY: SUNY Press.

Keynes, J. M. (1935). *The general theory of employment, interest, and money.* New York, NY: Harcourt, Brace.

King, P. M., & Kitchener, K. S. (1994). *Developing reflective judgment: Understanding and promoting intellectual growth and critical thinking in adolescents and adults.* San Francisco, CA: Jossey-Bass.

King, P. M., & Shuford, B. C. (1996). A multicultural view is a more cognitively complex view. *American Behavioral Scientist, 40,* 153–164.

Kirkwood-Tucker, T. F. (1998). A tribute to Jan Tucker. In L. Swartz, L. Warner, & D. L. Grossman (Eds.), *Intersections: A professional development project in multicultural and global education, Asian and Asian American studies* (pp. 193–208). Boston, MA: Children's Museum.

Kirkwood-Tucker, T. F. (2009). Tales from the field: Possibilities and processes leading to global education reform in the Miami-Dade County Public Schools. In T. F. Kirkwood-Tucker (Ed.), *Visions in global education: The globalization of curriculum and pedagogy in teacher education and schools* (pp. 116–136). New York, NY: Peter Lang.

Knight, J. (1994). *Internationalization: Elements and checkpoints.* Retrieved from ERIC database. (ED549823)

Knight, J. (2003). Updated internationalization definition. *International Higher Education, 33,* 2–3.

Knight, J. (2004). Internationalization remodeled: Definition, approaches, and rationales. *Journal of Studies in International Education, 8,* 5–31.

Koenig, R. (2016, January 27). U.S. colleges raise $40 billion; Stanford tops list at $1.6 billion. *Chronicle of Philanthropy.* Retrieved from http://www.philanthropy.com/article/US-Colleges-Raise-40/235059

Kolesnikov-Jessop, S. (2007, January 5). Spotlight: Jack Ma, co-founder of Alibaba.com. *New York Times.* Retrieved from http://www.nytimes.com/2007/01/05/business/worldbusiness/05iht-wbspot06.4109874.html

Kolossov, V., & Scott, J. (2013). Selected conceptual issues in border studies. *Belgeo, 1,* 2–16.

Krishnamurti, J. (2017). *Commentaries on living: Second series.* Login, England: PublishDrive.

Kuh, G. D. (1996). Guiding principles for creating seamless learning environments for undergraduates. *Journal of College Student Development, 37,* 135–148.

Laird, T. F. N. (2005). College students' experiences with diversity and their effects on academic self-confidence, social agency, and disposition toward critical thinking. *Research in Higher Education, 46,* 365–387.

Landorf, H., & Doscher, S. (2013a). *Assessing global learning: Lessons from the field.* Retrieved from http://www.nafsa.org/_/File/_/case_study_flintl.pdf

Landorf, H., & Doscher, S. P. (2013b). Global learning for global citizenship. In M. Walker and A. Boni (Eds.), *Universities and human development. A sustainable imaginary for the XXI century* (pp. 162–177). New York, NY: Routledge.

Landorf, H., & Doscher, S. P. (2015). Defining global learning at Florida International University. *Diversity and Democracy, 18*(3), 24–25.

Lane, J. E., & Owens, T. L. (2014). *State engagement in higher education internationalization efforts: What should international officers know?* Retrieved from http://www.aieaworld.org/assets/docs/Issue_Briefs/issue%20brief-%20state%20engagement%20in%20higher%20education.pdf

Lane, J. E., Owens, T. L., & Ziegler, P. (2014). *States go global: State government engagement in higher education internationalization.* Retrieved from http://www.rockinst.org/pdf/education/2014-05-28-States_Go_Global.pdf

Lasker, R. D., Weiss, E. S., & Miller, R. (2001). Partnership synergy: A practical framework for studying and strengthening the collaborative advantage. *Milbank Quarterly, 79*, 179–205.

Lawson, E., & Price, C. (2003). The psychology of change management. *McKinsey Quarterly, 4*, 30–41.

Leask, B. (2013). Internationalizing the curriculum in the disciplines—imagining new possibilities. *Journal of Studies in International Education, 17*, 103–118.

Leask, B. (2015). *Internationalizing the curriculum.* Abingdon, England: Routledge.

Leask, B., & Beelen, J. (2010). *Engaging academic staff in international education in Europe and Australia: Enhancing the engagement of academic staff in international education.* Retrieved from https://www.ieaa.org.au/documents/item/41

Lee, P. R., & Estes, C. L. (2003). *The nation's health.* Boston, MA: Jones & Bartlett.

Leithwood, K., & Mascall, B. (2008). Collective leadership effects on student achievement. *Educational Administration Quarterly, 44*, 529–561.

Lent, R. C. (2012). *Overcoming textbook fatigue: 21st century tools to revitalize learning.* Alexandria, VA: Association for Supervision and Curriculum Development.

Leonard, G. (1968). *Education and ecstasy.* Berkeley, CA: North Atlantic Books.

Levin Institute. (2016). *What is globalization?* Retrieved from http://www.globalization101.org/what-is-globalization/

Lewis, E., & Cantor, N. (2016). The value of diversity for democracy and a prosperous society. In E. Lewis & N. Cantor (Eds.), *Our compelling interests: The value of diversity for democracy and a prosperous society* (pp. 1–15). Princeton, NJ: Princeton University Press.

Lumina Foundation. (2014). *The degree qualifications profile.* Retrieved from http://www.luminafoundation.org/files/resources/dqp.pdf

Machonis, P. (Ed.). (2008). *Shatter the glassy stare: Implementing experiential learning in higher education.* Lincoln, NE: National Collegiate Honors Council.

Maddox, K. B. (2006). *Rethinking racial stereotyping, prejudice, and discrimination.* Retrieved from http://www.apa.org/science/about/psa/2006/04/maddox.aspx

Maki, P. (2010). *Assessing for learning: Building a sustainable commitment across the institution.* Sterling, VA: Stylus.

Map. (n.d.). Encyclopedia entry. Retrieved from https://www.nationalgeographic.org/encyclopedia/map/

Markham, B. (1942). *West with the night*. Boston, MA: Houghton Mifflin Company.

Markham, T. (2016, November 16). Why empathy holds the key to transforming 21st century learning. *KQED News*. Retrieved from https://ww2.kqed.org/mindshift/2016/11/16/why-empathy-holds-the-key-to-transforming-21st-century-learning/

Massey, C. (2011). *The originalist*. Retrieved from http://podcast.uctv.tv/web documents/legally-speaking/11_01LegallySpeaking_Scalia.pdf

Mathews, S. A. (2016). Using digital participatory research to foster glocal competence: Constructing multimedia projects as a form of global and civic citizenship. *Journal of Social Studies Education Research, 7*(2), 1–29.

Matthews, D. (2017). *Academics "fail to change teaching due to fear of looking stupid."* Retrieved from http://www.timeshighereducation.com/news/academics-fail-change-teaching-due-fear-looking-stupid

May, T. (2016, October 5). *Theresa May's keynote speech at Tory conference in full*. Retrieved from http://www.independent.co.uk/news/uk/politics/theresa-may-speech-tory-conference-2016-in-full-transcript-a7346171.html

Mazzei, P. (2014, May 20). Miami-Dade commissioners: PortMiami off-limits for David Beckham soccer stadium. *Miami Herald*. Retrieved from http://miamiherald.com/news/local/community/miami-dade/article1964701.html

McDonald, J. P. (1992). *Teaching: Making sense of an uncertain craft*. New York, NY: Teachers College Press.

McKenney, A. (2015). "Vorrei prendere il treno!" (I want to take the train): A narrative about how one inclusive recreation services study abroad course helped students to understand challenges people with disabilities confront while traveling abroad. *American Journal of Recreation Therapy, 14*(1), 13–22.

McNair, T. B. (2016). The time is now: Committing to equity and inclusive excellence. *Diversity & Democracy, 19*(1), 4–7.

Measurement. (n.d.). In *Merriam-Webster's online dictionary* (11th ed.). Retrieved from http://www.merriam-webster.com/dictionary/measurement

Meier, B. P., Moller, A. C., Chen, J. J., & Riemer-Peltz, M. (2011). Spatial metaphor and real estate: North-South location biases housing preference. *Social Psychological and Personality Science, 2*, 547–553.

Merryfield, M. M. (1992). Preparing social studies teachers for the twenty-first century: Perspectives on program effectiveness from a study of six exemplary programs in the United States. *Theory and Research in Social Education, 20*, 17–46.

Mezirow, J. (1978). Perspective transformation. *Adult Education, 28*, 100–110.

Mezirow, J. (1990). How critical reflection triggers transformative learning. In J. Mezirow & Associates (Eds.), *Fostering critical reflection in adulthood: A guide to transformative and emancipatory learning* (pp. 1–20). San Francisco, CA: Jossey-Bass.

Mezirow, J. (1991). *Transformative dimensions of adult learning.* San Francisco, CA: Jossey-Bass.

Mezirow, J. (1997). Transformative learning: Theory to practice. *New Directions for Adult and Continuing Education, 74,* 5–12.

Michaelsen, L. K., Knight, A. B., & Fink, L. D. (2004). *Team-based learning: A transformative use of small groups in college teaching.* Sterling, VA: Stylus.

Michaelsen, L. K., & Sweet, M. (2008). The essential elements of team-based learning. *New Directions for Teaching and Learning, 116,* 7–27.

Milem, J. F., Chang, M. J., & Antonio, A. L. (2005). *Making diversity work on campus: A research-based perspective.* Washington DC: Association of American Colleges & Universities.

Miller, R., & Leskes, A. (2005). *Levels of assessment: From the student to the institution.* Washington DC: Association of American Colleges & Universities.

Mokre, J. (2000). *The symbolism of the globe—past and present.* Retrieved from https://www.academia.edu/14735863/The_Symbolism_of_the_Globe_Past_and_Present

Morrill, R. (2013). Collaborative strategic leadership and planning in an era of structural change: Highlighting the role of the governing board. *Peer Review, 15*(1), 12.

Mueller, J. (2014). *Authentic assessment toolbox.* Retrieved from http://jfmueller.faculty.noctrl.edu/toolbox/tasks.htm

NAFSA: Association of International Educators. (2017). *Professional resources: Models for program financing.* Retrieved from http://www.nafsa.org/findresources/Default.aspx?id=17348

National Council for the Social Studies. (2013). *The college, career, and civic life (C3) framework for social studies state standards: Guidance for enhancing the rigor of K–12 civics, economics, geography, and history.* Silver Spring, MD: Author.

National Institute for Transformation & Equity. (2017). *CECE surveys at a glance.* Retrieved from https://www.indiana.edu/~cece/wordpress/surveys-at-a-glance/

National Research Council. (2010). *1: How are we changing the physical environment of Earth's surface?* Retrieved from https://www.nap.edu/read/12860/chapter/6

National Survey of Student Engagement. (2015). *Topical module: Global learning (experimental version).* Retrieved from http://nsse.indiana.edu/pdf/modules/2016/NSSE_2016_Global_Learning_Module.pdf

Neft, N., & Levine, A. D. (1998). *Where women stand: An international report on the status of women in 140 countries.* New York, NY: Random House.

Newcomb, T. L. (1943). *Personality and social change: Attitude formation in a student community.* New York, NY: Dryden Press.

Newcomb, T. L., Koenig, K. E., Flacks, R., & Warwick, D. P. (1967). *Persistence and change: Bennington College and its students after 25 years.* New York, NY: Wiley.

Nussbaum, M. (2004). Liberal education and global community. *Liberal Education, 90*(1), 42–48.

Nussbaum, M. (2006). Education and democratic citizenship: Capabilities and quality education. *Journal of Human Development and Capabilities, 7*, 385–395.

Nussbaum, M. C. (2000). *Women and human development: The capabilities approach.* Cambridge, England: Cambridge University Press.

Nussbaum, M. C., & Glover, J. (Eds.). (2001). *Women, culture, and economic development: A study of human capabilities.* Oxford, England: Oxford University Press.

Nye, J. S. (2004). *Soft power: The means to success in world politics.* New York, NY: Public Affairs.

O'Brien, J. G., Millis, B. J., & Cohen, M. W. (2008). *The course syllabus: A learning-centered approach.* San Francisco, CA: Wiley.

Olsen, C. L., Green, M. F., & Hill, B. A. (2006). *A handbook for advancing comprehensive internationalization: What institutions can do and what students should learn.* Washington DC: American Council on Education.

O'Neill, D. (2014, April 25). FIU's Graduation Success Initiative gaining national attention as it boosts on-time graduation rates. *FIU Magazine.* Retrieved from https://news.fiu.edu/2014/04/fiu-effort-to-boost-graduation-rates-delivering-results/77401

O'Neill, N. (2012). *Promising practices for personal and social responsibility: Findings from a national research collaborative.* Washington DC: Association of American Colleges & Universities.

Orbán, V. (2017, February 10). Prime minister Viktor Orbán's state of the nation address. Retrieved from http://www.kormany.hu/en/the-prime-minister/the-prime-minister-s-speeches/prime-minister-viktor-orban-s-state-of-the-nation-address-20170214

Orleans, L. A., Mirra, N., Garcia, A., & Morrell, E. (2016). *Doing participatory action research: Transforming inquiry with researchers, educators, and students.* New York, NY: Routledge.

Owen, J. M., & Lambert, F. C. (1998). Evaluation and the information needs of organizational leaders. *American Journal of Evaluation, 19*, 355–365.

Ozaki, C. C., & Hornak, A. M. (2014). Excellence within student affairs: Understanding the practice of integrating academic and student affairs. *New Directions for Community Colleges, 166*, 79–84.

Page, S. (2007). *The difference: How the power of diversity creates better groups, firms, schools, and societies.* Princeton, NJ: Princeton University Press.

Page, S. (2011). *Diversity and complexity.* Princeton, NJ: Princeton University Press.

Page, S. E. (2017). *The diversity bonus: How great teams pay off in the knowledge economy.* Princeton, NJ: Princeton University Press.

Park, S., Hironaka, S., Carver, P., & Nordstrum, L. (2013). *Continuous improvement in education.* Retrieved from http://www.carnegiefoundation.org/wp-content/uploads/2014/09/carnegie-foundation_continuous-improvement_2013.05.pdf

Parker, W. C. (2003). *Teaching democracy: Unity and diversity in public life.* New York, NY: Teachers College Press.

Parker, W. C. (2007). *Imagining a cosmopolitan curriculum* (Working paper). Seattle, WA: University of Washington.

Parkinson, C. N. (1957). *Parkinson's law and other studies in administration.* Boston, MA: Houghton Mifflin.

Pascarella, E. T., & Terenzini, P. T. (2005). *How college affects students* (Vol. 2). San Francisco, CA: Jossey-Bass.

Patten, E. (2016, July 1). *Racial, gender wage gaps persist in U.S. despite some progress.* Retrieved from http://www.pewresearch.org/fact-tank/2016/07/01/racial-gender-wage-gaps-persist-in-u-s-despite-some-progress

Paulson, M. (2017, March 8). What do 'Hamilton,' 'Amélie' and 'Great Comet' have in common? Phillipa Soo. *The New York Times.* Retrieved from https://www.nytimes.com/2017/03/08/theater/what-do-hamilton-amelie-and-great-comet-have-in-common-phillipa-soo.html

Peace Corps. (n.d.-a). *About: Changing lives the world over.* Retrieved from https://www.peacecorps.gov/about

Peace Corps. (n.d.-b). *Make the most of your world.* Retrieved from https://www.peacecorps.gov

Peace Corps. (2016). *2016 Peace Corps Prep invitation to participate.* Retrieved from https://www.peacecorps.gov/documents/457/PC_Prep_2016_Invitation_to_Participate.pdf

PechaKucha. (n.d.). *About.* Retrieved from http://www.pechakucha.org/faq

Pelletier, S. G. (2012). *Rethinking revenue.* Retrieved from http://www.aascu.org/WorkArea/DownloadAsset.aspx?id=5569

Perry, C. (1972). *The first thousand days.* Retrieved from ERIC database. (ED071592)

Perry, C. (1973, January 1). *We have only begun* [Convocation: Final draft]. Series 1, President's Office, Florida International University Archives (Box 10, Folder 17), Florida International University Libraries, Miami, FL.

Peterson, M. W., & Einarson, M. K. (1997). *Analytic framework of institutional support for student assessment.* Stanford, CA: National Center for Postsecondary Improvement.

Pettigrew, T. F. (1998). Intergroup contact theory. *Annual Review of Psychology, 49,* 65–85.

Pettigrew, T. F., & Tropp, L. R. (2006). A meta-analytic test of intergroup contact theory. *Journal of Personality and Social Psychology, 90,* 751–783.

Pew Charitable Trusts. (2015). *Federal and state funding of higher education: A changing landscape.* Retrieved from http://www.pewtrusts.org/~/media/assets/2015/06/federal_state_funding_higher_education_final.pdf

Pew Research Center. (2015). *Race and multiracial Americans in the U.S. census.* Retrieved from http://www.pewsocialtrends.org/2015/06/11/chapter-1-race-and-multiracial-americans-in-the-u-s-census

Pew Research Center. (2016). *Demographic trends and economic well-being.* Retrieved from http://www.pewsocialtrends.org/2016/06/27/1-demographic-trends-and-economic-well-being

Pike, G. R., & Kuh, G. D. (2006). Relationships among structural diversity, informal peer interactions and perceptions of the campus environment. *Review of Higher Education, 29*, 425–450.

Pinkerton, J. P. (2016, August 7). *The worldwide trumpian majority: Lessons from Brexit, Britain, and the United States.* Breitbart. Retrieved from http://www.breitbart.com/big-government/2016/08/07/worldwide-trumpian-majority-lessons-brexit-britain-united-states/

Ploman, E. W. (1986). Global learning: A challenge. In A. Thomas & E. W. Ploman (Eds.), *Learning and development: A global perspective* (pp. xix–xxvi). Toronto, Ontario, Canada: Ontario Institute for Studies in Education.

Podolsky, M. L. (1997). *Cures out of chaos.* Amsterdam, The Netherlands: Harwood Academic.

Post, M. A., Ward, E., Longo, N. V., & Saltmarsh, J. (2016). *Publicly engaged scholars: Next generation engagement and the future of higher education.* Sterling, VA: Stylus.

Prestamo, A. (2017). *Dean's message: Welcome to the FIU libraries.* Retrieved from http://library.fiu.edu/about-us/deans-message

Prewitt, K. (2001). Census 2000: As a nation, we are the world. *Carnegie Reporter, 1*(3), 3–11.

Purdie-Vaughns, V., & Eibach, R. P. (2008). Intersectional invisibility: The distinctive advantages and disadvantages of multiple subordinate-group identities. *Sex Roles, 59*, 377–391.

Purdue, K. (1999). *Shackled women: Abuses of a patriarchal world* [DVD]. United States: Films Media Group.

Ravitch, D. (2016). *The death and life of the great American school system.* New York, NY: Basic Books.

Rawls, J. (1987). The idea of an overlapping consensus. *Oxford Journal of Legal Studies, 7*, 1–25.

Read, B., Archer, L., & Leatherwood, C. (2003). Challenging cultures? Student conceptions of "belonging" and "isolation" at a post-1992 university. *Studies in Higher Education, 28*, 261–277.

Redden, E. (2009, February 9). Students help students study abroad. *Inside Higher Ed.* Retrieved from http://www.insidehighered.com/news/2009/02/09/studyabroad

Regents of the University of California v. Bakke, 438 U.S. 265 (1978).

Revell, K. (2017). *PAD3802: Introduction to urban and regional studies.* Retrieved from https://goglobal.fiu.edu/resources/syllabi-assessments

Rhodes, F. H. T. (1998). The university and its critics. In W. G. Bowen & H. T. Shapiro (Eds.), *Universities and their leadership* (pp. 3–14). Princeton, NJ: Princeton University Press.

Roffe, I. A. (1998). Conceptual problems of continuous quality improvement and innovation in higher education. *Quality Assurance in Education, 6*(2), 74–82.

Rogers, E. M. (2003). *Diffusion of innovations.* New York, NY: The Free Press.

Rowland, S. (2006). *The enquiring university: Compliance and contestation in higher education.* Maidenhead, Berkshire, England: Open University.

Santamaria, C. (2015). Carla's global learnings [Web log post]. Retrieved from http://carlatheglobalcitizen.blogspot.com/p/other-activities.html

Schiel, J. (1996). *Student effort and performance on a measure of postsecondary educational development* (ACT Report No. 96–9). Iowa City, IA: American College Testing Program.

Schneider, C. G. (1995). Higher education and the contradictions of American pluralism. In E. K. Minnich (Ed.), *The drama of diversity and democracy: Higher education and American commitments* (pp. xxii–xxx). Washington DC: Association of American Colleges & Universities.

Schneider, C. G. (2015). The LEAP challenge: Transforming for students, essential for liberal education. *Liberal Education, 101*(1/2), 6–15.

Schneider, C. G. (2016). Making excellence inclusive: Roots, branches, futures. *Liberal Education, 102*(2), 2–5.

Seltzer, R. (2016, July 15). Foundering finances, the faculty role: A survey of business officers. *Inside Higher Ed.* Retrieved from http://www.insidehighered.com/news/survey/foundering-finances-faculty-role-survey-business-officers

Sen, A. (1999). *Development as freedom.* New York, NY: Oxford University Press.

Sen, A. (2009). *The idea of justice.* Boston, MA: Belknap Press of Harvard University Press.

Shaffer, B. (2017, March 20). *Arriving at Boston public schools: More accurate—and inclusive—world maps.* Retrieved from http://www.wbur.org/edify/2017/03/16/world-maps-boston-public-schools

Shaw, E. J. (2005). *Researching the educational benefits of diversity.* Retrieved from http://research.collegeboard.org/publications/content/2012/05/researching-educational-benefits-diversity

Smith, B. L., & MacGregor, J. T. (1992). What is collaborative learning? In A. S. Goodsell, M. R. Maher, & V. Tinto (Eds.), *Collaborative learning: A sourcebook for higher education* (pp. 10–30). University Park, PA: National Center on Postsecondary Teaching, Learning, and Assessment.

Snyder, S. (2013*). The simple, the complicated, and the complex: Educational reform through the lens of complexity theory* (OECD Education Working Papers No. 96). Retrieved from http://www.oecd.org/edu/ceri/WP_The%20Simple,%20Complicated,%20and%20the%20Complex.pdf

Soedjatmoko. (1985). *Development as learning.* Retrieved from http://www.nfdindia.org/lec10.htm

Soedjatmoko, & Newland, K. (1987). The United Nations University: A new kind of university. *Washington Quarterly, 10*, 215–224.

Southern Association of Colleges and Schools Commission on Colleges. (2012). *Quality enhancement plan guidelines.* Retrieved from http://www.sacscoc.org/pdf/Quality%20Enhancement%20Plan%20Guidelines.pdf

Spiro, R. J., Coulson, R. L., Feltovich, P. J., & Anderson, D. (1988). *Cognitive flexibility theory: Advanced knowledge acquisition in ill-structured domains.* Retrieved from ERIC database. (ED302821)

Steenburgen, B. V. (1994). *The condition of citizenship.* London, England: Sage.

Steven J. Green School of International and Public Affairs. (n.d.). *Broad series lectures: About the Ruth K. and Shepard Broad Distinguished Lecture Series*. Retrieved from http://sipa.fiu.edu/about-us/lectures

Stohl, M. (2007). We have met the enemy and he is us: The role of the faculty in the internationalization of higher education in the coming decade. *Journal of Studies in International Education, 11*, 359–372.

Support Our Law Enforcement and Safe Neighborhoods Act, SB. 1070. 111th Cong. (2010).

Suskie, L. (2004). *Assessing student learning: A common sense guide*. Bolton, MA: Anker.

Taylor, T. E., Milem, J. F., & Coleman, A. L. (2016). *Bridging the research to practice gap: Achieving mission-driven diversity and inclusion goals*. Retrieved from http://www.aacu.org/sites/default/files/BridgingResearchPracticeGap.pdf

Tejedor, C. (2015, July 10). At student-led workshops, children learn about Haitian roots. *FIU News*. Retrieved from https://news.fiu.edu/2015/07/at-student-led-workshops-children-learn-about-haitian-roots/90078

Tejedor, C. (2017). *A different world map makes classroom debut*. Retrieved from https://news.fiu.edu/2017/03/a-different-world-map-makes-classroom-debut/110071

Temponi, C. (2005). Continuous improvement framework: Implications for academia. *Quality Assurance in Education, 13*, 17–36.

Thalheim, B. (2008). *Collaboration: 3C = C^3 = communication + coordination + coordination*. Retrieved from http://www.is.informatik.uni-kiel.de/thalheim/CollaborationManagement.pdf

Thelin, J. (2011). *A history of American higher education*. Baltimore, MD: Johns Hopkins University Press.

Thomas, D. A., & Ely, R. J. (1996). Making differences matter: A new paradigm for managing diversity. *Harvard Business Review, 74*(5), 79–80.

Thompson, C. (2017). From Ptolemy to GPS, the brief history of maps. *Smithsonian Magazine, 48*(4), 16–22.

Tienda, M. (2013). Diversity ≠ inclusion: Translating access into equity in higher education. *Educational Researcher, 42*, 467–475.

Transcript of arguments in Grutter v. Bollinger. (2003, April 1). *New York Times*. Retrieved from http://www.nytimes.com/2003/04/01/politics/transcript-of-arguments-in-grutter-v-bollinger.html

Treasure Valley Education Partnership. (2013). *2013 baseline report card*. Retrieved from http://www.idahotvep.org/wp-content/uploads/2017/02/2013-TVEP-Report-Card.pdf

Trochim, W. M. K. (2006). *The planning-evaluation cycle*. Retrieved from http://www.socialresearchmethods.net/kb/pecycle.php

Tropp, L. R., & Pettigrew, T. F. (2005). Relationships between intergroup contact and prejudice among minority and majority status groups. *Psychological Science, 16*, 951–957.

Tucker, J. L. (1979). Global education moves ahead. *Trends in Social Education, 25*(2/3), 6–9.

Tucker, J. L. (1982). Developing a global dimension in teacher education: The Florida International University experience. *Theory Into Practice, 21*, 212–217.

Tucker, J. L. (1991a). Global education is essential to secondary school social studies. *NASSP Bulletin, 75*(531), 43–51.

Tucker, J. L. (1991b). Global education partnerships between schools and universities. In K. A. Tye (Ed.), *Global education: From thought to action* (pp. 109–124). Alexandria, VA: Association for Supervision and Curriculum Development.

Turner, S., Merchant, K., Kania, J., & Martin, E. (2012). Understanding the value of backbone organizations in collective impact: Part 4. [Web log post]. Retrieved from https://ssir.org/articles/entry/understanding_the_value_of_backbone_organizations_in_collective_impact_4

Tye, K. A. (2009). A history of the global education movement in the United States. In T. F. Kirkwood-Tucker (Ed.), *Visions in global education: The globalization of curriculum and pedagogy in teacher education and schools* (pp. 3–24). New York, NY: Peter Lang.

United Nations. (n.d.-a). *Charter of the United Nations University.* Retrieved from http://i.unu.edu/media/unu.edu/page/299/UNU-Charter-2014.pdf

United Nations. (n.d.-b). *The United Nations University (UNU): Origins and background.* Retrieved from www.un-ngls.org/orf/documents/publications.en/ngls.handbook/a25unu.htm

United Nations. (1981). *Annual report of the council of the United Nations University and report of the director-general.* Retrieved from http://unesdoc.unesco.org/images/0004/000454/045499eo.pdf

University of Illinois at Urbana-Champaign. (2017). *Student funding opportunities.* Retrieved from http://www.international.illinois.edu/students/student-funding.html

University of Texas at Austin International Office. (2012). *UT study abroad office celebrates 25 years of connecting students to the world.* Retrieved from https://world.utexas.edu/about/features/25-years

U.S. Agency for International Development. (2015). *Global health fellows II.* Retrieved from http://www.ghfp.net

VoiceThread. (2017). *What is VoiceThread?* Retrieved from http://voicethread.com/products/highered

Walters, J. (2017). *Boston public schools map switch aims to amend 500 years of distortion.* Retrieved from https://www.theguardian.com/education/2017/mar/19/boston-public-schools-world-map-mercator-peters-projection

Wang, C., & Burris, M. A. (1997). Photovoice: Concept, methodology, and use for participatory needs. *Health Education & Behavior, 24*, 369–387.

Wang, Y. (2015, November 12). A course originally called "The Problem of Whiteness" returns to Arizona State. *The Washington Post.* Retrieved from http://www.washingtonpost.com/news/morning-mix/wp/2015/11/12/a-course-originally-called-the-problem-of-whiteness-returns-to-asu-as-racial-tensions-boil-over-on-campuses/?utm_term=.5b09e50dd8ca

Washington and Lee University. (2013). *Dyson Foundation makes $2.5 million grant to W&L for center for global learning* [Press release]. Retrieved from http://news.blogs.wlu.edu/2013/01/14/dyson-foundation-makes-2-5-million-grant-to-wl-for-center-for-global-learning/

Wehlburg, C. M. (2011). A scholarly approach to assessing learning. *International Journal for the Scholarship of Teaching and Learning, 5*(2), 1–4.

Wenger, E., McDermott, R., & Snyder, W. (2002). *Cultivating communities of practice: A guide to managing knowledge.* Boston, MA: Harvard Business School Press.

Westermann, M. (2012, March 9). *Internationalizing higher education: Can American philanthropy play a role?* [Video file]. Retrieved from www.iie.org/Who-We-Are/News-and-Events/Events/2012/Best-Practices-Conference-2012/Multimedia/Conference-Presentations#.V5aM8I4T_Vo

Westheimer, J., & Kahne, J. (2004). What kind of citizen? The politics of educating for democracy. *American Educational Research Journal, 41*, 237–269.

Wiggins, G. (1989). A true test: Toward a more authentic and equitable assessment. *Phi Delta Kappan, 70*, 703–713.

Wiggins, G. (1993). Assessment: Authenticity, context, and validity. *Phi Delta Kappan, 75*, 200–214.

Wiggins, G., & McTighe, J. (2005). *Understanding by design.* Upper Saddle River, NJ: Pearson.

Wise, S., & Demars, C. (2005). Low examinee effort in low-stakes assessment: Problems and potential solutions. *Educational Assessment, 10*, 1–17.

Wong, D., & Branham, D. S. (2016). Potential, not problem: An expanded view of cultural difference. *Diversity & Democracy, 19*(2), 22–23.

Woodhouse, K. (2015, August 25). Discounting grows again. *Inside Higher Ed.* Retrieved from http://www.insidehighered.com/news/2015/08/25/tuition-discounting-grows-private-colleges-and-universities

Young, I. M. (1994). Gender as seriality: Thinking about women as a social collective. *Signs, 19*, 713–738.

Zbick, J. (2017, January 10). The future of the world is in my classroom today. Retrieved from https://www.tnonline.com/2017/jan/10/future-world-my-classroom-today

Zook, G. F. (1947). *Higher education for American democracy: A report* (Vol. 1). Washington, DC: U.S. Government Printing Office.

This book is a copublication of NAFSA: Association of International Educators and Stylus Publishing, LLC.